Interactive Read–Alouds

Linking Standards, Fluency, and Comprehension

2–3

Linda Hoyt

*first*hand

HEINEMANN

DEDICATED TO TEACHERS

Heinemann, Portsmouth, NH

*first*hand
An imprint of Heinemann
361 Hanover Street
Portsmouth, NH 03801-3912
www.firsthand.heinemann.com

Offices and agents throughout the world

Library of Congress Cataloguing-in-Publications Data
CIP data is on file with the Library of Congress

ISBN 0-325-01030-7 (Lesson Book)
    0-325-01113-3 (Teachers Guide)
    0-325-01057-9 (set)

Printed in the United States of America on acid-free paper

10   09   ML   2   3   4   5   6

TABLE OF CONTENTS

SECTION 1: *Standards for Comprehension*

SECTION 2: *Standards for Story Elements*

SECTION 3: *Standards for Vocabulary/ Literary Language*

SECTION 4: *Standards for Literary Elements and Devices*

SECTION 5: *Standards for Genre*

SECTION 6: *Standards for Writing Traits*

ACKNOWLEDGMENTS

A project such as this is always the work of many. I feel especially honored to have had input from teachers whose shared thinking, willingness to pilot lessons, and advocacy for children have helped to shape and mold this resource. Special thanks go to Sally Wells, Marie Govro, Leah Shook, Katy Taylor, Kathryn McInnis, Ellen Arnold, Nick Gelbard, Kathryn Welch, Linda Watson, Jan Woodbury, Mary Hurliman, Teresa Therriault, and Gretchen Nelson.

Jan McCall has been a key player in the development of this concept over the last four years. Her knowledge of children's books, commitment to developmentally appropriate practice, and her love of literacy have been a guiding light as this project has evolved. We spent many hours joyfully reading and thinking together while selecting books for the lessons and the Booklinks.

Pat Dragan, Heinemann author and wonderful primary teacher, shared her thinking and book suggestions guaranteed to delight young children.

Lynnette Brent has become my pen pal and trusted writing colleague. She has deep knowledge of literacy instruction, is one of those rare individuals who understands how to shepherd reading development from emergent to fluent readers, and has an uncanny ability to craft language that will entice and extend the thinking of children. Her humorous poetry and several smartly crafted Readers Theater scripts grace this resource.

Many thanks go to the Heinemann *first*hand team, along with Cynthia Nye, for their expertise and careful shepherding of the manuscript as it moved through production. Lesa Scott, Tina Miller, and Michael Cirone in particular have been instrumental in turning the vision into reality.

Lesson Matrix

This chart identifies the mentor text used in the model lesson for each standard. (Standards for Writing Traits have two mentor texts and model lessons.) Booklinks are other wonderful books that help children expand and practice the standard. Use the lesson planner provided in the guide and on the *Printable Resources* CD-ROM to create your own lessons using the Booklinks.

LESSON MATRIX							
Standards for COMPREHENSION							
Page Ref	Standard	2/3 Mentor Text	Booklink 1	Booklink 2	Booklink 3	Booklink 4	Booklink 5
1	Use prior knowledge	*Stellaluna* ✓	Alexander and the Wind-Up Mouse	Snowflake Bentley	The Dinosaurs of Waterhouse Hawkins	Alexander and the Terrible, Horrible, No Good, Very Bad Day	Diary of a Worm
5	Ask/answer questions	*Officer Buckle and Gloria* ✓	Owl Moon	Grandfather's Journey	Duke Ellington	Annie and the Old One	Knots on a Counting Rope
9	Make connections	*The Relatives Came* ✓	The Stray Dog	All the Places to Love	If I Were in Charge of the World	The Velveteen Rabbit	Shrek!
13	Connect to experiences of others	*Grandfather's Journey* ✓	Cheyenne Again	The Girl Who Loved Wild Horses	Crow Boy	Wilfrid Gordon McDonald Partridge	The Relatives Came
17	Analyze and evaluate	*It Could Always Be Worse*	Chicken Sunday	Wilma Unlimited	Casey at the Bat	A Chair for My Mother	Martin's Big Words
21	Interpret through explanation	*What Do You Do With a Tail Like This?* ✓	Seven Blind Mice	Snowflake Bentley	Stellaluna	Free Fall	Where the Wild Things Are
25	Interpret through performance	*Snow*	Owl Moon	The Great Kapok Tree	The Story of Jumping Mouse	Jumanji	The Popcorn Book
29	Infer	*Where the Wild Things Are* ✓	Three Little Pigs	The Polar Express	Seven Blind Mice	Annie and the Old One	Mirette on the High Wire
33	Predict	*Tuesday*	Sleeping Ugly	The Ghost-Eye Tree	Sylvester and the Magic Pebble	Mufaro's Beautiful Daughters	Sam, Bangs & Moonshine
37	Draw conclusions	*Crow Boy*	Chicken Sunday	The Story of Jumping Mouse	The True Story of the Three Little Pigss	When I Was Young in the Mountains	Sam, Bangs & Moonshine
41	Compare and contrast	*Lon Po Po* and *Little Red Riding Hood*	The Velveteen Rabbit and Alexander and the Wind-Up Mouse	Martin's Big Words and My Brother Martin	Saint George and the Dragon and The Paper Bag Princess	The Three Pigs and The True Story of the Three Little Pigs	Grandfather's Journey
45	Identify cause and effect	*The Stray Dog*	Crow Boy	Miss Nelson Is Missing!	A River Ran Wild	It Could Always Be Worse	The Little House
49	Identify main ideas and supporting details	*The Art Lesson*	What Do You Do With a Tail Like This?	The Important Book	Knots on a Counting Rope	Sam, Bangs & Moonshine	Amos and Boris
53	Rank important vs. unimportant information	*The Biggest Bear*	Diary of a Worm	Seven Blind Mice	The Man Who Walked Between the Towers	The Dinosaurs of Waterhouse Hawkins	The Story of Jumping Mouse

continued

LESSON MATRIX

Standards for COMPREHENSION, continued

Page Ref	Standard	2/3 Mentor Text	Booklink 1	Booklink 2	Booklink 3	Booklink 4	Booklink 5
57	Represent text graphically	*The Dinosaurs of Waterhouse Hawkins*	Jumanji	Puss In Boots	The Mitten	What Do You Do With a Tail Like This?	Tomorrow's Alphabet
61	Read classic and contemporary works	*Make Way for Ducklings*	The Velveteen Rabbit	The Great Kapok Tree	The Biggest Bear	Don't Let the Pigeon Drive the Bus!	The Polar Express
67	Read for a purpose	*What Do You Do With a Tail Like This?*	The Ugly Duckling	Working Cotton	Martin's Big Words	Q is for Duck	If I Were In Charge of the World
71	Use pictures to support comprehension	*The Ghost-Eye Tree*	Diary of a Worm	Chicken Sunday	Doctor De Soto	Stellaluna	Officer Buckle and Gloria
77	Summarize	*Hansel and Gretel*	The Dinosaurs of Waterhouse Hawkins	The Boy of the Three-Year Nap	The Man Who Walked Between the Towers	Inch by Inch	Seven Blind Mice
81	Distinguish real from make-believe	*Stellaluna*	The Popcorn Book	Snowflake Bentley	Sam, Bangs & Moonshine	What Do You Do With a Tail Like This?	Dogteam

Standards for STORY ELEMENTS

Page Ref	Standard	2/3 Mentor Text	Booklink 1	Booklink 2	Booklink 3	Booklink 4	Booklink 5
85	Distinguish fiction/ nonfiction	*The Man Who Walked Between the Towers*	How Many Days To America?	Saint George and the Dragon	Martin's Big Words	Snowflake Bentley	The Polar Express
89	Sequence of events/plot	*Goggles!*	Alexander and the Wind-Up Mouse	The Story of Jumping Mouse	The Velveteen Rabbit	The Great Kapok Tree	Chicken Little
95	Initiating event and conclusion	*Cheyenne Again*	The Ghost-Eye Tree	Mirandy and Brother Wind	Knots on a Counting Rope	Duke Ellington	Jumanji
101	Climax and falling action	*Casey at the Bat*	Little Red Riding Hood	Puss In Boots	The Biggest Bear	Officer Buckle and Gloria	Saint George and the Dragon
107	Main idea	*Snowflake Bentley*	Amos and Boris	A Chair for My Mother	What Do You Do With a Tail Like This?	Martin's Big Words	It Could Always Be Worse
111	Setting	*Owl Moon*	Snowflake Bentley	Tuesday	Miss Rumphius	How Many Days to America?	Dogteam
117	Character development	*Mufaro's Beautiful Daughters*	Alexander and the Terrible, Horrible, No Good, Very Bad Day	Mirandy and Brother Wind	Shrek!	Song and Dance Man	Annie and the Old One
121	Narration and dialogue	*When Sophie Gets Angry—Really, Really Angry*	Mufaro's Beautiful Daughters	The Polar Express	The Lorax	The Frog Prince Continued	Sleeping Ugly
125	Theme and author's purpose	*The Ugly Duckling*	The True Story of the Three Little Pigs	Ashanti to Zulu	Chicken Sunday	Dogteam	Miss Rumphius
131	Culture in literature	*Cheyenne Again*	Grandfather's Journey	The Girl Who Loved Wild Horses	Lon Po Po	Going Home	Mufaro's Beautiful Daughters
135	Problem/solution	*Puss In Boots*	Wilma Unlimited	Chicken Sunday	Inch by Inch	Lon Po Po	It Could Always Be Worse

continued

LESSON MATRIX

Standards for VOCABULARY/LITERARY LANGUAGE

Page Ref	Standard	2/3 Mentor Text	Booklink 1	Booklink 2	Booklink 3	Booklink 4	Booklink 5
141	Vocabulary	*Sylvester and the Magic Pebble*	Dogteam	Mirandy and Brother Wind	Doctor De Soto	Snowflake Bentley	Lilly's Purple Plastic Purse
145	Context clues	*Mufaro's Beautiful Daughters*	Chrysanthemum	Sylvester and the Magic Pebble	Owen	Stellaluna	Lon Po Po
151	Literary/figurative language leads	Leads: *Mirandy and Brother Wind, Frederick, Stellaluna,* and *Shrek!*	Endings: The Polar Express, The Story of Jumping Mouse, Owl Moon, Annie and the Old One	Home Place	Endings: Make Way for Ducklings, Goldilocks and the Three Bears, Little Red Riding Hood, Martin's Big Words	Saint George and the Dragon	The Snowy Day, Where the Wild Things Are
155	Multiple-meaning words	*A Chocolate Moose for Dinner*	The King Who Rained	Dandelion	Amelia Bedelia	The True Story of the Three Little Pigs	Jim and the Beanstalk
161	Alliteration	*Some Smug Slug*	Chicken Little	Possum Magic	Shrek!	Dr. Seuss's ABC	How the Grinch Stole Christmas
167	Onomatopoeia	*Kitten's First Full Moon*	Mirandy and Brother Wind	Blueberries for Sal	Click, Clack, Moo: Cows That Type	Peter Rabbit	Too Much Noise
173	Transition words	*Goldilocks and the Three Bears*	Stone Soup	Rotten Ralph	The Mitten	The Bremen-Town Musicians	Make Way for Ducklings

Standards for LITERARY ELEMENTS AND DEVICES

Page Ref	Standard	2/3 Mentor Text	Booklink 1	Booklink 2	Booklink 3	Booklink 4	Booklink 5
179	Point of view	*The True Story of the Three Little Pigs*	The Girl Who Loved Wild Horses	Wilfrid Gordon McDonald Partridge	Where the Wild Things Are	Tuesday	Don't Let the Pigeon Drive the Bus!
183	Personification	*Little Bear's Visit*	The Ghost-Eye Tree	Officer Buckle and Gloria	Frederick	Rotten Ralph	Doctor De Soto
187	Foreshadowing	*Strega Nona*	The Biggest Bear	Lon Po Po	Grandfather's Journey	Miss Rumphius	Alexander and the Wind-Up Mouse
191	Flashback	*The True Story of the Three Little Pigs*	The Dinosaurs of Waterhouse Hawkins	Home Place	The Keeping Quilt	The Day Jimmy's Boa Ate the Wash	Roxaboxen
197	Simile/metaphor	*Seven Blind Mice*	Quick as A Cricket	The Girl Who Loved Wild Horses	Snowflake Bentley	The Polar Express, The Night Before Christmas	Metaphor: Tar Beach; Encounter; White Snow, Bright Snow
201	Allusion	*Sleeping Ugly*	Goldilocks Returns	Jim and the Beanstalk	Each Peach Pear Plum	The Frog Prince Continued	The True Story of the Three Little Pigs
207	Repetition	*When I Was Young in the Mountains*	Rain Makes Applesauce	Alexander and the Terrible, Horrible, No Good, Very Bad Day	Click, Clack, Moo: Cows That Type	The Important Book	King Bidgood's in the Bathtub
211	Exaggeration	*Cloudy With a Chance of Meatballs*	Click, Clack, Moo: Cows That Type	Millions of Cats	May I Bring A Friend?	The Boy of the Three-Year Nap	Rotten Ralph

continued

Standards for LITERARY ELEMENTS AND DEVICES, continued

Page Ref	Standard	2/3 Mentor Text	Booklink 1	Booklink 2	Booklink 3	Booklink 4	Booklink 5
217	Poetic justice	*Doctor De Soto*	Mufaro's Beautiful Daughters	The Quicksand Book	Inch by Inch	Why Mosquitoes Buzz in People's Ears	Strega Nona
223	Irony	*The Frog Prince Continued*	Petunia	Pinkerton, Behave!	Four Dollars and Fifty Cents	The Amazing Bone	Frederick

Standards for GENRE

Page Ref	Standard	2/3 Mentor Text	Booklink 1	Booklink 2	Booklink 3	Booklink 4	Booklink 5
229	Distinguishing features of genres (poetry)	*Heartland*	Mirandy and Brother Wind	Jumanji	The Dinosaurs of Waterhouse Hawkins	Stellaluna	The Ugly Duckling
233	Nonfiction genres	*Tomorrow's Alphabet*	(a textbook or nonfiction resource)	What Do You Do With a Tail Like This?	Martin's Big Words	The Popcorn Book	Snowflake Bentley
237	Biography	*Martin's Big Words*	Grandfather's Journey	Duke Ellington	The Man Who Walked Between the Towers	The Dinosaurs of Waterhouse Hawkins	Wilma Unlimited
243	Fantasy	*Jumanji*	Roxaboxen	Possum Magic	Where the Wild Things Are	Sector 7	Tuesday
249	Fairy tales	*Rumpelstiltskin*	The Frog Prince Continued	The Paper Bag Princess	Lon Po Po	The Ugly Duckling	Puss In Boots
255	Alphabet book	*Ashanti to Zulu*	Q is for Duck	The Z was Zapped	A, My Name Is Alice	Tomorrow's Alphabet	The Ocean Alphabet Book

Standards for WRITING TRAITS

Page Ref	Standard	2/3 Mentor Text	2/3 Mentor Text	Booklink 1	Booklink 2	Booklink 3	Booklink 4
261	Ideas	*Snowflake Bentley*	*When I Was Young in the Mountains*	A Tree Is Nice	Grandfather's Journey	What Do You Do With a Tail Like This?	(a Gail Gibbons book)
271	Organization	*Tuesday*	*The Important Book*	So Far from the Sea	Snowflake Bentley	Tomorrow's Alphabet	Jumanji
281	Voice	*Officer Buckle and Gloria*	*Heartland*	Gleam and Glow	Diary of a Worm	If I Were in Charge of the World	I'm in Charge of Celebrations
289	Word Choice	*Owl Moon*	*Jumanji*	Sylvester and the Magic Pebble	Q is for Duck	The Polar Express	The Snowman
299	Sentence Fluency	*Dogteam*	*The Relatives Came*	Stellaluna	Amos and Boris	The Important Book	Chicken Sunday
311	Conventions	*Yo! Yes?*	*The Ghost-Eye Tree*	Where the Wild Things Are	No, David!	Wilfrid Gordon McDonald Partridge	Officer Buckle and Gloria

Title List

This chart will help you locate lessons that fit each title. Mentor Lessons use the title as a mentor text. Booklinks list standards for which the title is an excellent extension text. Use the lesson planner in this guide and on the *Printable Resources* CD-ROM to create lessons for Booklinks. "Strand" identifies the tabbed section in which you will find each lesson in the lesson book. "Standard" identifies the lesson's focus.

TITLE LIST		
Book Title, Author, and Publisher	Mentor Lessons Strand/Standard	Booklinks Strand/Standard
A, My Name is Alice Jane E. Bayer Dial		Genre/Alphabet book
Alexander and the Terrible, Horrible, No Good, Very Bad Day Judith Viorst Atheneum		Comprehension/Use prior knowledge Story Elements/Character development Literary Elements and Devices/Repetition
Alexander and the Wind-Up Mouse Leo Lionni Pantheon		Comprehension/Use prior knowledge Comprehension/Compare and contrast Story Elements/Sequence of events/plot Literary Elements and Devices/Foreshadowing
All the Places to Love Patricia MacLachlan Joanna Cotler		Comprehension/Make connections
Amazing Bone, The William Steig Farrar, Straus and Giroux		Literary Elements and Devices/Irony
Amelia Bedelia Peggy Parish HarperFestival		Vocabulary/Literary Language/ Multiple-meaning words
Amos and Boris William Steig Farrar, Straus and Giroux		Comprehension/Identify main ideas and details Story Elements/Main idea Writing Traits/Sentence fluency
Annie and the Old One Miska Miles Little, Brown Young Readers		Comprehension/Ask/answer questions Comprehension/Infer Story Elements/Character development Vocabulary/Literary Language/Literary/ figurative language endings

	TITLE LIST	
Book Title, Author, and Publisher	Mentor Lessons Strand/Standard	Booklinks Strand/Standard
Art Lesson, The Tomie dePaola Trumpet	Comprehension/Identify main ideas and details	
Ashanti to Zulu Margaret Musgrove Dial	Genre/Alphabet book	Story Elements/Theme and author's purpose
Biggest Bear, The Lynd Ward Houghton	Comprehension/Rank important vs. unimportant information	Comprehension/Read classic and contemporary works Story Elements/Climax and falling action Literary Elements and Devices/Foreshadowing
Blueberries for Sal Robert McCloskey Viking		Vocabulary/Literary Language/Onomatopoeia
Boy of the Three-Year Nap, The Dianne Snyder Houghton Mifflin		Comprehension/Summarize Literary Elements and Devices/Exaggeration
Bremen-Town Musicians, The Ilse Plume Doubleday		Vocabulary/Literary Language/Transition words
Casey at the Bat Ernest Thayer Handprint	Story Elements/Climax and falling action	Comprehension/Analyze and evaluate
Chair for My Mother, A Vera B. Williams Greenwillow		Comprehension/Analyze and evaluate Story Elements/Main idea
Cheyenne Again Eve Bunting Clarion Books	Story Elements/Initiating event and conclusion Story Elements/Culture in literature	Comprehension/Connect to experiences of others
Chicken Little Steven Kellogg HarperTrophy		Story Elements/Sequence of events/plot Vocabulary/Literary Language/Alliteration
Chicken Sunday Patricia Polacco Philomel		Comprehension/Analyze and evaluate Comprehension/Draw conclusions Comprehension/Use pictures to support comprehension Story Elements/Theme and author's purpose Story Elements/Problem/solution Writing Traits/Sentence fluency
Chocolate Moose for Dinner, A Fred Gwynne Aladdin	Vocabulary/Literary Language/ Multiple-meaning words	

TITLE LIST

Book Title, Author, and Publisher	Mentor Lessons Strand/Standard	Booklinks Strand/Standard
Chrysanthemum Kevin Henkes Greenwillow		Vocabulary/Literary Language/Context clues
Click, Clack, Moo: Cows That Type Doreen Cronin Simon & Schuster		Vocabulary/Literary Language/Onomatopoeia Literary Elements and Devices/Repetition Literary Elements and Devices/Exaggeration
Cloudy With a Chance of Meatballs Judy Barrett Aladdin	Literary Elements and Devices/Exaggeration	
Crow Boy Taro Yashima Viking	Comprehension/Draw conclusions	Comprehension/Connect to experiences of others Comprehension/Identify cause and effect
Dandelion Don Freeman Viking		Vocabulary/Literary Language/Multiple-meaning words
Day Jimmy's Boa Ate the Wash, The Trinka Hakes Noble Dial		Literary Elements and Devices/Flashback
Diary of a Worm Doreen Cronin Joanna Cotler		Comprehension/Use prior knowledge Comprehension/Rank important vs. unimportant information Comprehension/Use pictures to support comprehension Writing Traits/Voice
Dinosaurs of Waterhouse Hawkins, The Barbara Kerley Scholastic	Comprehension/Represent text graphically	Comprehension/Use prior knowledge Comprehension/Rank important vs. unimportant information Comprehension/Summarize Literary Elements and Devices/Flashback Genre/Distinguishing features of genre Genre/Biography
Doctor De Soto William Steig Farrar	Literary Elements and Devices/Poetic justice	Comprehension/Use pictures to support comprehension Vocabulary/Literary Language/Vocabulary Literary Elements and Devices/Point of view
Dogteam Gary Paulsen Bantam	Writing Traits/Sentence fluency	Comprehension/Distinguish real from make-believe Story Elements/Setting Story Elements/Theme and author's purpose Vocabulary/Literary Language/Vocabulary

	TITLE LIST	
Book Title, Author, and Publisher	**Mentor Lessons** **Strand/Standard**	**Booklinks** **Strand/Standard**
Don't Let the Pigeon Drive the Bus! Mo Willems Hyperion		Comprehension/Read classic and contemporary works Literary Elements and Devices/Point of view
Dr. Seuss's ABC Dr. Seuss Random House		Vocabulary/Literary Language/Alliteration
Duke Ellington Andrea Davis Pinkney Jump at the Sun		Comprehension/Ask/answer questions Story Elements/Initiating event and conclusion Genre/Biography
Each Peach Pear Plum Janet and Allan Ahlberg Viking		Literary Elements and Devices/Allusion
Encounter Jane Yolen Harcourt		Literary Elements and Devices/Simile/metaphor
Four Dollars and Fifty Cents Eric A. Kimmel Holiday House		Literary Elements and Devices/Irony
Frederick Leo Lionni Pantheon	Vocabulary/Literary Language/Literary/ figurative language leads	Literary Elements and Devices/Point of view Literary Elements and Devices/Irony
Free Fall David Wiesner HarperCollins		Comprehension/Interpret through explanation
Frog Prince Continued, The Jon Scieszka Puffin	Literary Elements and Devices/Irony	Story Elements/Narration and dialogue Literary Elements and Devices/Allusion Genre/Fairy tale
Ghost-Eye Tree, The Bill Martin, Jr., and John Archambault Henry Holt and Co.	Comprehension/Use pictures to support comprehension Writing Traits/Conventions (the ellipse)	Comprehension/Predict Story Elements/Initiating event and conclusion Literary Elements and Devices/Point of view
Girl Who Loved Wild Horses, The Paul Goble Atheneum		Comprehension/Connect to experiences of others Story Elements/Culture in literature Literary Elements and Devices/Point of view Literary Elements and Devices/Simile/metaphor
Gleam and Glow Eve Bunting Harcourt		Writing Traits/Voice

	TITLE LIST	
Book Title, Author, and Publisher	Mentor Lessons Strand/Standard	Booklinks Strand/Standard
Goggles! Ezra Jack Keats Macmillan	Story Elements/Sequence of events/plot	
Going Home Eve Bunting Trophy		Story Elements/Culture in literature
Goldilocks and the Three Bears James Marshall Dial	Vocabulary/Literary Language/Transition words	Vocabulary/Literary Language/Literary/figurative language endings
Goldilocks Returns Lisa Campbell Ernst Simon & Schuster		Literary Elements and Devices/Allusion
Grandfather's Journey Allen Say Houghton	Comprehension/Connect to experiences of others	Comprehension/Ask/answer questions Comprehension/Compare and contrast Story Elements/Culture in literature Literary Elements and Devices/Foreshadowing Genre/Biography Writing Traits/Ideas
Great Kapok Tree, The Lynne Cherry Gulliver Green		Comprehension/Interpret through performance Comprehension/Read classic and contemporary works Story Elements/Sequence of events/plot
Hansel and Gretel Rika Lesser Dodd	Comprehension/Summarize	
Heartland Diane Siebert HarperCollins	Genre/Distinguishing features of genre (poetry) Writing Traits/Voice	
Home Place Crescent Dragonwagon Atheneum		Vocabulary/Literary Language/Literary/figurative language Literary Elements and Devices/Flashback
How Many Days to America? Eve Bunting Clarion		Story Elements/Distinguish fiction/nonfiction Story Elements/Setting
How the Grinch Stole Christmas Dr. Seuss Random House		Vocabulary/Literary Language/Alliteration
If I Were in Charge of the World Judith Viorst Atheneum		Comprehension/Make connections Comprehension/Read for a purpose Writing Traits/Voice

	TITLE LIST	
Book Title, Author, and Publisher	Mentor Lessons Strand/Standard	Booklinks Strand/Standard
I'm in Charge of Celebrations Byrd Baylor Aladdin		Writing Traits/Voice
Important Book, The Margaret Wise Brown HarperTrophy	Writing Traits/Organization (main idea and details)	Comprehension/Identify main ideas and details Literary Elements and Devices/Repetition Writing Traits/Sentence fluency
Inch by Inch Leo Lionni HarperTrophy		Comprehension/Summarize Story Elements/Problem/solution Literary Elements and Devices/Poetic justice
It Could Always Be Worse Margot Zemach Farrar	Comprehension/Analyze and evaluate	Comprehension/Identify cause and effect Story Elements/Main idea Story Elements/Problem/solution
Jim and the Beanstalk Raymond Briggs Putnam		Vocabulary/Literary Language/ Multiple-meaning words Literary Elements and Devices/Allusion
Jumanji Chris Van Allsburg Houghton Mifflin	Genre/Fantasy Writing Traits/Word choice	Comprehension/Interpret through performance Comprehension/Represent text graphically Story Elements/Initiating event and conclusion Genre/Distinguishing features of genre Writing Traits/Organization
Keeping Quilt, The Patricia Polacco Simon & Schuster		Literary Elements and Devices/Flashback
King Bidgood's in the Bathtub Audrey Wood Harcourt		Literary Elements and Devices/Repetition
King Who Rained, The Fred Gwynne Aladdin		Vocabulary/Literary Language/ Multiple-meaning words
Kitten's First Full Moon Kevin Henkes Greenwillow	Vocabulary/Literary Language/Onomatopoeia	
Knots on a Counting Rope Bill Martin, Jr., and John Archambault Henry Holt and Co.		Comprehension/Ask/answer questions Comprehension/Identify main ideas and details Story Elements/Initiating event and conclusion
Lilly's Purple Plastic Purse Kevin Henkes Greenwillow		Vocabulary/Literary Language/Vocabulary

TITLE LIST

Book Title, Author, and Publisher	Mentor Lessons Strand/Standard	Booklinks Strand/Standard
Little Bear's Visit Else H. Minarik Harper	Literary Elements and Devices/Personification	
Little House, The Virginia Lee Burton Houghton Mifflin		Comprehension/Identify cause and effect
Little Red Riding Hood Trina Schart Hyman Holiday House	Comprehension/Compare and contrast	Story Elements/Climax and falling action Vocabulary/Literary Language/Literary/ figurative language endings
Lon Po Po Ed Young Philomel	Comprehension/Compare and contrast	Story Elements/Culture in literature Story Elements/Problem/solution Vocabulary/Literary Language/Context clues Literary Elements and Devices/Foreshadowing Genre/Fairy tale
Lorax, The Dr. Seuss Random House		Story Elements/Narration and dialogue
Make Way for Ducklings Robert McCloskey Viking	Comprehension/Read classic and contemporary works	Vocabulary/Literary Language/Literary/figurative language endings Vocabulary/Literary Language/Transition words
Man Who Walked Between the Towers, The Mordicai Gerstein Roaring Brook Press/Millbrook Press	Story Elements/Distinguish fiction/nonfiction	Comprehension/Rank important vs. unimportant information Comprehension/Summarize Genre/Biography
Martin's Big Words Doreen Rapport Jump at the Sun/Hyperion	Genre/Biography	Comprehension/Analyze and evaluate Comprehension/Compare and contrast Comprehension/Read for a purpose Story Elements/Distinguish fiction/nonfiction Story Elements/Main idea Vocabulary/Literary Language/Literary/ figurative language endings Genre/Nonfiction genres
May I Bring a Friend? Beatrice Schenk De Regniers Aladdin		Literary Elements and Devices/Exaggeration
Millions of Cats Wanda Gag Putnam		Literary Elements and Devices/Exaggeration
Mirandy and Brother Wind Patricia C. McKissack Knopf	Vocabulary/Literary Language/Literary/ figurative language leads	Story Elements/Initiating event and conclusion Story Elements/Character development Vocabulary/Literary Language/Vocabulary Vocabulary/Literary Language/Onomatopoeia Genre/Distinguishing features of genre

Book Title, Author, and Publisher	Mentor Lessons Strand/Standard	Booklinks Strand/Standard
TITLE LIST		
Mirette on the High Wire Emily Arnold McCully Putnam		Comprehension/Infer
Miss Nelson Is Missing! Harry Allard Houghton Mifflin		Comprehension/Identify cause and effect
Miss Rumphius Barbara Cooney Viking		Story Elements/Setting Story Elements/Theme and author's purpose Literary Elements and Devices/Foreshadowing
Mitten, The Jan Brett Scholastic		Comprehension/Represent text graphically Vocabulary/Literary Language/Transition words
Mufaro's Beautiful Daughters John Steptoe Lothrop	Story Elements/Character development Vocabulary/Literary Language/Context clues	Comprehension/Predict Story Elements/Narration and dialogue Story Elements/Culture in literature Literary Elements and Devices/Poetic justice
My Brother Martin Christine King Farris Simon & Schuster		Comprehension/Compare and contrast
Night Before Christmas, The Clement Clarke Moore Little, Brown		Literary Elements and Devices/Simile/metaphor
No, David! David Shannon Scholastic		Writing Traits/Conventions
Ocean Alphabet Book, The Jerry Pallotta Charlesbridge Publishing		Genre/Alphabet book
Officer Buckle and Gloria Peggy Rathmann Putnam	Comprehension/Ask/answer questions Writing Traits/Voice	Comprehension/Use pictures to support comprehension Story Elements/Climax and falling action Literary Elements and Devices/Point of view Writing Traits/Conventions
Owen Kevin Henkes Greenwillow		Vocabulary/Literary Language/Context clues
Owl Moon Jane Yolen Philomel	Story Elements/Setting Writing Traits/Word choice	Comprehension/Ask/answer questions Comprehension/Interpret through performance Vocabulary/Literary Language/Literary/figurative language endings

TITLE LIST

Book Title, Author, and Publisher	Mentor Lessons Strand/Standard	Booklinks Strand/Standard
Paper Bag Princess, The Robert N. Munsch Scholastic		Comprehension/Compare and contrast Genre/Fairy tale
Peter Rabbit Beatrix Potter Grosset & Dunlap		Vocabulary/Literary Language/Onomatopoeia
Petunia Roger Duvoisin Knopf		Literary Elements and Devices/Irony
Pinkerton, Behave! Steven Kellogg Puffin		Literary Elements and Devices/Irony
Polar Express, The Chris Van Allsburg Houghton Mifflin		Comprehension/Infer Comprehension/Read classic and contemporary works Story Elements/Distinguish fiction/nonfiction Story Elements/Narration and dialogue Vocabulary/Literary Language/Literary/ figurative language endings Literary Elements and Devices/Simile/ metaphor Writing Traits/Word choice
Popcorn Book, The Tomie dePaola Holiday House		Comprehension/Interpret through performance Comprehension/Distinguish real from make-believe Genre/Nonfiction genres
Possum Magic Mem Fox Gulliver		Vocabulary/Literary Language/Alliteration Genre/Fantasy
Puss In Boots Malcolm Arthur Di Capua/Farrar	Story Elements/Problem/solution	Comprehension/Represent text graphically Story Elements/Climax and falling action Genre/Fairy tale
Q is for Duck Mary Elting and Michael Folsom Clarion		Comprehension/Read for a purpose Genre/Alphabet book Writing Traits/Word choice
Quick as a Cricket Audrey Wood Child's Play		Literary Elements and Devices/Simile/metaphor

	TITLE LIST	
Book Title, Author, and Publisher	**Mentor Lessons** Strand/Standard	**Booklinks** Strand/Standard
Quicksand Book, The Tomie dePaola Holiday House		Literary Elements and Devices/Poetic justice
Rain Makes Applesauce Julian Scheer Holiday House		Literary Elements and Devices/Repetition
Relatives Came, The Cynthia Rylant Bradbury	Comprehension/Make connections Writing Traits/Sentence fluency	Comprehension/Connect to experiences of others
River Ran Wild, A Lynne Cherry Voyager		Comprehension/Identify cause and effect
Rotten Ralph Jack Gantos Houghton Mifflin		Vocabulary/Literary Language/Transition words Literary Elements and Devices/Point of view Literary Elements and Devices/Exaggeration
Roxaboxen Alice McLerran HarperCollins		Literary Elements and Devices/Flashback Genre/Fantasy
Rumpelstiltskin Paul O. Zelinsky Dutton	Genre/Fairy tale	
Saint George and the Dragon Margaret Hodges Little, Brown		Comprehension/Compare and contrast Story Elements/Distinguish fiction/nonfiction Story Elements/Climax and falling action Vocabulary/Literary Language/Literary/ figurative language
Sam, Bangs & Moonshine Evaline Ness Henry Holt and Co.		Comprehension/Predict Comprehension/Draw conclusions Comprehension/Identify main ideas and details Comprehension/Distinguish real from make-believe
Sector 7 David Wiesner Clarion		Genre/Fantasy
Seven Blind Mice Ed Young Philomel	Literary Elements and Devices/Simile/metaphor	Comprehension/Interpret through explanation Comprehension/Infer Comprehension/Rank important vs. unimportant information Comprehension/Summarize

TITLE LIST

Book Title, Author, and Publisher	Mentor Lessons Strand/Standard	Booklinks Strand/Standard
Shrek! William Steig Farrar	Vocabulary/Literary Language/Literary/ figurative language leads	Comprehension/Make connections Story Elements/Character development Vocabulary/Literary Language/Alliteration
Sleeping Ugly Jane Yolen Putnam	Literary Elements and Devices/Allusion	Comprehension/Predict Story Elements/Narration and dialogue
Snow Uri Shulevitz Farrar	Comprehension/Interpret through performance	
Snowflake Bentley Jacqueline Briggs Martin Houghton	Story Elements/Main idea Writing Traits/Ideas	Comprehension/Use prior knowledge Comprehension/Interpret through explanation Comprehension/Distinguish real from make-believe Story Elements/Distinguish fiction/nonfiction Story Elements/Setting Vocabulary/Literary Language/Vocabulary Literary Elements and Devices/Simile/metaphor Genre/Nonfiction genres Writing Traits/Organization
Snowman, The Raymond Briggs Random House		Writing Traits/Word choice
Snowy Day, The Ezra Jack Keats Viking		Vocabulary/Literary Language/ Literary/figurative language
So Far from the Sea Eve Bunting Clarion		Writing Traits/Organization
Some Smug Slug Pamela Duncan Edwards HarperTrophy	Vocabulary/Literary Language/Alliteration	
Song and Dance Man Karen Ackerman Knopf		Story Elements/Character development
Stellaluna Janell Cannon Harcourt	Comprehension/Use prior knowledge Comprehension/Distinguish real from make-believe Vocabulary/Literary Language/Literary/ figurative language leads	Comprehension/Interpret through explanation Comprehension/Use pictures to support comprehension Vocabulary/Literary Language/Context clues Genre/Distinguishing features of genre Writing Traits/Sentence fluency
Stone Soup Marcia Brown Aladdin		Vocabulary/Literary Language/Transition words

	TITLE LIST	
Book Title, Author, and Publisher	Mentor Lessons Strand/Standard	Booklinks Strand/Standard
Story of Jumping Mouse, The John Steptoe HarperTrophy		Comprehension/Interpret through performance Comprehension/Draw conclusions Comprehension/Rank important vs. unimportant information Story Elements/Sequence of events/plot Vocabulary/Literary Language/Literary/ figurative language endings
Stray Dog, The Marc Simont HarperCollins	Comprehension/Identify cause and effect	Comprehension/Make connections
Strega Nona Tomie dePaola Simon & Schuster	Literary Elements and Devices/Foreshadowing	Literary Elements and Devices/Poetic justice
Sylvester and the Magic Pebble William Steig Windmill Books	Vocabulary/Literary Language/Vocabulary	Comprehension/Predict Vocabulary/Literary Language/Context clues Writing Traits/Word choice
Tar Beach Faith Ringgold Crown Books		Literary Elements and Devices/Simile/metaphor
Three Pigs, The David Wiesner Clarion		Comprehension/Infer Comprehension/Compare and contrast
Tomorrow's Alphabet George Shannon Scholastic	Genre/Nonfiction genres	Comprehension/Represent text graphically Genre/Alphabet book Writing Traits/Organization
Too Much Noise Ann McGovern Houghton Mifflin		Vocabulary/Literary Language/Onomatopoeia
Tree is Nice, A Janice May Udry HarperTrophy		Writing Traits/Ideas
True Story of the Three Little Pigs, The Jon Scieszka Viking	Literary Elements and Devices/Point of view Literary Elements and Devices/Flashback	Comprehension/Draw conclusions Comprehension/Compare and contrast Story Elements/Theme and author's purpose Vocabulary/Literary Language/ Multiple-meaning words Literary Elements and Devices/Allusion
Tuesday David Wiesner Clarion	Comprehension/Predict Writing Traits/Organization (passage of time)	Story Elements/Setting Literary Elements and Devices/Point of view Genre/Fantasy
Ugly Duckling, The Jerry Pinkney Morrow	Story Elements/Theme and author's purpose	Comprehension/Read for a purpose Genre/Distinguishing features of genre Genre/Fairy tale

Book Title, Author, and Publisher	TITLE LIST	
	Mentor Lessons Strand/Standard	Booklinks Strand/Standard
Velveteen Rabbit, The Margery Williams Doubleday		Comprehension/Make connections Comprehension/Compare and contrast Comprehension/Read classic and contemporary works Story Elements/Sequence of events/plot

What Do You Do With a Tail Like This?
Steve Jenkins and Robin Page
Houghton Mifflin
	Comprehension/Interpret through
	  explanation
	Comprehension/Read for a purpose
		Comprehension/Identify main ideas and details
		Comprehension/Represent text graphically
		Comprehension/Distinguish real from
		  make-believe
		Story Elements/Main idea
		Genre/Nonfiction genres
		Writing Traits/Ideas

When I Was Young in the Mountains Cynthia Rylant Dutton	Literary Elements and Devices/Repetition Writing Traits/Ideas	Comprehension/Draw conclusions
When Sophie Gets Angry—Really, Really Angry Molly Bang Scholastic	Story Elements/Narration and dialogue	
Where the Wild Things Are Maurice Sendak HarperCollins	Comprehension/Infer	Comprehension/Interpret through explanation Vocabulary/Literary Language/Literary/ figurative language Literary Elements and Devices/Point of view Genre/Fantasy Writing Traits/Conventions
White Snow, Bright Snow Alvin Tresselt HarperCollins		Literary Elements and Devices/Simile/metaphor
Why Mosquitoes Buzz in People's Ears Verna Aardema Puffin		Literary Elements and Devices/Poetic justice
Wilfred Gordon McDonald Partridge Mem Fox Kane/Miller		Comprehension/Connect to experiences of others Literary Elements and Devices/Point of view Writing Traits/Conventions
Wilma Unlimited Kathleen Krull Harcourt		Comprehension/Analyze and evaluate Story Elements/Problem/solution Genre/Biography
Working Cotton Sherley Anne Williams Harcourt		Comprehension/Read for a purpose
Yo? Yes! Richard Jackson Orchard	Writing Traits/Conventions (punctuation)	
Z was Zapped, The Chris Van Allsburg Houghton Mifflin		Genre/Alphabet book

READERS THEATER INDEX

Page Ref	Readers Theater Title	Genre: Topic	Teaching Points to Consider	Associated Book Title
148	Approaching the City	Fiction: retell	Context clues, word meaning, theme	*Mufaro's Beautiful Daughters*
52	Art Lesson, The	Fiction: retell	Main idea, sequence	*The Art Lesson*
258	Ashanti to Zulu	Alphabet book: Africa	Alphabet book, culture	*Ashanti to Zulu: African Traditions*
84	Bats	Nonfiction: bats, mammals	Distinguish real from make-believe, summarize	*Stellaluna*
220	Beautiful Day in the Woods, A	Nonfiction: environment, opinion	Poetic justice, point of view, description	*Doctor De Soto*
56	Biggest Bear, The	Fiction: retell	Important vs. unimportant information, main idea, poetry	*The Biggest Bear*
210	Blue Whale	Nonfiction: whales	Repetition, nonfiction	*When I Was Young in the Mountains*
104	Casey at the Bat	Poetry: baseball	Climax, sequence	*Casey at the Bat*
204	Cast of Characters, A	Fiction: retell, fairy tale, folktale	Allusion, inference, connections	*Sleeping Ugly*
144	Celebration of Words, A	Poetry: word choice	Vocabulary, word choice	*Sylvester and the Magic Pebble*
292	Chocolate and Frog	Poetry: chocolate, frog	Word choice, imagery	*Owl Moon*
64	Classic and Contemporary Poems	Poetry: wind, skirts, dinosaurs	Classic and contemporary works	*Make Way for Ducklings*
214	Clouds . . . and Weather	Nonfiction: weather	Exaggeration, summarize	*Cloudy with a Chance of Meatballs*
240	Continuing the Dream	Nonfiction: Martin Luther King, Jr.	Biography, repetition	*Martin's Big Words*
20	Could It Be Worse?	Fiction: retell, folktale	Analyze and evaluate, onomatopoeia, sequence	*It Could Always Be Worse*
40	Crow Boy	Fiction: retell	Draw conclusions, summarize	*Crow Boy*
74	Designed to Survive	Nonfiction: polar bears	Use pictures to support comprehension, summarize, determine importance	*The Ghost-Eye Tree*
60	Dinosaurs of Waterhouse Hawkins, The	Nonfiction: biography, dinosaurs	Represent text graphically, sequence	*The Dinosaurs of Waterhouse Hawkins*
16	Divided Heart	Poetry: multilingual	Connect to experience of other, cultures, point of view	*Grandfather's Journey*
246	Fantasy?	Fiction: animals, weather	Fantasy, interpretation, imagery, word choice	*Jumanji*
296	Favorite Jokes	Fiction: jokes	Word choice, multiple-meaning words, inference	*Jumanji*
268	Field Trip Fiasco	Fiction: retell	Ideas, cause/effect	*When I Was Young in the Mountains*
120	Finding Courage	Fiction: dialogue	Character development, dialogue	*Mufaro's Beautiful Daughters*

continued

READERS THEATER INDEX

Page Ref	Readers Theater Title	Genre: Topic	Teaching Points to Consider	Associated Book Title
124	Fish for Dinner?	Fiction: dialogue, fishing	Narration and dialogue, point of view	*When Sophie Gets Angry—Really, Really Angry . . .*
236	Flight	Nonfiction: airplanes	Nonfiction genre, vocabulary	*Tomorrow's Alphabet*
284	Four-Legged Friend	Poetry: dogs, pets	Voice, connections	*Officer Buckle and Gloria*
36	Frog Song	Fiction: song, frogs	Predict	*Tuesday*
288	Frog, Frog	Poetry: frogs	Voice, point of view	*Heartland*
92	Goldilocks and the Cops	Fiction: retell	Sequence, transition words	*Goggles!*
252	Goldilocks and the Three Bears	Fiction: retell, folktale	Fairy tales, summarize	*Rumpelstiltskin*
80	Hansel and Gretel	Fiction: retell	Summarize, problem/solution	*Hansel and Gretel*
158	Have You Ever Seen?	Fiction: word play	Multiple-meaning words, compound words, question/answer	*A Chocolate Moose for Dinner*
114	Hiding	Poetry: jungle	Setting, imagery, tension	*Owl Moon*
164	Interview with a Slug and . . . a Snail	Fiction: interview, slug and snail facts	Alliteration, compare/contrast	*Some Smug Slug*
318	Jack and Jill	Fiction: retell	Conventions, dialogue, allusion	*The Ghost-Eye Tree*
154	Leads	Poetry: leads	Literary language, writing craft	*Mirandy and Brother Wind, Frederick, Stellaluna,* and *Shrek!*
44	Lion, The	Nonfiction: lions	Compare/contrast	*Lon Po Po and Little Red Riding Hood*
88	Man Who Walked Between the Towers, The	Poetry: biography	Distinguish fiction/nonfiction, imagery, cause/effect	*The Man Who Walked Between the Towers*
278	Octopus, The	Nonfiction: oceans	Organization, text features, summarize	*The Important Book*
8	Officer Buckle and Gloria	Fiction: retell	Questioning	*Officer Buckle and Gloria*
226	Oh, NO!	Fiction: action figures	Irony, climax	*The Frog Prince Continued*
176	On the Beach	Nonfiction: sea turtles	Transition words, sequence	*Goldilocks and the Three Bears*
314	Punctuation Song	Nonfiction: song, punctuation	Conventions	*Yo! Yes?*
138	Puss In Boots	Fiction: retell, fairy tales	Problem/solution, story structure, characterization	*Puss In Boots*
232	Rainbows: A Magic Mix	Nonfiction: weather	Distinguishing features of genres, main idea, summarize	*Heartland*
12	Relatives Came, The	Fiction: retell	Connections	*The Relatives Came*
32	School Day	Poetry: school	Inference, imagery, sequence	*Where the Wild Things Are*
302	Silver Tranquility	Nonfiction: fish	Sentence fluency, imagery, word choice	*Dogteam*

continued

READERS THEATER INDEX

Page Ref	Readers Theater Title	Genre: Topic	Teaching Points to Consider	Associated Book Title
110	Snakes	Nonfiction: reptiles	Main idea	*Snowflake Bentley*
28	Snow	Poetry: snow	Interpret through drama, imagery, verbs	*Snow*
264	Snowflake Bentley	Nonfiction: biography, snow, science	Ideas, sequence	*Snowflake Bentley*
4	Stellaluna: A Poem for Three Voices	Poetry: bats	Using prior knowledge	*Stellaluna*
274	Storm	Poetry: weather, sounds	Organization, passage of time, onomatopoeia	*Tuesday*
48	Stray Dog, The	Fiction: retell	Cause/effect, sequence	*The Stray Dog*
70	Sugar Cookie Song	Nonfiction: song, recipe	Reading for a purpose, read directions, rhyming	*What Do You Do With a Tail Like This?*
186	Sun	Poetry: sun	Personification, compare/contrast, imagery	*Little Bear's Visit*
308	Tadpole	Nonfiction: frogs	Sentence fluency, sentence length, transitions.	*The Relatives Came*
200	This Classroom	Poetry: school	Simile, imagery, description	*Seven Blind Mice*
170	Three Billy Goats, The	Fiction: retell, folktale	Onomatopoeia, compare/contrast	*Kitten's First Full Moon*
98	Trial of Jack . . . and the Beanstalk, The	Fiction: trial transcript, fairy tales	Initiating event and conclusion, point of view	*Cheyenne Again*
194	Trial, The	Fiction: trial	Flashback, point of view	*The True Story of the Three Little Pigs*
128	Ugly Duckling, The	Fiction: retell, fairy tales	Theme, author's purpose, sequence	*The Ugly Duckling*
24	What is Special About an Animal?	Nonfiction: animals	Interpret, summarize	*What Do You Do With a Tail Like This?*
190	What Should We Make?	Poetry: ingredients	Foreshadowing, inference	*Strega Nona*
182	Wolves and Pigs	Nonfiction: wolves, pigs	Point of view, compare/contrast	*The True Story of the Three Little Pigs*
134	Young Bull	Poetry: Native Americans, history	Culture in literature, experiences of others	*Cheyenne Again*

Comprehension

This strand—from utilizing prior knowledge and asking questions to summarizing and distinguishing real from make-believe—focuses on strategies that help learners negotiate the meaning of texts. Within this strand, you will find familiar terms such as *main idea, cause* and *effect, analyze,* and *evaluate* that commonly appear in lists of standards for comprehension.

Stellaluna
Janell Cannon

FOCUS THE LEARNING

Introduction: *Stellaluna* by Janell Cannon is about a baby bat who tries to live with a family of birds. To understand this story, we need to use our prior knowledge about bats and birds to help us understand what is happening.

Think together for a minute. What do you know about bats? What do you know about birds? How are they alike and how are they different? We will write your thinking on a chart to help ourselves remember ways they are alike and different.

Bats   Both   Birds

INTERACTIVE READ-ALOUD
Model and Guide Practice

READ PAGE 1. I am trying to use my prior knowledge about bats now. I remember that bats often eat fruit, and it says here that this is a mother fruit bat. I am going to add "eat fruit" on the chart under "bats." I am also remembering that bats don't have feathers. Their wings have skin and fur but no feathers. As I look at the picture, I can almost see through the mother's wings. I am going to add "skin on wings" to the chart. My prior knowledge reminds me that bats sleep in the day and fly at night. How is this matching with your prior knowledge about bats?

READ TO WHERE STELLALUNA CAN HOLD ON NO LONGER. Wow. I need to really use my prior knowledge here. I am trying to remember if owls eat bats. Is that why the owl attacked the mother? I am noticing, too, that Stellaluna is hanging upside down from the branch. That reminds me that bats sleep upside down. That is definitely different than birds, because prior knowledge reminds me that many birds sleep in nests.

Think together. Use your prior knowledge. Is there anything else you know about bats and birds?

READ TO WHERE STELLALUNA GETS THE GRASSHOPPER. Wait! I know that Stellaluna's mother was a fruit bat. This grasshopper might taste good to a bird, but I wonder what she thinks!

I am also noticing in the picture how the mother bird has a beak and Stellaluna has a mouth and a nose more like a mouse. I knew birds had beaks. This reminds me I should write that on our chart.

Think together. Have you learned anything new that you can add to your prior knowledge so you will know more about bats and birds?

CONTINUE TO THE END. Stop frequently to talk about prior knowledge. Ask: When do you use your prior knowledge to help you understand? Have you learned something to add to your prior knowledge? Should something be added to the chart?

END OF STORY REFLECTION

I am thinking about places where my prior knowledge helped me understand the story better. (Turn to the pages where Stellaluna tries to land on a branch and can't.) My prior knowledge really helped me in this part because I know that bats don't stand on their feet. They hang from their feet so it's no wonder that Stellaluna couldn't land on a branch.

 Think together. Where were you able to use your prior knowledge to understand the story better?

🎭 SHARE THE LEARNING
Focus on Using Prior Knowledge

Tip for Share the Thinking

Guide the students to use their prior knowledge to reflect on what they know about birds and bats without looking at the book. Encourage them to add information to the Venn diagram using their prior knowledge, now that they have added to it with the information in the book.

Use your prior knowledge to decide which attributes go with birds and which ones go with bats.

	Birds	Bats
Eat bugs		
See at night		
Sleep upside down		
Land on a branch		
Eat fruit		
Build a nest		
Have feathers		
Have fur		

Tip for Readers Theater Script

Divide the group into three teams. Each team rehearses their lines. Then all the lines are threaded together. Help teams to focus on reading "Stellaluna: A Poem for Three Voices" with expression and at a rate of fluency that matches the natural rhythms of the language. With increased proficiency, students can meet in teams of three to enjoy the poem.

Stellaluna: A Poem for Three Voices
Readers Theater Adaptation by Linda Hoyt

Team 1	Team 2	Team 3
Stellaluna is a bat.	She can fly at night.	
		And hang by her feet.
She likes to eat fruit	But doesn't like meat.	She was raised by a bird
In a nest with rules.	Now she knows that bats	Are nobody's fools!
Stellaluna	Stellaluna	Stellaluna

EXTEND THE LEARNING

☆ Encourage students to use the term *prior knowledge* when they are recalling information to help them label the action of consciously activating what they know.

☆ Have students draw or write to show what they know on a topic before you read a book to them. After reading, have them add information to show what they have added to their prior knowledge.

☆ Read nonfiction selections on bats and then read *Stellaluna* again. Ask: Did the additional information help make the story easier to understand?

☆ During independent reading, have students use sticky notes to mark places in a text where they realize they are able to activate prior knowledge to assist comprehension. After reading, have partners share their thinking with each other.

☆ Before reading a selection in science or social studies, pause and give students time to meet with partners and share prior knowledge on the topic.

ASSESS THE LEARNING

➤ During small group instruction, take time to ask students about prior knowledge they may have on the topic that will help them understand the story. Then assess their ability to apply what they know while they read.

➤ Confer with readers during independent reading to see if they are consciously applying prior knowledge in an independent setting.

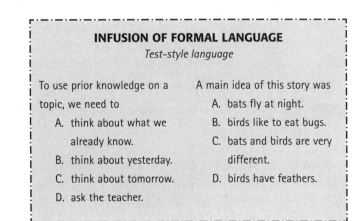

INFUSION OF FORMAL LANGUAGE
Test-style language

To use prior knowledge on a topic, we need to
   A. think about what we already know.
   B. think about yesterday.
   C. think about tomorrow.
   D. ask the teacher.

A main idea of this story was
   A. bats fly at night.
   B. birds like to eat bugs.
   C. bats and birds are very different.
   D. birds have feathers.

Use your prior knowledge to decide which attributes go with birds and which go with bats.

	Birds	Bats
Eat bugs		
See at night		
Sleep upside down		
Land on a branch		
Eat fruit		
Build a nest		
Have feathers		
Have fur		

Stellaluna: A Poem for Three Voices

Readers Theater Adaptation by Linda Hoyt

Team 1	Team 2	Team 3
Stellaluna is a bat.	She can fly at night	
		And hang by her feet.
She likes to eat fruit		
	But doesn't like meat.	She was raised by a bird
In a nest with rules.		
	Now she knows that bats	Are nobody's fools!
Stellaluna	Stellaluna	Stellaluna

Officer Buckle and Gloria
Peggy Rathmann

INTERACTIVE READ-ALOUD
Model and Guide Practice

READ PAGE 1. I wonder why Officer Buckle needs so many rules for safety. There are really a lot of rules up here on his bulletin board. I would think it would be hard to remember that many rules. And, look! It says rule #77 is "Never stand on a swivel chair." It looks like he is hanging in space, and when I look at the other page, there goes the swivel chair. It rolled right out from under his feet. I wonder why he would make up a rule and then break his own rule.

READ PAGE 2. I wonder why the kids are snoring and shooting paper airplanes. Why do you think they aren't listening to him?

Think together. What might be wrong?

READ TO WHERE OFFICER BUCKLE NOTICES HOW FUNNY SAFETY TIPS COULD BE.

Turn to your thinking partner. What are you wondering? Talk to each other and use "I wonder..." to start your thinking together.

READ TO WHERE OFFICER BUCKLE IS WATCHING HIMSELF ON TV. Oh, my. I wonder what he is going to think when he sees Gloria's antics on TV.

What do you think will happen? Remember to say: "I wonder...."

CONTINUE TO THE END. Pause occasionally to give partners time to share their "I wonder..." questions.

END OF STORY REFLECTION

If we were lucky enough to have Peggy Rathmann, the author of this book, come to visit, what questions would we have for her? What would you want to know?

Partners, think together. What "I wonder..." questions would you have? What would you want to ask the author who wrote this funny book?

SHARE THE LEARNING
Focus on Questioning

Tip for Share the Thinking

Have the children look at the photo of the surfer and think of questions they have. Help them remember to use the stem "I wonder...." Jot their questions on the transparency right next to the picture of the surfer. Ensure that children are sticking to questions and not beginning to tell stories. Repeat with the photo of the firefighters.

Tip for Readers Theater Script

For emergent readers, read "Officer Buckle and Gloria" to the children to model fluent expression. Encourage them to ask questions and to consider how the script compares to the original book. With developing and fluent readers, divide the group into narrator teams and present the script as a performance.

EXTEND THE LEARNING

☆ Generate "I wonder..." questions about many stories as well as nonfiction selections so the students see that this is a strategy that helps them engage with any kind of text.

☆ During small group instruction, take time for "I wonder..." questions about selections the children can read themselves.

☆ Invite a guest speaker to class and have the children use "I wonder..." questions to keep them focused on questioning vs. storytelling.

☆ Have partners ask each other questions about books, about what they read at home over the weekend and so on.

☆ Bring children to the Author's Chair with their writing and have the class ask "I wonder..." questions.

☆ Have students keep a log of questions that come to mind during independent reading and share them with partners.

ASSESS THE LEARNING

> During small group instruction, have children generate questions about the text so you can determine how effectively they are using the strategy.

> Confer with readers during independent reading to see if they can generate questions about their independent reading selections.

> Have students jot questions on sticky notes about photographs in books. Then assess the questions to see if they are using question structure or reverting to statements.

INFUSION OF FORMAL LANGUAGE
Test-style language

Why did Officer Buckle fall down at the beginning of the story?
- A. He was giving a speech.
- B. His shoelaces were untied.
- C. He was standing on a chair.
- D. He was watching the kids.

What was the author's message in this story?
- A. Dogs are funnier than policemen.
- B. Officer Buckle and Gloria made a good team.
- C. Kids at school don't listen.
- D. There should be lots of rules.

I wonder . . .

I wonder . . .

Officer Buckle and Gloria

Readers Theater Adaptation by Linda Hoyt

Narrator 1:   Officer Buckle really liked safety tips, and he knew a lot of them.

Narrator 2:   He liked to write them on pieces of paper and put them on his bulletin board.

Narrator 3:   Then he would go to schools and read the safety tips to children.

Narrator 4:   But Officer Buckle put the children to sleep. No one listened to his safety tips

Narrator 1:   even when they were good ones.

Narrator 3:   Then, the police department bought a police dog named Gloria and Officer Buckle took her to the school.

Narrator 2:   While Officer Buckle shared his safety tips, Gloria did all kinds of funny things to act out the safety tips.

Narrator 4:   Officer Buckle didn't see what she was doing.

Narrator 1:   The children loved it and they remembered the safety tips.

Narrator 3:   But Officer Buckle didn't know that Gloria was the star of his show.

Narrator 2:   One day a television news team videotaped Officer Buckle.

Narrator 4:   When he watched himself on TV that night, he saw how funny Gloria was while he was reading his tips.

Narrator 1:   He was so sad that he stopped giving speeches.

Narrator 2:   Gloria tried to do it alone,

Narrator 3:   but it just wasn't the same.

Narrator 4:   They were a team and learned Safety Tip #101.

Everyone: "Always stick with your buddy."

The Relatives Came
Cynthia Rylant

FOCUS THE LEARNING

Introduction: Relatives are family members. Sometimes they live with us and sometimes they don't. Are some of you lucky enough to have grandparents? Do any of you have aunts, uncles, or cousins? Do you get to visit them or have them come to visit you?

Partners, tell each other about your relatives.

INTERACTIVE READ-ALOUD
Model and Guide Practice

LOOK AT THE TITLE PAGE. I am already making connections. Looking at these suitcases and sleeping bags and boxes reminds me of what it was like when my husband and I took our kids on a trip. We had so much stuff we had to pile some of it on top of the car!

READ THE FIRST AND SECOND PAGE OF TEXT. Look at their car. This looks like our car when we had to put things on top. I am also connecting to how much work it is to get ready to go on a trip. I am also making a connection to the food they took. They had an ice chest of pop, crackers, and sandwiches. When we go on a long trip, we take snacks, too.

Have you ever gone somewhere where you had to pack things for a long ride in the car? Did you take snacks and a suitcase of clothes? Share your connections.

READ TO WHERE IT SAYS YOU WOULD HAVE TO GO THROUGH AT LEAST FOUR HUGS TO GET THROUGH THE KITCHEN. This part brings lots of connections for me too. Look at the people on the porch and in the windows. I remember when I was little and our relatives came over. They even messed up my hair! I am also remembering at holiday time, when the house was so full there was nowhere to sit and there was so much noise. It was kind of crazy. It would be hard to be in a place where it was that busy for a long time.

Think together. Have you ever been in a place that was this full of people? Can you make a connection here?

READ TO "ALL THAT NEW BREATHING IN THE HOUSE." Have you ever tried to go to sleep in a strange place or with extra people in your room?

Can you make a connection here? The girl found it hard to sleep. How would it be for you?

CONTINUE TO THE END. Pause occasionally to give partners time to make connections and share them.

END OF STORY REFLECTION

Connections are important when they help us understand a story better. I am thinking about the connections I made and which ones helped me understand this story. I think the most important connections I made were the ones about having a house full of people with the noise and the food and all of the action. It helped me realize what it would have been like to have relatives stay for a really long time.

You made a lot of connections, too. Now you need to think about which connections helped you understand the story better. Think together now. Which connections were important?

Tip for Share the Thinking

Read aloud the list poem "Relatives" with expression. Then ask the children to make connections between the words in the poem and what they remember from the story. Help them to make text-to-self connections as they consider each line. Do they remember times when they were with relatives and people were smiling and laughing? Invite them to add more words or to write their own list poems about the story or about personal experiences with relatives.

Relatives
By Linda Hoyt

Relatives
Smiling
Laughing
Eating
Talking
Loving
Feeling
Relatives!

Tip for Readers Theater Script

For emergent readers, read "The Relatives Came" Readers Theater script to the children, asking them to visualize as you read the script. Read it again, asking the children to dramatize the action to solidify the sequence. Developing readers can read along chorally, read in teams, or read in small groups. As they gain confidence, have them read with fluency and expression, turning the script into a performance.

The Relatives Came
Readers Theater Adaptation by Linda Hoyt

Narrator 1:	It was summer and time for the relatives to come for a visit.
Narrator 2:	They packed up their car, their ice chest, and a pile of bologna sandwiches.
Narrator 3:	They drove for miles and miles and finally arrived at our house.
Narrator 4:	Once they arrived, the house was filled with hugging and laughing
Narrator 5:	and even some crying.
Narrator 6:	Luckily, the relatives would sleep almost anywhere.
Narrator 7:	Some were on the floor,
Narrator 8:	some squeezed in with us, but no one seemed to mind,
Narrators 1 and 2:	except it was hard to go to sleep.
Narrators 3 and 4:	The relatives helped us to fix things that were broken,
Narrators 5 and 6:	pulled weeds in our garden,
Narrators 7 and 8:	and played music on the lawn.
Everyone:	We can't wait for next summer so we can do it all again.

EXTEND THE LEARNING

☆ To help children avoid random connections that take them away from the goal of understanding the story, practice making connections with lots of selections, but always wrap up with thinking about which connections best helped them to understand more deeply.

☆ Support text-to-text connections by reading several versions of a familiar tale, such as *The Three Little Pigs,* or reading a fiction and a nonfiction book on the same topic.

☆ Integrate conversations about connections into small group instruction.

☆ Have learners draw and write about connections they can make with a story.

☆ Encourage students to justify how their connections help them as a learner.

ASSESS THE LEARNING

➤ Listen in as partners tell each other about connections to see if they are retaining their focus on understanding the story.

➤ Confer with readers during independent reading to see if they are able to make meaningful connections.

➤ Ask students to write their most important connections and tell why the connections helped them understand the story.

INFUSION OF FORMAL LANGUAGE
Test-style language

Which line *best* tells how crowded the house became?

    A. You had to go through four hugs to get through the kitchen.

    B. The house was full.

    C. The relatives stayed for weeks.

    D. There were a lot of them.

A conclusion you could draw from this story was

    A. they had animals.

    B. they didn't want to leave.

    C. they liked sleeping on the floor.

    D. the relatives lived a long way away.

Relatives

By Linda Hoyt

Relatives

Smiling

Laughing

Eating

Talking

Loving

Feeling

Relatives!

The Relatives Came

Readers Theater Adaptation by Linda Hoyt

Narrator 1: It was summer and time for the relatives to come for a visit.

Narrator 2: They packed up their car, their ice chest, and a pile of bologna sandwiches.

Narrator 3: They drove for miles and miles and finally arrived at our house.

Narrator 4: Once they arrived, the house was filled with hugging and laughing

Narrator 5: and even some crying.

Narrator 6: Luckily, the relatives would sleep almost anywhere.

Narrator 7: Some were on the floor,

Narrator 8: some squeezed in with us, but no one seemed to mind,

Narrators 1 and 2: except it was hard to go to sleep.

Narrators 3 and 4: The relatives helped us to fix things that were broken,

Narrators 5 and 6: pulled weeds in our garden,

Narrators 7 and 8: and played music on the lawn.

Everyone: We can't wait for next summer so we can do it all again.

© 2007 by Linda Hoyt from *Interactive Read-Alouds, 2–3* (Portsmouth, NH: Heinemann). This page may be reproduced for classroom use only.

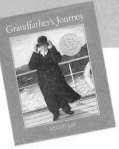

Grandfather's Journey
Allen Say

FOCUS THE LEARNING

Introduction: *Grandfather's Journey* by Allen Say is a true story of a man who had the courage to leave his country and live in a new place. Each country was special to him, and he appreciated each of them. Have any of you ever moved to a new place? Do you have memories of where you used to live that you can share?

 Talk to your thinking partner. Share a memory about where you used to live. Compare your previous home to where you live today. How is it different?

INTERACTIVE READ-ALOUD
Model and Guide Practice

READ PAGES 4–6. I am going to stop reading and look back at these pages so I can think for a moment. I am already noticing how different his clothing is. When he was in Japan, he wore a traditional kimono. When he headed for the United States, he wore a suit and tie. This is a good reminder. People in different cultures dress in different ways. In Japanese culture, he wore a kimono. In American culture, he wore a shirt and tie.

For those of you lucky enough to have lived in another country, what did you notice about the cultural differences in clothing between here and there?

READ TO PAGE 11. I am thinking about culture and the changes he is experiencing. He is dressed in a way that is very different from his homeland. The language is different. He is alone, and yet he has the courage to travel and see so much. I would imagine that he felt really alone. I wonder who helped him with his English.

Think together. What would be the challenges of traveling in a different culture alone? What would you do to help yourself? Do you think he is happy? What evidence do you see that he is having a good time in this new culture?

READ TO PAGE 15.

Talk to your thinking partner. What evidence can we find that he is feeling successful in this new culture?

READ TO PAGE 18. I am thinking again about culture. He has been very successful in America. But he is missing his old friends and the Japanese culture. It says, "He surrounded himself with songbirds, but he could not forget." I wonder if there had been a lot of songbirds in Japan.

Think together. What might we infer about his feelings of having two cultures and two places that are deeply important to him?

CONTINUE TO THE END. Pause occasionally to give partners time to talk about being bicultural and having a love of two places and two cultures in your heart. What would this be like?

END OF STORY REFLECTION

Many people in our world are bicultural. They have lived in and experienced two different countries, two different languages, and two different ways of doing things. What are the advantages of experiencing more than one culture? What are the challenges of moving into a foreign place?

Think together about being bicultural. Think about the story and how it helped us understand what it is like to have two cultures and two very different sets of experiences. If you have had an experience like this, be sure to share.

🙂🙂 SHARE THE LEARNING
Focus on Connecting to Experiences of Others

Tip for Share the Reading	Tip for Readers Theater Script

Read the poem fluently with expression. Then ask the students to join you in a shared reading that might include unison reading, trading every other line, or reading from a whisper with increasing volume until the last line is at full volume. Guide a conversation about this poem. What does this tell us about the author? How is he handling his experiences with two cultures? What are the benefits he is experiencing? What are the challenges?

> I am proud that I can speak both English and Spanish.
>
> But I feel like jelly in a sandwich.
>
> Or a river between two mountains.
>
> I feel my head is filled with words.
>
> It makes me feel smart.
>
> Sometimes I feel as if the Spanish speakers were on one mountain
>
> And the English speakers on another.
>
> I wish we could all be together.
>
> Adapted from Juan Manuel García, 11 years old, from *I Am of Two Places* (Rigby, 1997).

Read "Divided Heart" to the children with soothing, quiet music in the background. Support a conversation about the message of the writer. Then ask the children to read the poem with you, focusing on expressive interpretation. For this selection, pauses and dramatic reading will assist emphasis on the meaning. As children are ready, encourage them to read with partners and independently. If learners feel a connection to the topic, they may enjoy writing poems of their own.

Divided Heart
By Lorena Losada, 8 years old, from *I Am of Two Places* (Rigby, 1997)

> I feel my heart beating.
> It gives me a life full of feelings.
> I think I am two people inside.
> I speak another language
> And I imagine my father's country.
> I know I am from there.
> I dream that my grandmother
> Carries me in her heart.
> There . . . here, always in my soul,
> My family is with me
> And I love them.
> I want to be there
> But I like it better here.
> I feel like my heart is divided.

EXTEND THE LEARNING

☆ Read the various poems in *I Am of Two Places* (Rigby, 1997). Have students analyze them and write their own poetry.

☆ Read *A Day's Work* by Eve Bunting. Discuss truth and how it crosses culture.

☆ Read *Going Home* by Eve Bunting. Focus on the concept of having a home where you live and a home where your relatives and memories are based.

☆ Guide writers in crafting repetitive language focused on their families. "In my family…" could be the lead on each page and would create a predictable structure that even emergent readers and writers could follow.

ASSESS THE LEARNING

> Listen in as partners interpret the story to determine their levels of understanding.

> During small group instruction, read and discuss selections in which culture plays a role.

> Have students write about culture or about the benefits and challenges of being bicultural.

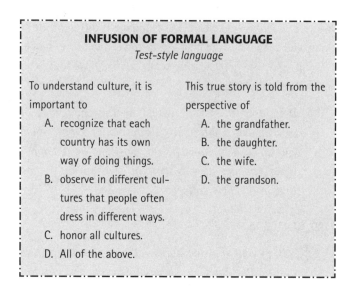

INFUSION OF FORMAL LANGUAGE
Test-style language

To understand culture, it is important to

A. recognize that each country has its own way of doing things.

B. observe in different cultures that people often dress in different ways.

C. honor all cultures.

D. All of the above.

This true story is told from the perspective of

A. the grandfather.

B. the daughter.

C. the wife.

D. the grandson.

I am proud that I can speak both English and Spanish.

But I feel like jelly in a sandwich.

Or a river between two mountains.

I feel my head is filled with words.

It makes me feel smart.

Sometimes I feel as if the Spanish speakers were on one mountain

And the English speakers on another.

I wish we could all be together.

Adapted from Juan Manuel Garcia, 11 years old, from *I Am of Two Places* (Rigby, 1997).

Divided Heart

By Lorena Losada, 8 years old, from *I Am of Two Places* (Rigby, 1997)

I feel my heart beating.

It gives me a life full of feelings.

I think I am two people inside.

I speak another language

And I imagine my father's country.

I know I am from there.

I dream that my grandmother

Carries me in her heart.

There . . . here, always in my soul,

My family is with me

And I love them.

I want to be there

But I like it better here.

I feel like my heart is divided.

It Could Always Be Worse

Margot Zemach

(Handwritten notes, upside-down: "Art Amund us — Quest Cabins", "What Pet Should You Get?", "(H) Goats Are Good")

LEARNING

...have opinions. We analyze things and select our favorites: favorite people, places, and games, ...and what toppings we like on our pizza. Opinions are good as they help us to think critically, to ...aluate things around us. This kind of critical thinking is going to help us as we read *It Could Always Be Worse* by Margot Zemach. Get ready to analyze and evaluate the things that happen.

INTERACTIVE READ-ALOUD
Model and Guide Practice

READ THE FIRST PAGE OF TEXT. I am thinking about this poor man with all of these children in a one-room hut. I wonder why he doesn't get a bigger house or add another room to his hut. It says that he went to the Rabbi for advice, but it makes me wonder if he should have talked to some friends first to see if they would help him add more space.

 What is your opinion of this? What should the man do to solve the problem?

READ THE SECOND PAGE OF TEXT. In my opinion, adding chickens, a rooster, and a goose into a tiny one-room hut that is already overcrowded is not very good advice. I am thinking that the hut will be even more crowded and the poor man will be even more miserable.

 Think together. What opinion do you have? If the man asked you for advice, what would you tell him to do?

READ TO WHERE THE RABBI TELLS HIM TO ADD A GOAT. As I analyze the writing of this author, I realize that she is doing a really good job of showing how frustrated the man is feeling. She is using words that really show emotion and frustration. I can just see the man begging the Rabbi for help.

 Share your opinions about the author's ability to help us understand the man and his feelings. Do you have any other opinions about the story?

READ TO WHERE THE RABBI TELLS HIM TO ADD A COW. This is getting crazy.

 Think together. How would you evaluate this situation? What do you think the man should do?

CONTINUE TO THE END OF THE STORY. Pause occasionally to give partners time to offer opinions and to evaluate the behavior of the characters.

END OF STORY REFLECTION

When we evaluate and give opinions, we can also think about the story as a whole. How would you rate this story? Did you think it was one of the best you have ever read? Was it medium or not so great? Take a minute to think about your evaluation of this story.

 Share your evaluation with your thinking partner. How would you rate this story and why? Share your opinions.

SHARE THE LEARNING
Focus on Analyzing and Evaluating

Tip for Share the Reading

Read the passage fluently showing different voices for the Rabbi and the man. Invite opinions about what the writer did to help us understand what the man was feeling. Underline words and phrases the author used to communicate emotion. As learners evaluate the passage, encourage them to offer suggestions for making emotions even stronger by trying different verbs or adding adjectives.

"Help me!" screamed the man. "My house is a nightmare."

"The Chickens, the rooster, and the goat are going wild!"

"Go home," said the Rabbi calmly.

"Take the cow into your hut. Do it now."

"What is the Rabbi thinking?" wondered the man.

But home he went with heavy feet and a stunned face.

And the cow joined the family and all the other animals in the very loud, busy, messy one-room hut.

Tip for Readers Theater Script

Read "Could It Be Worse?" to the children inviting them to join in on making the sounds. Then invite them to join you in reading chorally. As they are ready, shift to reading the roles in teams or as individuals.

Could It Be Worse?
Readers Theater Adaptation by Linda Hoyt

A long time ago a lady lived in a very old house with her cat.
The door squeaked. Creak, creak.
The window leaked. Drip, drip.
The cat scratched. Scratch, scratch.
The lady thought it was too noisy and went to see a wise man.
The wise man told her to get the cow from the barn and bring it inside.
Now, the door squeaked. Creak, creak.
The window leaked. Drip drip.
The cat scratched. Scratch, scratch.
The cow said, "Moo, moo."
"Too noisy," said the lady and went back to the wise man.
"Get a frog and a donkey and a rooster. Bring them all into your house tonight," said the wise man.
Now, the door squeaked. Creak, creak.
The window leaked. Drip, drip.
The cat scratched. Scratch, scratch.
The cow said, "Moo, moo."
The frog said, "Ribbit, ribbit."
The donkey said, "Hee haw."
The rooster said, "Cockadoodledoo!"
The lady left the animals in the house and went to the barn where she had a very good night's sleep.

EXTEND THE LEARNING

☆ Have students rate each book that you read aloud to them on a scale of 1 to 5. Invite them to share their opinions about why the book deserved the rating.

☆ Evaluate a movie that you watch together, sharing opinions and evaluating the action.

☆ Engage in critical thinking about a problem in the classroom. Use the opinions of the children to guide the group toward a solution.

☆ Rate books you read during small group instruction. Justify ratings with opinions.

ASSESS THE LEARNING

➤ Listen in as partners evaluate the story to determine their levels of understanding.

➤ During small group instruction, invite opinions and assess understanding.

➤ Have students evaluate independent reading books and report on their thinking.

INFUSION OF FORMAL LANGUAGE
Test-style language

In your opinion, which *best* tells about the problem?
  A. A man had too many children.
  B. A poor man lived with his wife and mother.
  C. A one-room hut isn't big enough for a family of nine.
  D. Animals don't belong in houses.

If you were to evaluate the man, you could say he was
  A. a good father.
  B. very frustrated.
  C. happy.
  D. mad.

"Help me!" screamed the man. "My house is a nightmare."

"The chickens, the rooster, and the goat are going wild!"

"Go home," said the Rabbi calmly.

"Take the cow into your hut. Do it now."

"What is the Rabbi thinking?" wondered the man.

But home he went with heavy feet and a stunned face.

And the cow joined the family and all the other animals in the very loud, busy, messy one-room hut.

Could It Be Worse?

Readers Theater Adaptation by Linda Hoyt

A long time ago a lady lived in a very old house with her cat.

The door squeaked. *Creak, creak.*

The window leaked. *Drip, drip.*

The cat scratched. *Scritch, scratch.*

The lady thought it was too noisy and went to see a wise man.

The wise man told her to get the cow from the barn and bring it inside.

Now, the door squeaked. *Creak, creak.*

The window leaked. *Drip drip.*

The cat scratched. *Scritch, scratch.*

The cow said, *"Moo, moo."*

"Too noisy," said the lady and went back to the wise man.

"Get a frog and a donkey and a rooster. Bring them all into your house tonight," said
    the wise man.

Now, the door squeaked. *Creak, creak.*

The window leaked. *Drip, drip.*

The cat scratched. *Scritch, scratch.*

The cow said, *"Moo, moo."*

The frog said, *"Ribbit, ribbit."*

The donkey said, *"Hee haw."*

The rooster said, *"Cockadoodledoo!"*

The lady left the animals in the house and went to the barn where she had a very good
    night's sleep.

What Do You Do With a Tail Like This?
Steve Jenkins and Robin Page

FOCUS THE LEARNING

Introduction: In *What Do You Do With a Tail Like This?* by Steve Jenkins and Robin Page, we are going to look at clues about animal body parts and then try to explain how the animal uses that part of its body.

INTERACTIVE READ-ALOUD
Model and Guide Practice

SHOW THE PAGE WITH THE VARIOUS NOSES. Look at these noses. I am trying to figure out which animal goes with each nose. I need to try to explain what I know about these animals. Right away I know this is the elephant's trunk. To explain how he uses it, I would say that he uses his trunk like we use our arms. He uses his trunk to move things. An elephant can also use his trunk to get water and bring it to his mouth. How did I do at explaining? Let's look at more noses.... How about this long green nose on the left?

 What animal does this long green nose belong to? Think together. What can you explain about the way this animal uses its nose?

READ THE NEXT PAGE WITH THE EXPLANATIONS ABOUT NOSES. The explanations on this page really helped me to interpret the pictures. If I had just looked at the alligator, I wouldn't have thought about how he hides under the water with just his nose sticking out.

 Think together. Did you learn anything new on these pages? Explain your new learning to your partner.

TURN TO THE PAGE WITH THE EARS. Look at these ears. I recognize a rabbit in the middle. I am thinking that this might be a horse on the left.... And I am wondering why a leg is on a page about ears. Do some animals hear with their legs? Can anyone explain this?

 Talk to your thinking partner. What do you know about ears? Can anyone explain which animals might have such interesting ears?

READ THE PAGE OF EXPLANATION ABOUT EARS. This is so interesting! I never knew that rabbits use their ears to stay cool or that crickets have their ears on their knees! If I were to interpret this for someone who hadn't read this book today, I could say animals use their ears in many interesting ways. Rabbits' ears help them stay cool, and crickets' ears are on their knees.

 Think together. What could you tell your family about ears? Think together how you could explain what you know so someone else would understand.

CONTINUE TO THE END. Pause to make guesses about animals and practice explaining and interpreting the learning.

END OF STORY REFLECTION
Explaining helps us to interpret what we read. Think about the whole book. What did you learn? If you were going to explain your learning to someone, what details would you include? We will begin by drawing. Your job is to interpret your learning by drawing about one of the animals. Your drawing needs to explain how the animal uses a body part. Your drawing also needs to include details that will help your partner understand what you have learned.

SHARE THE LEARNING
Focus on Interpreting Through Explanation

Tip for Share the Thinking	Tip for Readers Theater Script

Invite students to look closely at this photograph and interpret what they see. They need to contribute descriptions, possible explanations, and details as they work with their partners. Record their interpretations next to the photograph.

For emergent readers, enjoy "What Is Special About an Animal?" as an echo poem: teacher reads and children echo. For developing readers, enjoy the script as a three-team experience. (You might have learners who need extra support pose the questions, as there is more

predictability in the format.) With increased proficiency, create teams of three to read the poem for fluency and expression.

EXTEND THE LEARNING

☆ Read a wide range of poetry and ask the students to interpret or explain what is happening in each poem.

☆ Look at *The Mysteries of Harris Burdick* by Chris Van Allsburg and have students interpret the pictures.

☆ Have students interpret photographs in nonfiction selections before reading the text.

☆ Guide students as they write interpretations and then share them with each other.

ASSESS THE LEARNING

➤ Listen in as partners interpret a story to determine their levels of understanding.

➤ During small group instruction, ask students to explain things that are not directly stated in the text, adding descriptions and details as needed.

➤ Engage in charades, and pantomime familiar activities while the students interpret what is happening. Assess understanding.

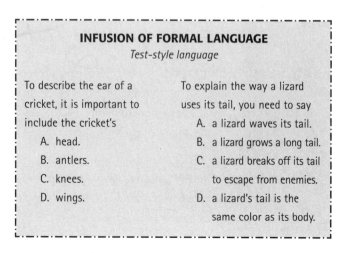

INFUSION OF FORMAL LANGUAGE
Test-style language

To describe the ear of a cricket, it is important to include the cricket's

  A. head.

  B. antlers.

  C. knees.

  D. wings.

To explain the way a lizard uses its tail, you need to say

  A. a lizard waves its tail.

  B. a lizard grows a long tail.

  C. a lizard breaks off its tail to escape from enemies.

  D. a lizard's tail is the same color as its body.

What Is Special About an Animal?

By Linda Hoyt

Team 1	Team 2	Team 3
What is special about an animal's nose?	An elephant uses it like a hose!	A platypus can dig in the mud, mud, mud.
What is special about an animal's ears?	A cricket hears with its ears on its knees.	A rabbit's ears keep it cool as a breeze!
What is special about an animal's tail?	A monkey can hang by its tail from a tree.	A scorpion can sting worse than a bee!
What is special about an animal's mouth?	A pelican can scoop up fish in a pouch.	An anteater has a long sticky tongue—yum, yum!
What is special about the animal world?		
Everything!	Everything!	Everything!

INTERPRET THROUGH PERFORMANCE

Snow
Uri Shulevitz

FOCUS THE LEARNING

Introduction: One of the ways that we can understand books is to act out what we think is happening. As we read *Snow* by Uri Shulevitz, our job is to visualize what is happening and then *SHOW* what it might look like.

INTERACTIVE READ-ALOUD
Model and Guide Practice

READ UNTIL GRANDFATHER SAYS: "IT'S ONLY A SNOWFLAKE." I am trying to visualize what is happening. I visualize that everything is gray. The sky, the buildings, and everything are gray. When a snowflake falls, the boy with his dog is watching really closely. Then I visualize the grandfather, who isn't very excited about just ONE snowflake. If I were the boy, I would act like _____, and if I were the grandfather, I would act like _____. (Act out the possible behavior of the two characters.)

 Turn to your thinking partner. How did I do? Did I act like you think they would have acted?

READ UNTIL YOU COME TO THE LADY WITH THE UMBRELLA. I am going to stop reading for a minute and visualize what is happening. I visualize this really excited boy and the adults who really don't think anything will happen. I think the adults are acting like they are too busy to notice.

 Turn to your thinking partner. Show your partner the face of the boy. Show your partner what the face of the lady would look like.

READ TO WHERE THE LADY, THE MAN, AND THE "RADIO" ARE WALKING WITH SNOW ON THEIR BACKS.

 You know what to do. Turn to your thinking partner. Think together. What do their faces look like now? Show each other. Stand up and show me what you would do if you saw that much snow!

READ TO "FALLING, FALLING EVERYWHERE."

 If you were a snowflake and there was a little bit of wind, what would happen to you? Talk to your partner about how you would float through the air. Now show me…you are a snowflake floating, floating through the air.

CONTINUE TO THE END.

END OF STORY REFLECTION

As readers, we create sensory images to help ourselves understand what is happening. Drama helps us turn our visualizations into action and deepen our understanding.

 Turn and talk to your partner. What was your favorite part of this story? What part would you like to act out?

(Invite partners to dramatize their favorite parts.)

SHARE THE LEARNING
Focus on Interpreting

Tip for Share the Reading

Place the text on the overhead projector and read it aloud with expression, making your voice shift clearly from speaker to narration. After modeling, have the children join you with an emphasis on shifting their voices dramatically. Then have partner teams agree who will be Mom and who will be Andrew. While you read, have partners act out the roles. Trade roles and do it again.

Andrew was really unhappy. He couldn't believe his mom would tell him he couldn't have a dog. He thought it was a sure thing, but now he wasn't so sure.

"Mom, I really want this puppy. He is free. He is cute, and Alex said he will help me train him. Please, Mom!"

Andrew's mom sighed. "Honey, I am sorry, but we just don't have room. Besides, who will walk him every day, feed him, and make sure he has lots of attention?"

"What if I do it? I can feed him . . . and everything. I can do it. I know I can. You won't have to do a thing!"

Andrew knew in a moment that he had won. His mom broke out in a big smile and said, "Okay, my friend. But I am really counting on you! The dog is yours if you promise not to let me down."

Tip for Readers Theater Script

For emergent readers, enjoy "Snow" as an echo poem: teacher reads and children echo. Have children dramatize the poem. Read it again for expression and fluency. The children then could create illustrations to show that the snow in stanza one is different from the snow in stanza two. For developing readers, enjoy "Snow" as a partner drama or small team experience, where one student reads and two or three others act it out.

Snow
By Linda Hoyt

Twirling
Floating
Landing gently on my nose

Beating
Stinging
Going down my neck

EXTEND THE LEARNING

☆ Have children write descriptions of snow, or extend their thinking into poetry. Have them read their writing with expression and dramatic action.

☆ Confer with readers, asking them to visualize and share their thinking about how they might dramatize various selections.

☆ Ask: If this were to become a play, which scenes would be important to include? How might characters act?

ASSESS THE LEARNING

➤ Listen in as partners converse about how to dramatize the selection.

➤ Confer with readers during guided and independent reading to see if they can visualize and transfer their thinking to drama.

INFUSION OF FORMAL LANGUAGE
Test-style language

What is most likely to happen after the end of the story?
- A. The boy and the dog will play in the snow.
- B. The adults will play in the snow.
- C. Everyone will have a party.
- D. The dog will get a bone.

In this selection, *swirling* means
- A. sitting down.
- B. adding more snow.
- C. floating and spinning in the air.
- D. None of the above.

Andrew was really unhappy. He couldn't believe his mom would tell him he couldn't have a dog. He thought it was a sure thing, but now he wasn't so sure.

"Mom, I really want this puppy. He is free. He is cute, and Alex said he will help me train him. Please, Mom!"

Andrew's mom sighed. "Honey, I am sorry, but we just don't have room. Besides, who will walk him every day, feed him, and make sure he has lots of attention?"

"What if I do it? I can feed him . . . and everything. I can do it. I know I can. You won't have to do a thing!"

Andrew knew in a moment that he had won. His mom broke out in a big smile and said, "Okay, my friend. But I am really counting on you! The dog is yours if you promise not to let me down."

Snow

By Linda Hoyt

Twirling

Floating

Landing gently on my nose

Beating

Stinging

Going down my neck

Where the Wild Things Are
Maurice Sendak

FOCUS THE LEARNING

Introduction: Inferences are something we create in our minds when we notice clues and think about what those clues might mean. For example: When my dog scratches at the door, I can infer that he needs to go outside. If I see it is raining, I can infer that I will get wet if I go outside. Today as we read *Where the Wild Things Are,* by Maurice Sendak, we will be watching for clues and making inferences. Remember, when we infer we are using clues in the book and thinking about what they might mean.

INTERACTIVE READ-ALOUD
Model and Guide Practice

READ THE FIRST PAGE; THEN CLOSE THE BOOK SO IT IS CLEAR YOU ARE NOT READING. I am going to stop reading for a minute and think about clues that might help me to infer. I remember that Max is wearing a wolf suit and chasing his dog. I can infer that Max is pretending to be a wolf. I can also infer that Max likes to dress up and pretend things. Inferring helps me understand what is happening.

OPEN THE BOOK AND READ THE NEXT PAGE; THEN CLOSE IT. On the second page, the book said that Max was sent to bed without eating anything. I know that parents sometimes send their children to their bedrooms when they are naughty. I can infer that he was sent to his bedroom because he was being naughty.

What can you and your partner infer? Think together. Why would his mother have sent him to his room?

READ TO WHERE THE WILD THINGS MAKE MAX KING. CLOSE THE BOOK. Hmm...Max is king of the wild things. I can infer that means he gets to tell the wild things what to do.

Think together. What can you infer here?

LOOKING AT THE PAGES WITH THE WILD RUMPUS ...

What can you infer about the rumpus? What might be happening? If they made Max king, what can we infer the wild things think of him?

READ TO WHERE MAX SENDS THE WILD THINGS TO BED WITHOUT SUPPER AND SMELLS SOMETHING GOOD TO EAT. I can infer he is acting like his mom since he sent the wild things to bed. It says that Max wanted to be where someone loved him best of all. I could infer that he was sad and didn't want to be with the wild things anymore. I also see that it says he smelled good things to eat. I could infer that he is hungry because he didn't have any dinner.

Think of an inference you can make together.

READ TO THE END.

His supper is waiting for him in his room. What can we infer about his mother? Is she still unhappy with him?

END OF STORY REFLECTION

We have been able to make so many inferences with this book. Max had quite an adventure, but was it real or a dream? What can we infer? What clues can we find?

Turn and talk to your partner. What was your favorite inference in this book?

SHARE THE LEARNING
Focus on Inferring

Tip for Share the Thinking

Place the photographs on an overhead projector. Expose them one at a time and guide the children in using the "I can infer..." stem to share their observations for each photo. Encourage them to look closely at elements of the environment, the structure, and the person's clothing to make inferences about weather, location, kind of building, age of the building, what is happening, and so on.

Tip for Readers Theater Script

For emergent readers, read "School Day" to the children straight through and talk about what is happening. Then read it again, line by line, making inferences with each line. Be sure to help learners make inferences about point of view in each line. As children become familiar with the poem, invite them to join in reading chorally. For developing readers, guide a conversation about inferences they can make from the poem and then read it chorally, with partners, and independently, emphasizing the snappy pacing that is natural to this selection.

EXTEND THE LEARNING

☆ Link conversations about inference to small group reading instruction, helping the students to find places where they can infer in books they are reading.

☆ Look for inferences in other read-alouds. Ask students to use the "I can infer..." stem to share their observations.

☆ Have students focus on characteristics of individuals in a favorite story and make inferences about the characters.

ASSESS THE LEARNING

> Listen in as partners converse about inferences they were able to make while listening to *Where the Wild Things Are*. Check to be sure they use the "I can infer..." stem.

> Confer with readers to see if they can make inferences within the classroom about a drawing or about a reading selection.

INFUSION OF FORMAL LANGUAGE
Test-style language

We could infer that Max's mother

  A. wanted him to settle down.

  B. loved him enough to bring him supper.

  C. sent him to his room because he was naughty.

  D. All of the above.

In *Where the Wild Things Are*, the central problem was

  A. Max was naughty and his mother sent him to his bedroom.

  B. Max was hungry.

  C. Max wanted to act like a wolf.

  D. the wild things made him king.

School Day

By Linda Hoyt

Big step up

A noisy greeting

The bus rolls on its way.

Chattering kids

Stops and starts

"Sit down and be quiet!"

Running in

School bags flying

Breakfast and some play.

Teachers smiling

Books are out

The best part of our day.

Tuesday
David Wiesner

INTERACTIVE READ-ALOUD
Model and Guide Practice

EXAMINE THE ILLUSTRATIONS THAT APPEAR BEFORE THE TITLE PAGE. These pictures are so great. In the first one, three frogs are sleeping on their lily pads. In the second illustration, I can predict that if this frog could talk, he would say something like "What is goin' on! Hey guys, look. I'm floating!"

 Look at the third picture and talk together. What can you predict they could be saying to each other?

READ TO "TUESDAY EVENING, AROUND EIGHT." These three illustrations are like zooming in with a camera. First, we are far away from the turtle, and then we get closer and closer. I notice that the turtle is looking up and he looks worried or scared. I predict that the frogs on the lily pads are coming!

TURN TO THE PAGE THAT SHOWS THE FROGS FLYING OVER THE TURTLE. Look at the turtle! His eyes are huge, and he looks scared. Remember, there were three frogs earlier. Look! There are four now! All flying on lily pads.

 Talk to your thinking partner. What do you predict will happen? Predict together. What would the turtle or the frogs be thinking or saying?

SHOW THE PAGE WITH THE FROGS AND THE BIRDS, COVERING THE LAST INSET WITH YOUR HAND OR A PIECE OF PAPER. I am looking at this first illustration. This frog looks like he is having fun! He is flying sideways. Once the frogs learn to steer their lily pads, imagine the mischief they can cause! Look how many frogs and lily pads are in the sky. Notice their shadows in the background. There are really a lot of frogs.

 Think together. What do you predict will happen with the birds? Share your ideas, and then I will show you the last picture on this page.

CONTINUE TO THE END. Pause occasionally to give partners time to predict. Prompt with questions such as: What might the frogs and people be thinking? How will this end? How will the frogs feel at the end? Encourage students to use the "I predict…" stem as they share with partners. (Be sure they notice the frog with the remote control on the page with the television set and the shadow on the side of the barn at the end.)

END OF STORY REFLECTION
(Gather three or four books with covers and titles that give clear clues to the story line. A few suggestions include *My Friend Rabbit, The Bremen-Town Musicians, The Biggest Bear, Song and Dance Man,* and *Mufaro's Beautiful Daughters.*) I am lining these books up so you can look closely at their covers. As I read the titles, think together about predictions you can make about each book. Predict who the main character might be, if this is real or make-believe, where the story takes place, and so on. After we have had time to think together, I will write our predictions on sticky notes that we can save with each book. Then, when we have time to read these selections, we can remember your great predictions.

 Think together. What predictions can you make from the cover and the title of these books?

SHARE THE LEARNING
Focus on Predicting

Tip for Share the Reading

Cover the text so that only the photograph and the title show on the overhead projector. Ask the students to predict words they think are likely to appear in a passage that is written about this picture. Record their predictions on a chart or somewhere easily visible. Next, uncover the passage and read it with expression, helping the students to find their predicted words in the passage. Invite the students to share the reading for fluency and enjoyment.

The Winning Goal

The game had been a tie since halftime and players from both teams were determined to score. As the soccer ball passed the center of the field, a strong kick sent it flying to a forward. The coach was screaming on the sideline as the player dribbled, turned, and shot to the corner of the goal. The goalie jumped as high as he could, but the ball slipped through his fingers and flew into the quivering net.

Tip for Readers Theater Script

For emergent readers, sing "Frog Song" several times so the children learn the lyrics and can enjoy the musical retelling of the selection. For developing readers, read and sing the script chorally. Then shift to partner pairs and independent reading/singing. Emphasize smooth, fluent movement through the text.

EXTEND THE LEARNING

☆ Read *Joseph Had a Little Overcoat* by Simms Taback and predict using the content and the cutouts.

☆ Read several nonfiction selections after predicting words the students expect to appear in the text.

☆ Predict the weather based on looking at the sky.

☆ Take a walk to the cafeteria and see if the students can predict what is for lunch using their sense of smell.

☆ Have children illustrate one prediction before reading and then create a postreading illustration to share with a partner and compare.

☆ Read *Puss In Boots* by Charles Perrault, stopping often so students can predict what will happen.

ASSESS THE LEARNING

➤ Listen in as partners make predictions to determine their levels of understanding.

➤ During small group instruction, have students make predictions before and during reading.

➤ During independent reading, confer with learners to assess their ability to predict.

INFUSION OF FORMAL LANGUAGE
Test-style language

If *Tuesday* were to continue, we could predict that

  A. the detective would figure out which frogs were flying.

  B. the frogs would fly again.

  C. pigs would have a flying adventure.

  D. cows would fly.

On the page where a frog had the remote control to the TV, we could predict that

  A. the frog was going to change the channel.

  B. the frogs woke up the lady.

  C. the frogs were about to leave.

  D. the television had a long cord.

The Winning Goal

The game had been a tie since halftime and players from both teams were determined to score. As the soccer ball passed the center of the field, a strong kick sent it flying to a forward. The coach was screaming on the sideline as the player dribbled, turned, and shot to the corner of the goal. The goalie jumped as high as he could, but the ball slipped through his fingers and flew into the quivering net.

Frog Song

By Linda Hoyt

(to the tune of "Here We Go 'Round the Mulberry Bush")

Who would have thought a frog could fly,
frog could fly,
frog could fly . . .
Who would have thought a frog could fly,
Early in the morning.

Who would have thought they'd watch TV,
watch TV,
watch TV . . .
Who would have thought they'd watch TV,
Early in the morning.

Who would have thought they'd chase a dog,
chase a dog,
chase a dog . . .
Who would have thought they'd chase a dog,
Early in the morning.

Who would have thought that pigs might fly,
pigs might fly,
pigs might fly . . .
Who would have thought that pigs might fly—
What a crazy morning.

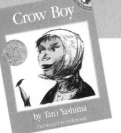

Crow Boy
Taro Yashima

FOCUS THE LEARNING

Introduction: As we read *Crow Boy* by Taro Yashima, we are going to use the clues in the story and what we know in our heads to infer and draw conclusions.

 Let's practice. If I told you that you needed to put on your tennis shoes and line up, what conclusion could you draw?

INTERACTIVE READ-ALOUD
Model and Guide Practice

READ THE FIRST TWO PAGES OF PRINT. I noticed that Chibi was hiding under the schoolhouse. I could conclude that he was afraid to go inside so he was hiding. I see a man walking around the outside of the building.

 We know this story is about Chibi. What can you conclude the man is doing?

READ TO WHERE IT SAYS HE WAS A FORLORN LITTLE TAG-ALONG. Chibi is always alone. I can conclude that he must be lonely without any friends. It says that he is afraid of the teacher and afraid of the other students. I could conclude that they aren't helping him fit in...they aren't making him feel good about being at school.

 Think together. What would it be like to be so alone? What can you conclude about his feelings at school?

READ TO WHERE IT SAYS THEY WERE IN SIXTH GRADE, THE LAST CLASS IN SCHOOL. This makes me really sad. I can conclude that he had so much trouble understanding what was happening in school that he needed other things to keep his mind busy, but how amazing that he always came.

 Talk to your thinking partner. It says he had a raincoat made from zebra grass. A grass coat? What conclusion can you make about that?

READ TO WHERE IT SAYS THE TEACHER TALKED TO CHIBI WHEN NO ONE WAS AROUND.

 Think together. What can you conclude about this teacher and the way he was paying attention to Chibi?

READ ABOUT THE TALENT SHOW. This is amazing. I can conclude that Chibi must have spent a lot of time listening to crows and practicing his calls. To be able to hear that well, I can conclude that Chibi must live in a very quiet place away from a city.

CONTINUE TO THE END. Pause occasionally to give partners time to share conclusions.

END OF STORY REFLECTION

What conclusions can we draw about why Chibi had the best attendance even though he had to walk so far? What conclusions can we draw about how the students felt when they thought about how mean they had been? Why can we conclude that he made a happy crow call at the end?

 Think together. What can you conclude about this story?

SHARE THE LEARNING
Focus on Drawing Conclusions

Tip for Share the Reading

Read each quote with expression. Then work with the students to generate conclusions that can be drawn from each. Record the conclusions in the box. Share the reading, infusing meaning and expression into each section.

On the playground if he closed his eyes and listened, Chibi could hear many different sounds, near and far.

Conclusions we can draw

The other children called him stupid and slowpoke.

Conclusions we can draw

Day after day Chibi came trudging to school. He always carried the same lunch, a rice ball wrapped in a radish leaf. Even when it rained or stormed he still came trudging along, wrapped in a raincoat made from dried zebra grass.

Conclusions we can draw

Tip for Readers Theater Script

For emergent readers, read "Crow Boy" to the students to model expressive reading. For developing readers, have teams or individual students plan for expressive reading of individual parts. Focus the readers on expressive, fluent reading that supports the central message in "Crow Boy." Present the script as a performance with music playing softly in the background.

EXTEND THE LEARNING

☆ Read poems and draw conclusions about their meaning.

☆ Read other books by Taro Yashima, such as *Umbrella* and *The Wave,* and draw conclusions about his artistic style.

☆ Read *Leo the Late Bloomer* by Robert Kraus and draw conclusions about Leo.

☆ Read *Lilly's Purple Plastic Purse* or *Julius, The Baby of the World* by Kevin Henkes and draw conclusions about Lilly or Julius.

☆ Have students draw conclusions in small group and independent reading times.

ASSESS THE LEARNING

> Listen in as partners draw conclusions to assess their levels of understanding.

> Have children illustrate a conclusion they can draw from a reading selection.

> During small group instruction, ask students to generate conclusions about their reading.

INFUSION OF FORMAL LANGUAGE
Test-style language

There is enough evidence to conclude that

A. Chibi grew to be very tall.

B. Chibi was happy at the end.

C. Chibi sold charcoal for the rest of his life.

D. Chibi loved the school.

We could conclude that Mr. Isobe

A. was a good teacher.

B. cared about Chibi.

C. found things that Chibi was good at.

D. All of the above.

On the playground if he closed his eyes and listened, Chibi could hear many different sounds, near and far.

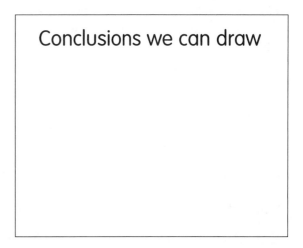
Conclusions we can draw

The other children called him stupid and slowpoke.

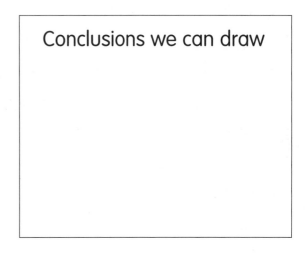
Conclusions we can draw

Day after day Chibi came trudging to school. He always carried the same lunch, a rice ball wrapped in a radish leaf. Even when it rained or stormed he still came trudging along, wrapped in a raincoat made from dried zebra grass.

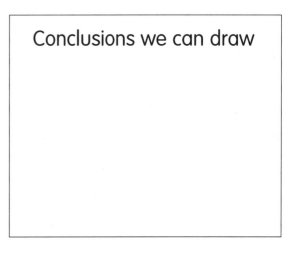
Conclusions we can draw

Crow Boy

Readers Theater Adaptation by Linda Hoyt

Narrator 1:   There once was a boy called Chibi.

Narrator 2:   He was tiny and very afraid of the teacher

Narrator 4:   and the other children.

Narrator 3:   He was always alone so he found interesting things to watch

Everyone: and to hear.

Narrator 1:   He sat by himself.

Narrator 2:   The students called him stupid and slowpoke,

Narrator 3:   But no matter what, Chibi came to school,

Narrator 4:   wrapped in a coat of dried zebra grass.

Everyone: When he was in sixth grade,

Narrator 1:   his teacher noticed that Chibi knew a lot.

Narrator 2:   He saw Chibi's knowledge of flowers and things that grew.

Narrator 3:   He spent time talking with Chibi when no one was around.

Narrator 4:   When Chibi appeared in the talent show,

Everyone: everyone was amazed that he could imitate the voices of crows—

Narrator 1:   crows that were happy,

Narrator 3:   crows that were sad,

Narrator 2:   crows that were old,

Narrator 4:   and crows that were young.

Everyone: Everyone saw Chibi in a new way.

Narrator 1:   They understood that he lived in a very different place.

Narrator 2:   They began to call him Crow Boy.

Narrator 3:   And they were sorry

Narrator 4:   for the way they had treated him.

Lon Po Po
Ed Young

Little Red Riding Hood
Trina Schart Hyman

FOCUS THE LEARNING

Read *Little Red Riding Hood* to the students before conducting this lesson.

Introduction: We compare things every day. We compare the weather yesterday with the weather today. We compare the taste of grilled cheese sandwiches and tuna fish sandwiches. We compare the size of the apples that we may get in the cafeteria. Today we will be comparing two stories: *Little Red Riding Hood* and *Lon Po Po.*

Turn to your partner and tell something you remember about Little Red Riding Hood.

Lon Po Po is a similar story. It came from China and has many similarities. Listen closely and be ready to think about ways the stories are alike and different.

INTERACTIVE READ-ALOUD
Model and Guide Practice

BEGIN READING LON PO PO. Pause to think aloud and make comparisons. I am thinking about the beginning of the stories. In *Little Red Riding Hood,* the little girl left home to take something to her grandmother. In *Lon Po Po,* the mother left home to visit the grandmother and left three children home alone. The beginnings both tell about someone leaving but in one the little girl leaves and in the other, the mother leaves!

Turn to your partner and share your thinking about the beginning of these two stories.

READ A FEW MORE PAGES. I am thinking about the wolves in the stories. In *Little Red Riding Hood,* the wolf is in the forest and waits for Little Red Riding Hood to come by. In *Lon Po Po* the wolf is much braver and goes right up to the house and knocks on the door. I am also beginning to notice things that are different because of the cultures the stories represent.

What comparisons can you make?

READ TO WHERE SHANG ASKS IF THE WOLF IS HUNGRY. I can't believe that Shang is so smart! She has convinced the wolf that a special food can be found at the top of the gingko tree and gets the other children to safety at the top of the tree!

What do you think about Shang? How does Shang compare to Little Red Riding Hood??

CONTINUE TO THE END. Pause occasionally to think aloud and give partners time to exchange ideas.

END OF STORY REFLECTION

There are so many comparisons I can make. I can think about the wolf, the grandma, the mother, and the girls in *Little Red Riding Hood* and *Lon Po Po.* I know that when we compare and contrast things, we think about how they are alike and different. When I compare these stories, I can say that the problem is the same. The wolf wants to eat the girls. I can say that the setting is different because one is in the woods and one is in China, but both stories have a house.

Think together about ways the stories are alike and different. While you do that, I am going to write a few of my ideas on a chart.

(Start a Venn diagram to record students' thinking. Then have partners make suggestions for additions to the chart.)

SHARE THE LEARNING
Focus on Comparing and Contrasting

Tip for Share the Reading

Read the *Lon Po Po* opening chorally at the overhead. Ask the children to close their eyes, visualize the scene, and share their images. Then, show the illustration on the opening page of *Lon Po Po*. Help the children notice that the house is sitting on the wolf's head and the mother is walking toward his nose. Help them notice the sun peeking through the clouds and consider the time of day. Repeat the process of visualizing with the *Little Red Riding Hood* passage. Compare the openings of the two stories.

> **Lon Po Po**
>
> Once, long ago, there was a woman who lived alone in the country with her three children, Shang, Tao, and Paotze. On the day of their grandmother's birthday, the good mother set off to see her, leaving the three children at home.
>
> **Little Red Riding Hood**
>
> Once upon a time, there was a little girl named Elisabeth who lived with her mother in a house on the edge of a village.... One day the grandmother sewed a red velvet cloak with a hood, and gave it to Elisabeth for her birthday. It looked so pretty, and she liked it so much that she would never wear anything else, and therefore everyone called her Little Red Riding Hood.

Tip for Readers Theater Script

Explain to the children that in this Readers Theater they will be focusing on comparing and contrasting voices. Read "The Lion" to the children using your voice to contrast the quiet and loud, strong voices of the poem. Invite the children to take over the part of the quiet voice while you read the loud, powerful voice. Be sure to notice that everyone reads the last line together.

> **The Lion**
> *By Linda Hoyt*
>
> | Quiet Voices | Loud Voices |
> |---|---|
> | I am a lion. | I am king of the beasts! |
> | I am a lion. | I watch for danger! |
> | I am a lion. | I care for my cubs! |
> | I am a lion. | I run like the wind! |
> | I am a lion. | I roar like thunder! |
> | I am king of the beasts. | I am king of the beasts! |

EXTEND THE LEARNING

☆ Have students fold a sheet of paper in half and label one side *Lon Po Po* and the other side *Little Red Riding Hood*. Have them draw and write about a comparison they can make between the two books. They could compare the beginnings, the characters, the wolves, and so on. Have them meet with partners to share their comparisons.

☆ Compare *Yeh-Shen: A Cinderella Story from China* by Ai-Ling Louie, *The Rough-Face Girl* by Rafe Martin and David Shannon, and a traditional version of *Cinderella*.

☆ Compare the cultures of two classrooms. Visit another classroom and notice how they have arranged their desks, how their classroom library is organized, where they have story time, and so on. Talk about the culture of your classroom and how it is like and different from the culture of the other classroom.

ASSESS THE LEARNING

> Listen to partner conversations to assess the children's ability to make comparisons.

> Confer with learners as they draw and write about comparisons they can make. Notice if they are able to compare elements of story structure (beginning, middle, end) as well as characters. Listen for evidence of understanding of cultural differences.

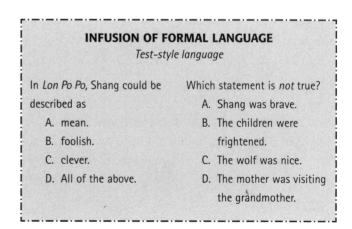

INFUSION OF FORMAL LANGUAGE
Test-style language

In *Lon Po Po*, Shang could be described as
  A. mean.
  B. foolish.
  C. clever.
  D. All of the above.

Which statement is *not* true?
  A. Shang was brave.
  B. The children were frightened.
  C. The wolf was nice.
  D. The mother was visiting the grandmother.

Lon Po Po

Once, long ago, there was a woman who lived alone in the country with her three children, Shang, Tao, and Paotze. On the day of their grandmother's birthday, the good mother set off to see her, leaving the three children at home.

Little Red Riding Hood

Once upon a time, there was a little girl named Elisabeth who lived with her mother in a house on the edge of a village .... One day the grandmother sewed a red velvet cloak with a hood, and gave it to Elisabeth for her birthday. It looked so pretty, and she liked it so much that she would never wear anything else, and therefore everyone called her Little Red Riding Hood.

The Lion

By Linda Hoyt

Quiet Voices	Loud Voices
I am a lion.	I am king of the beasts!
I am a lion.	I watch for danger!
I am a lion.	I care for my cubs!
I am a lion.	I run like the wind!
I am a lion.	I roar like thunder!
I am king of the beasts.	I am king of the beasts!

The Stray Dog
Marc Simont

FOCUS THE LEARNING
(Prepare a cause–and–effect chart as shown.)

Cause	Effect

Introduction: If I hold up a pencil and then let it go, what will happen? (Demonstrate.) Letting go of the pencil has the *effect* of causing the pencil to fall on the floor. I am going to write that in our chart. Let's try another one. If the custodian was to turn off the heat or the air-conditioning, what effect would that have on us? How can we show that in our chart? It is important to think about the effect our actions will have.

Can you think of something you could do that would cause something else to happen?

Today we are going to read *The Stray Dog* by Marc Simont. Our job will be to enjoy the story and notice cause-and-effect relationships as we read.

INTERACTIVE READ-ALOUD
Model and Guide Practice

READ PAGES 1–3 ("UNTIL IT IS TIME TO GO"). What a great picnic they must have had. That scruffy little dog is really cute, and he is so friendly. I am going to stop reading and think about cause and effect for a minute. I am thinking that the weather was nice, which had the effect of encouraging the family to go for a picnic. I will jot that on our chart. Nice weather…go for a picnic. Next, a little dog comes along who wants to play. The effect? The children give him a name and play with him until it is time to go. I am going to add that to our chart as well.

READ UNTIL IT SAYS "SATURDAY" AND THEY ARE BACK IN THE PARK. I am thinking about cause and effect. The children asked if they could take Willy home. I think that was caused because Willy was so much fun to play with. The book said that "all week they had Willy on their minds."

 Think together. Why did they keep thinking about him? What caused that to happen?

READ TO WHERE WILLY COMES RACING BY WITH THE DOG WARDEN BEHIND HIM.

What is causing Willy to run so fast? Why doesn't he stop to see the kids?

READ TO WHERE THE CHILDREN ARE TALKING TO THE DOG WARDEN.

Turn to your thinking partner. What caused them to take off their belt and hair ribbon? What was the effect of what they did?

CONTINUE TO THE END. Pause occasionally to give partners time to talk about cause and effect.

END OF STORY REFLECTION

I am thinking about the events in that story and the effect of different events. I am wondering…What if the kids hadn't been so smart and didn't think about taking off their belt and hair ribbon? What would the effect have been on Willy?

What would have happened?

SHARE THE LEARNING
Focus on Identifying Cause and Effect

Tip for Share the Reading

Model reading each line straight across, pausing between the cause and effect statements. Show the children how to slow down on the second part of the line to add dramatic effect. After they catch on, create two teams. One team reads the cause; the other reads the effect.

Cause	Effect
I put my hand in the garbage can . . .	And cut my finger on a tin lid.
I ran into the street to catch my ball . . .	And almost got hit by a car.
I pushed really hard on the book at the end . . .	And everything fell off the shelf.
I raced my bike as fast as I could . . .	And tipped over when I hit gravel.
I helped my mom carry groceries inside . . .	And she gave me her own special smile.
Everything in our world has a cause and effect . . .	We just have to think and to notice!

Tip for Readers Theater Script

For emergent readers, read "The Stray Dog" to the children, emphasizing the cause-and-effect structure. You might stand in one spot to read the cause and move to a different spot when you read the effect. As children gain confidence, read the cause and have the children join in on the effect. For developing readers, divide the group into two teams with one team reading the cause and the other reading the effect. Focus on fluent, expressive reading. Shift to having partners read the selection together for fluency.

The Stray Dog
Readers Theater Adaptation by Linda Hoyt
with assistance from Will, Frankie, Leilosi, Max, Patrick and Ms. McCabe

Cause	Effect
It was a beautiful day	So they went for a picnic
They played with Willy	So he stayed all day
They left Willy at the park	And they all missed him
They missed him so much	They went back to the park
Because the dog warden was trying to catch him	Willy ran by *fast*
The dog warden said Willy was a stray	So the boy took off his belt and called it a collar. The girl took off her hair ribbon and called it a leash.
Because Willy was dirty	They gave him a bath
Because they all loved him so much	Willy had a new home

EXTEND THE LEARNING

☆ Look for cause-and-effect relationships all day long. Encourage the students to use the terms "cause" and "effect" to describe events and classroom interactions.

☆ Consider cause-and-effect relationships in a variety of literature selections.

☆ Encourage students to find cause-and-effect relationships in small group reading experiences.

☆ Explore cause-and-effect relationships in science.

☆ Help writers to understand that our writing naturally involves cause-and-effect relationships.

ASSESS THE LEARNING

> Listen in as partners talk together about cause and effect in reading selections.

> Confer with readers during independent reading to see if they can identify cause and effect in independent reading.

> Have students illustrate a cause and an effect from a reading experience.

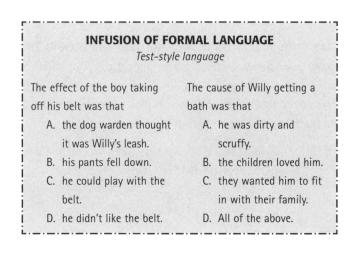

INFUSION OF FORMAL LANGUAGE
Test-style language

The effect of the boy taking off his belt was that
  A. the dog warden thought it was Willy's leash.
  B. his pants fell down.
  C. he could play with the belt.
  D. he didn't like the belt.

The cause of Willy getting a bath was that
  A. he was dirty and scruffy.
  B. the children loved him.
  C. they wanted him to fit in with their family.
  D. All of the above.

Cause	Effect
I put my hand in the garbage can . . .	And cut my finger on a tin lid.
I ran into the street to catch my ball . . .	And almost got hit by a car.
I pushed really hard on the book at the end . . .	And everything fell off the shelf.
I raced my bike as fast as I could . . .	And tipped over when I hit gravel.
I helped my mom carry groceries inside . . .	And she gave me her own special smile.
Everything in our world has a cause and effect . . .	We just have to think and to notice!

The Stray Dog

Readers Theater Adaptation by Linda Hoyt

with assisstance from Will, Frankie, Leticia, Max, Patrick and Ms. McCabe

Cause	Effect
It was a beautiful day	So they went for a picnic
They played with Willy	So he stayed all day
They left Willy at the park	And they all missed him
They missed him so much	They went back to the park
Because the dog warden was trying to catch him	Willy ran by *fast*
The dog warden said Willy was a stray	So the boy took off his belt and called it a collar. The girl took off her hair ribbon and called it a leash.
Because Willy was dirty	They gave him a bath
Because they all loved him so much	Willy had a new home

IDENTIFY MAIN IDEAS AND SUPPORTING DETAILS

The Art Lesson
Tomie dePaola

FOCUS THE LEARNING

Introduction: Main ideas and details help us understand the world around us. For example, a main idea about caterpillars is that they turn into butterflies. Their body changes completely and they eventually can fly. A detail is that caterpillars have many legs. Another detail is that caterpillars eat leaves. The main idea is that caterpillars turn into butterflies.

Think together. The main idea is that we are all students in this classroom. Talk about some details that you can share about our classroom.

As we read *The Art Lesson* by Tomie dePaola, we will be looking for main ideas and details about the story.

INTERACTIVE READ-ALOUD
Model and Guide Practice

READ TO WHERE IT SAYS TOMMY DREW AND DREW AND DREW. I am thinking about main ideas and details. Tommy is on the cover, and two of the first three pages tell how much Tommy likes to draw. I think a main idea is that Tommy really loves art. Now I am thinking of details. There are lots of details, but I want to think about details that support the main idea. The main idea is that Tommy really loves art. A detail that supports the main idea is that he wants to be an artist when he grows up.

READ TO WHERE TOMMY IS DRAWING ON HIS SHEETS. I am thinking about the main idea and the details that support the main idea. I still think the main idea is that Tommy really loves art. There are a lot of details here (flip through the previous pages slowly so the students can look again). I am looking for the details that go with our main idea.

Think together. What details support the main idea that Tommy really loves art?

READ TO WHERE THE PAINT BLEW OFF THE PAPER.

Talk to your thinking partner. Do you still think the main idea is about Tommy loving art? Have you found any supporting details that you think are important?

READ TO WHERE TOMMY WAS TOLD TO TAKE HIS CRAYONS HOME.

Think together. We have heard lots more details… Which ones support our main idea?

CONTINUE TO THE END. Pause occasionally to give partners time to talk and wonder if the main idea chosen in the beginning is still a good one and which details support that main idea.

END OF STORY REFLECTION

Sometimes stories have several main ideas. What do you think about this one? Was there more than one main idea, or did the one we selected work well for the whole book?

Let's make a chart of our main ideas and the details we think best support them.

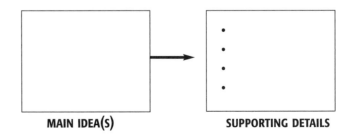

SHARE THE LEARNING
Focus on Identifying Main Ideas and Supporting Details

Tip for Share the Reading

Chorally read the recipe with the students, encouraging them to visualize the steps. Work with students to identify a main idea. Then read the passage again to find the details that support the main idea.

Recipe for a Peanut Butter & Jelly Sandwich

First, you open the jar of peanut butter. Then you open a jar of jelly. Next, you take a piece of bread and spread peanut butter on it with a knife. Your hands might get messy so be sure you have a napkin. Now you are ready for the jelly, which goes on top of the peanut butter. Finally, you put on a second slice of bread and take a big bite. Yum!

Tip for Readers Theater Script

Enjoy "The Art Lesson" as a two-team experience. Team 1 reads the left column and Team 2 reads the right column, ensuring they pause to give the other team a chance to read their line. With increased proficiency, partners can read the poem together for fluency and expression. Review the script to search for main ideas and supporting details.

The Art Lesson
Readers Theater Adaptation by Linda Hoyt

Team 1	Team 2
Tommy wanted to be an artist	And his parents were so proud.
He practiced and he practiced	And even drew their house.
Tommy wanted to be an artist	Art lessons were his dream.
When the teacher had him copy,	He felt like he could scream.
Tommy wanted to be an artist	And his parents were so proud.
Today, his books and art	Live on in books we love.
Tommy wanted to be an artist	
And his parents were so proud.	And his parents were so proud.

EXTEND THE LEARNING

☆ Read an array of fiction and nonfiction selections to the students to identify main ideas and details that support them. Keep in mind that many texts have more than one main idea.

☆ Model how to create an illustration and identify a main idea before you start to write. Show how you think of details to include in your writing by making sure they support your main idea.

☆ During interactive writing, help students craft a main idea statement and then add details that make the main idea more clear to a reader.

☆ Use *The Important Book* by Margaret Wise Brown as a model for writing about topics in science and math, characters in books, and even students in the classroom.

ASSESS THE LEARNING

➤ Listen in as partners identify main ideas to assess their understanding.

➤ During small group instruction, have students select supporting details that go with a main idea.

➤ Assess a piece of writing to determine the learner's ability to focus on a main idea and support it with details in the illustration and writing.

INFUSION OF FORMAL LANGUAGE
Test-style language

The detail that *best* supports our main idea is which of the following?
  A. Tommy drew all of the time.
  B. The paint blew off of his paper.
  C. He only got one piece of paper.
  D. His father took his pictures to the barber shop.

A main idea is an important idea that
  A. is the only idea.
  B. you need to learn.
  C. runs through the whole story.
  D. is funny.

Recipe for a Peanut Butter & Jelly Sandwich

First, you open the jar of peanut butter. Then you open a jar of jelly. Next, you take a piece of bread and spread peanut butter on it with a knife. Your hands might get messy so be sure you have a napkin. Now you are ready for the jelly, which goes on top of the peanut butter. Finally, you put on a second slice of bread and take a big bite. Yum!

The Art Lesson

Readers Theater Adaptation by Linda Hoyt

Team 1

Tommy wanted to be an artist

He practiced and he practiced

Tommy wanted to be an artist

When the teacher had him copy,

Tommy wanted to be an artist

Today, his books and art

Tommy wanted to be an artist

And his parents were so proud.

Team 2

And his parents were so proud.

And even drew their house.

Art lessons were his dream.

He felt like he could scream.

And his parents were so proud.

Live on in books we love.

And his parents were so proud.

RANK IMPORTANT VS. UNIMPORTANT INFORMATION

The Biggest Bear
Lynd Ward

FOCUS THE LEARNING

Introduction: *The Biggest Bear* by Lynd Ward is a really great book. It is filled with important information that helps us understand what is happening. Like all books, it also has some information that is not as important to the story. Let's start by looking at the cover.

Think together. What do you see on the cover that you think will be important to the story? Do you see anything that may not be so important?

INTERACTIVE READ-ALOUD
Model and Guide Practice

READ TO PAGE 4. I am thinking about what is important. It sounds like it is pretty important to Johnny to have a bearskin on the barn. I am thinking it is important that he lives on a farm; people who live in cities aren't likely to have barns or bears. I noticed a detail that isn't very important. It said that the apple orchard was on a hill. I don't think the hill is very important to this story.

READ TO PAGE 12. It seems to me that it is important that Johnny has a gun.

Think together. What do you think? What seems important so far? Can you name a detail that is unimportant?

READ TO PAGE 20.

Talk to your thinking partner. Think together. What is important here?

READ TO PAGE 42. Oh, my. This bear sure is hungry!

What is important? What is unimportant?

CONTINUE TO THE END. Pause occasionally to give partners time to talk about important vs. unimportant information.

END OF STORY REFLECTION

What a great story! So many important things happened. Let's make a list of the things in the story we think are the MOST important. Then we will use our list to retell the story focusing on the most important information.

Think together. What should we put on our list?

I am going to practice retelling the story using the ideas we have listed. Listen as I retell, and see if we have forgotten anything important.

Think together. How was my retell? Did I include the most important information? Is there anything else I should add?

It is your turn to plan a retell. Meet with your partner and talk about your retell. Your job is to decide what important information you will be sure to include and then practice your retell together. Later, we will form groups of four so you can do your retells for each other.

🗣️ SHARE THE LEARNING
Focus on Ranking Important vs. Unimportant Information

Tip for Share the Reading

🔧 Read the passage with frequent pauses to encourage students to visualize and identify important vs. unimportant information. Guide a conversation to identify first the most important ideas. Then point out unimportant information. Use the chart to record observations.

Elk are beautiful animals that are related to the deer family. People often stop along the side of a road to watch elk as they slowly move across a field eating grass and soaking up summer warmth. The elk usually ignore them. Some people even have a picnic in the field and watch the elk.

Male elk grow huge antlers that they use to protect themselves and their herd of cows. These antlers are wider than the elk's body and are so hard they can do battle with their antlers. In the spring the antlers fall off and some people like to collect them and use them for light fixtures and knife handles. New antlers grow again in the late summer and fall.

Most Important	Unimportant

Tip for Readers Theater Script

📋 For emergent readers, enjoy "The Biggest Bear" as an echo poem: the teacher reads and children echo. The children then could create illustrations that re-create the story line. For developing and fluent readers, have the students read the poem in unison, in partners, or in teams with each team reading every other line. Be sure to have them read the poem several times to emphasize improvements in fluency and expression.

The Biggest Bear
Readers Theater Adaptation by Linda Hoyt

Johnny found a baby bear
But he got really big.
He ate and ate and ate and ate—
He acted like a pig!

Johnny tried to send the bear away;
He always came right back
Until the day when Johnny found
Himself inside a trap.

The men who came were from a zoo,
They promised to be kind.
The bear would have all kinds of food
And Johnny knew he'd find
The people would enjoy him.
His life would be just fine.

EXTEND THE LEARNING

☆ In small group instruction, focus students on identifying important information in both fiction and nonfiction.

☆ Encourage writers to look at their illustrations before writing and identify the most important information they want to be sure to include in their writing.

☆ Model in many texts the way you can read a passage and think about important ideas rather than try to remember everything.

☆ After independent reading, have the children create an illustration of the most important idea that was in a story.

☆ Have readers use the VIP (Very Important Points) Strategy (Hoyt, 1999). After cutting sticky notes in strips, readers mark VIPs in a text and share with partners.

ASSESS THE LEARNING

> Listen in as partners identify important vs. unimportant information.

> During small group instruction, assess the children's ability to mark VIPs and to tell why they selected these points as most important.

> Assess a piece of writing to determine the writer's ability to focus on the most important points of information.

INFUSION OF FORMAL LANGUAGE
Test-style language

In this story, it was *important* to understand that
  A. in the beginning Johnny wanted a bearskin on the barn.
  B. he found a baby bear and cared for it.
  C. he was happy that the bear would be safe in a zoo.
  D. All of the above.

An *unimportant* detail in this story is that
  A. the bear grew to be really big.
  B. the bear caused trouble looking for food.
  C. the bear liked pancakes on Sunday.
  D. the bear went to the zoo.

Elk are beautiful animals that are related to the deer family. People often stop along the side of a road to watch elk as they slowly move across a field eating grass and soaking up summer warmth. The elk usually ignore them. Some people even have a picnic in the field and watch the elk.

Male elk grow huge antlers that they use to protect themselves and their herd of cows. These antlers are wider than the elk's body and are so hard they can do battle with their antlers. In the spring the antlers fall off and some people like to collect them and use them for light fixtures and knife handles. New antlers grow again in the late summer and fall.

Most Important	Unimportant

The Biggest Bear

Readers Theater Adaptation by Linda Hoyt

Johnny found a baby bear

But he got really big.

He ate and ate and ate and ate—

He acted like a pig!

Johnny tried to send the bear away;

He always came right back

Until the day when Johnny found

Himself inside a trap.

The men who came were from a zoo,

They promised to be kind.

The bear would have all kinds of food

And Johnny knew he'd find

The people would enjoy him.

His life would be just fine.

REPRESENT TEXT GRAPHICALLY

The Dinosaurs of Waterhouse Hawkins
Barbara Kerley

FOCUS THE LEARNING

Introduction: *The Dinosaurs of Waterhouse Hawkins* by Barbara Kerley is a biography. That means it is a true story. It tells the life of a man who was interested in dinosaurs and used his skills as an artist to make models that were as big as the real dinosaurs. This book tells the story of his life so we are going to make a time line to show the order in which things happened. (Show the two-page photo layout that is on pages 17 and 18 of the book.)

 Think together. What do you know about dinosaurs?

INTERACTIVE READ-ALOUD
Model and Guide Practice
(Hang a 12-foot-long piece of string horizontally near your read-aloud area. Have clothespins and 8½ x 11 sheets of tagboard easily at hand.)

READ THE FIRST TWO PAGES. I am going to put the year 1853 on the time line, as that is the first year we are given. I will write "1853" at the bottom of this card, and I will also write "workshop" to remind me that he had a workshop in that year.

READ THE NEXT TWO PAGES. Now we know that when he was young, he loved to draw and paint animals. I am going to put another card on the time line to show what he did before 1853. I don't know the year, but I can write "Loved to draw and paint animals." I will hang this card before 1853. Later, we are going to create illustrations to go on our time line.

 Talk to your thinking partner. We know he loved to draw animals. We know he had a workshop. He is called Dinosaur Hawkins. What do you think is in his workshop?

READ TO WHERE QUEEN VICTORIA COMES TO VISIT.

 Talk to your thinking partner. Think together. What is important here? Is there anything we should add to our time line around 1853?

READ ON TO HIS NEW YEAR'S EVE PARTY.

 Think together. What is important? What might we add to our time line?

CONTINUE TO THE END. Pause occasionally to add events to the time line and give partners time to talk. With each addition to the time line, remind the students that illustrations will be added to the time line so they need to think what they might draw that will show important events.

END OF STORY REFLECTION
What a great biography! So many important things happened. Let's go over our time line and think about all of the important events. (Review the time line, guiding learners as they retell the content.)

 Now it is time for the illustrations. Think together. What illustrations should we add for each card?

(You may want to have several partner pairs illustrating each card so that all students have the chance to participate. You may also want to assign a team to create front and back covers so the time line can be bound into a book at a later date.)

SHARE THE LEARNING
Focus on Representing Text Graphically

Tip for Share the Reading

Read the passage to the students and explain that you are going to pull out important ideas and place them on the chart. The chart will help connected ideas stay together. Think aloud for paragraph one showing how you decide which part of the chart this information

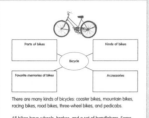

matches. Then jot down important facts in the "Kinds of bikes" box. Continue reading and jotting information, encouraging partners to read along and think with you about what to write on the chart. Cover the text and use the chart to generate a retell of what you have learned. Model how to use one section of the chart to generate an illustration and/or a piece of writing using the chart, not copying from the original text.

Tip for Readers Theater Script

For emergent readers, have them participate in the "All" segments of "The Dinosaurs of Waterhouse Hawkins" while you read the narrator sections. You might want to use the time line created during the reading of the book to support understanding. For developing readers, read the script once through to model fluent expression. Then divide the group into teams. Rehearse until the reading is smooth and fluent.

EXTEND THE LEARNING

☆ Provide blank versions of a spider map such as in Share the Reading and have students record important information they find in small group reading experiences.

☆ Have students use a spider map to record information gained from a weekly newsmagazine or a science or social studies text.

☆ Read another biography to the students and create a new time line. Illustrate the time line and turn it into a class book.

☆ Create a class time line showing something that happened in each month of the year.

☆ Have students create personal time lines showing the year they were born and just a few key events in their lives. The format might be something like: _____ was born in _____. When he was little, he _____ and _____ and _____. Today he is in _____ grade and goes to _____ school.

ASSESS THE LEARNING

> Listen in as partners discuss the time line for the life of Waterhouse Hawkins to determine if they understand the time order the line represents.

> During small group instruction, assess the children's ability to use a map or chart to represent ideas.

> Conduct an interactive writing to place important information on a spider chart and assess individual ability to select the correct area in which to place information.

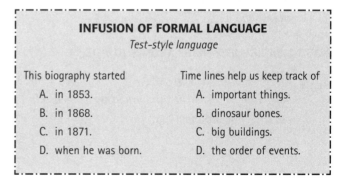

INFUSION OF FORMAL LANGUAGE
Test-style language

This biography started
  A. in 1853.
  B. in 1868.
  C. in 1871.
  D. when he was born.

Time lines help us keep track of
  A. important things.
  B. dinosaur bones.
  C. big buildings.
  D. the order of events.

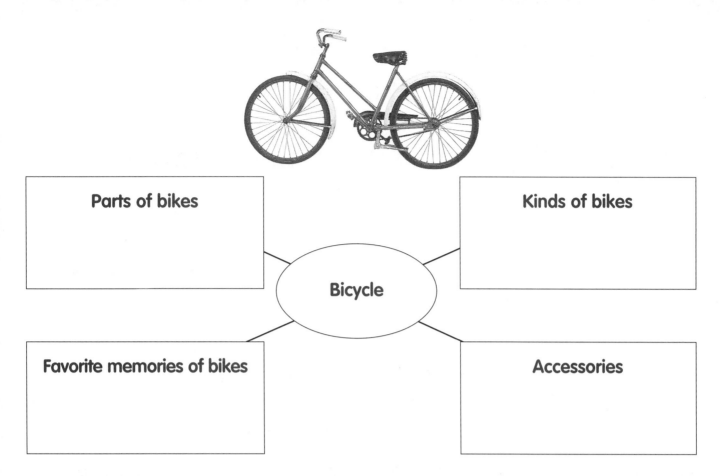

Parts of bikes		Kinds of bikes

Bicycle

Favorite memories of bikes		Accessories

There are many kinds of bicycles: coaster bikes, mountain bikes, racing bikes, road bikes, three-wheel bikes, and pedicabs.

All bikes have wheels, brakes, and a set of handlebars. Some bikes have brakes you push with your feet. Some bikes have brakes on the handlebars so you can operate them with your hands. Bikes have a chain that rotates when you pedal. The chain turns the gear and the gear makes the wheels turn.

To be safe, you need to wear special accessories. You need to have a helmet to protect your head. The helmet should fit down over your forehead and have a snug strap. Elbow pads and knee pads are good protection, too. Some people like to buy special seats, colorful pedals, and other accessories for their bikes.

The Dinosaurs of Waterhouse Hawkins

Readers Theater Adaptation by Linda Hoyt

All: Waterhouse Hawkins loved dinosaurs and art.

Narrator 1:   When he was young, he loved to paint, draw, and create sculptures of animals.

All: Waterhouse Hawkins loved dinosaurs and art.

Narrator 2:   In 1853, he had a workshop and was piecing dinosaur bones together to create models showing what they might have looked like.

All: Waterhouse Hawkins loved dinosaurs and art.

Narrator 1:   Queen Victoria came to visit his workshop, and he planned an amazing New Year's Eve party filled with huge dinosaur models.

All: Waterhouse Hawkins loved dinosaurs and art.

Narrator 2:   In 1854, his models were placed in the Crystal Palace in London.

All: Waterhouse Hawkins loved dinosaurs and art.

Narrator 1:   In 1868, he began to create dinosaur models in the United States. He continued working until 1871 when vandals entered his workshop and ruined all of his models.

All: Waterhouse Hawkins loved dinosaurs and art.

Narrator 2:   He didn't give up. He created dinosaurs for Princeton University in New Jersey and the Smithsonian Institute in Washington, D.C. He was 71 years old.

All: Waterhouse Hawkins loved dinosaurs and art.

Narrator 1:   People still come to the Crystal Palace in England to see the dinosaurs of Waterhouse Hawkins even though he died in 1878.

All: Waterhouse Hawkins loved dinosaurs and art.

READ CLASSIC AND CONTEMPORARY WORKS

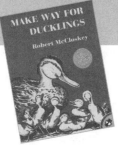

Make Way for Ducklings
Robert McCloskey

FOCUS THE LEARNING

Introduction: *Make Way for Ducklings* by Robert McCloskey was written in 1941. Let's think about how old this book might be. I am going to write this year's date and then subtract 1941 to see how long ago Robert McCloskey wrote this. Wow! That was a long time ago, maybe even before your parents were born...perhaps even before your grandparents were born. Let's look at some pictures and think about how things might have been when this book was written.

 Look at this page with the cars on it. Think together. What do you notice? Do these cars look like the cars we drive today? How are they different?

This book is called a classic because it was written a long time ago, but everyone still loves it because it is such a good story.

INTERACTIVE READ-ALOUD
Model and Guide Practice

READ TO WHERE THE DUCKS DECIDE TO SPEND THE NIGHT ON THE ISLAND. I am thinking about this story and I know that ducks today would be about the same. They fly around and look for safe places to sleep. I do notice that all of the pictures are brown. There isn't any color. I wonder if that is the way they made books back then.

READ TO WHERE THEY FOLLOW THE SWAN BOAT. I am thinking that people today enjoy feeding ducks. That is the same, but look at the way the people are dressed.

 Think together. What do you notice about their clothes?

CONTINUE TO THE END. Pause occasionally to give partners time to think about this classic story and notice clues that reflect the time in which it was written. Be sure the children notice additional cars, the cord on the phone in the phone booth, the whistle used by the policeman, the policeman's uniform, policemen directing traffic instead of using traffic lights, and so on.

END OF STORY REFLECTION

Wasn't that a great classic story? I can understand why people still love it. If we hadn't seen the copyright date and didn't know for sure how long ago the story was written, what clues could we have used to figure out that this is a classic story, not a new story?

 Think together. What clues did you notice in the book? What should we list as clues that this was written a long time ago?

Let's look at some of the books in our classroom library to see if we can find more books that are classics. Remember, there will be clues all through the book, not just on the copyright page.

SHARE THE LEARNING
Focus on Reading Classic and Contemporary Works

Tip for Share the Thinking

Show the photos on the overhead projector and tell the students that one of the photos was taken around the time that *Make Way for Ducklings* was written. Invite partners to think together. Which picture is a classic? Which picture is more like something we would see today? How do you know? What are the clues? What do we think we know about school for children of this era?

Tip for Readers Theater Script

Read "The Wind," "Auntie's Skirts," and "Dinosaur Stew" to the children, helping them to visualize what is happening. Guide them in understanding that in the time the first two poems were written, ladies wore long skirts all the way to the floor and the poems reflect those long noisy skirts. These are classic poems. Then read the more contemporary "Dinosaur Stew" and compare. For developing readers, involve them in choral and partner reading, comparing and contrasting the poems. Students may enjoy comparing these poems to contemporary works by Silverstein, Prelutsky, and other contemporary poets.

EXTEND THE LEARNING

☆ Gather an array of books by Robert McCloskey and read them to the children to enjoy the classic story lines as well as to analyze the backgrounds, art, and clues about life in the era in which they were written.

☆ Meet with your librarian to gather books by other authors that might be considered classic works and help your students develop an appreciation for these wonderful titles.

☆ Have children ask their parents about books they loved when they were children and see if any can be located to share with the students.

☆ Bring in books that you loved in your own childhood to share with your students.

☆ Provide time to consider the art in contemporary children's books. How does it compare to the art of the classic works?

ASSESS THE LEARNING

> Listen in as partners look for clues in illustrations to see if they understand the meaning of *classic*.

> During a small group time, provide an array of classic and contemporary titles. Ask the students to sort them. Assess which learners can identify classics and separate them from contemporary titles.

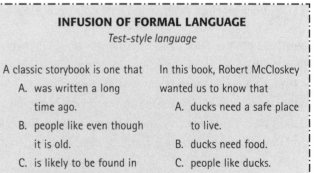

INFUSION OF FORMAL LANGUAGE
Test-style language

A classic storybook is one that
  A. was written a long time ago.
  B. people like even though it is old.
  C. is likely to be found in most libraries.
  D. All of the above.

In this book, Robert McCloskey wanted us to know that
  A. ducks need a safe place to live.
  B. ducks need food.
  C. people like ducks.
  D. All of the above.

Classic Poems from *A Child's Garden of Verses*
by Robert Louis Stevenson (Copyright © "1900. Rand, McNally and Co., Chicago.)

The Wind

By Robert Louis Stevenson

I saw you toss the kites on high
And blow the birds about the sky;
And all around I heard you pass,
Like ladies' skirts across the grass—
    O wind, a-blowing all day long!
    O wind, that sings so loud a song!

Auntie's Skirts

By Robert Louis Stevenson

Whenever Auntie moves around,
Her dresses make a curious sound,
They trail behind her up the floor,
And trundle after through the door.

Contemporary Poem

Dinosaur Stew

By Linda Hoyt

Dinosaur

Dinosaur

Dinosaur Stew

Aren't you glad they don't want to eat

YOU!

What Do You Do With a Tail Like This?
Steve Jenkins and Robin Page

FOCUS THE LEARNING
Introduction: We have a lot of reasons for reading. We read to learn things. We read because it is fun. We read because books and other texts are interesting. We even read to relax and just listen to a story. Today, as we read *What Do You Do With a Tail Like This?* by Steve Jenkins and Robin Page, our purpose will be to learn. We are going to focus on trying to learn something new that we didn't know before.

INTERACTIVE READ-ALOUD
Model and Guide Practice
We are going to use a strategy called "I remember...." I am going to read to you. Your job is to think and try to remember as much as you can. Ready?

READ THE PAGES ABOUT NOSES. I am remembering...I am going to look at the pictures and think. I remember that an elephant can give himself a bath with his nose. He doesn't need a shower!

 Use the "I remember..." stem and tell each other something you learned on these two pages.

TURN TO THE PAGES ABOUT EARS. It is your job to remember. Listen carefully while I read.

 Talk to your thinking partner. Share your thinking. What do you remember?

You are really catching on. I can tell you are listening carefully and really trying to learn. Here we go.

READ THE PAGES ABOUT TAILS.

 Okay, thinking partners, what do you remember?

CONTINUE TO THE END. Pause occasionally to give partners time to use the "I remember..." strategy and share their learning.

END OF STORY REFLECTION
The "I remember..." strategy is a great one when your purpose for reading is to learn and to remember. Let's think back on the whole book for a moment. If you were going to go home and do the "I remember..." strategy for your parents to share your learning in this book, what would you say? What learning would you share?

 Think together. What would you want your parents to learn from this book?

I am going to ask you to draw and write what you remember. Use your "I remember..." thinking to create illustrations and then write. Try to capture your learning in your picture and your writing.

 **SHARE THE LEARNING**

Reading for a Purpose

Tip for Share the Reading

Sing the song tracking under the line of print as you go to make it clear that you are reading the words. Engage the children in a conversation about your purpose for reading the song. How does your purpose for the song compare to the purpose for reading *What Do You Do With a Tail Like This?*

> Mary had a little lamb,
> Little lamb,
> Little lamb,
> Mary had a little lamb.
> Its fleece was white as snow.
>
> Everywhere that Mary went,
> Mary went,
> Mary went,
> Everywhere that Mary went,
> The lamb was sure to go.

Tip for Readers Theater Script

Invite the children to have some fun singing "The Sugar Cookies Song. . . ." Sing it together. Then talk about how the strategies might change if you were going to make the cookies.

EXTEND THE LEARNING

☆ Read a rich mixture of songs, poems, and nonfiction and fiction selections. With each one, pause to talk about your purpose for reading and how you are going to plan your reading to match your purpose. Will you read quickly or slowly? Will you relax, or will you sit up straight to help yourself think?

☆ Demonstrate skimming to find an answer using a nonfiction Big Book with an index. Explain that sometimes when we want an answer quickly, we use the index, skim the page indicated by the index, find our answer, and then move on. Our purpose changes our reading. Model the process of "toe dipping," looking just at the pages that help us to find an answer quickly.

ASSESS THE LEARNING

> During small group instruction, have the children survey a selection and then state a purpose for reading. Are they reading to learn, reading to answer a question, rereading for fluency, or reading to enjoy an entertaining poem? Assess their ability to match their purpose to the way they approach the text.

> Confer with readers during individual conferences to assess their understanding of their purposes for reading.

INFUSION OF FORMAL LANGUAGE
Test-style language

People read for many purposes. They read to

  A. relax.

  B. hear good stories.

  C. learn.

  D. All of the above.

When our purpose is reading to learn, we need to

  A. bounce a ball.

  B. sharpen our pencils.

  C. think about lunch.

  D. try hard to remember what is in the book.

Mary had a little lamb,

Little lamb,

Little lamb.

Mary had a little lamb.

Its fleece was white as snow.

Everywhere that Mary went,

Mary went,

Mary went,

Everywhere that Mary went,

The lamb was sure to go.

Sugar Cookies Song . . .

(to the tune of "Clementine")

Oh my darling, oh my darling,
Sugar cookies—you are fun.
You will soon be in the oven,
In my stomach when you're done.

Mix the butter with the sugar,
Stir it twenty times and then
Add the flour, baking powder,
Add the salt, and stir again.

Oh, my darling, oh, my darling,
Sugar cookies—you are fun.
You will soon be in the oven,
In my stomach when you're done.

Add the egg and then the milk, and
Add vanilla, if you please.
Stir and scrunch well with your fingers
Till you work the dough with ease.

Oh my darling, oh my darling,
Sugar cookies—you are fun.
You will soon be in the oven,
In my stomach when you're done.

Wash your hands and with a teaspoon
Round the dough on baking sheets.
Flatten each round with damp fingers.
Top with sugar for a treat.

Sugar Cookies

Mix:
I cup brown sugar
I cup soft butter
1 egg, slightly beaten
3 tablespoons milk
2 teaspoons vanilla

Add:
3 cups flour
1½ teaspoons baking powder
½ teaspoon salt

Bake at 350 degrees for 8 minutes.
Top with sugar after baking.

(Adapted from *Revisit, Reflect, Retell: Strategies for Improving Reading Comprehension.* Linda Hoyt: Heinemann 1999).

USE PICTURES TO SUPPORT COMPREHENSION

The Ghost-Eye Tree
Bill Martin, Jr., and John Archambault

FOCUS THE LEARNING

Introduction: Illustrations are really important. They help us understand more deeply and give important clues about a story. In *The Ghost-Eye Tree* by Bill Martin, Jr., and John Archambault, the illustrations are created by Ted Rand. Look at the cover that Ted Rand created and think about the title.

 Think together. What do you notice?

INTERACTIVE READ-ALOUD
Model and Guide Practice

SHOW THE ILLUSTRATIONS ON THE FIRST TWO PAGES. Let's just look at the pictures for a minute and think. I can tell from the pictures that the lady wants the boy to take a bucket. I can see she is handing it to him. I can also see the trees look bent over so I think it must be a windy night. Let's look at more pictures and think together. (Show the illustrations for the next four pages.)

Think together. What can you learn from the pictures?

SHOW THE REST OF THE ILLUSTRATIONS.

Talk to your thinking partner. Think together. What are you learning from the pictures? What do you think is happening?

RETURN TO THE BEGINNING AND READ THE FIRST PAGE. Oh, now I get it. I knew she wanted him to take the bucket. Now I know it was a bucket for milk. They must not have a grocery store close by. I like the phrase, "I dreaded to go...I dreaded the tree." That really fits with the dark, scary-looking tree. I can tell this boy really doesn't want to go.

READ TO WHERE IT LOOKS LIKE THE CHILDREN ARE DANCING. Here is a place where the words and the illustrations really work together. I thought they were dancing because they were happy. Now that I am reading the story, I can tell they are dancing because they are pretending not to be afraid. That is really different because they are afraid on the inside.

Talk to your thinking partner. Think together. Would you be afraid? If you were, what would you do?

CONTINUE TO THE END. Pause occasionally to give partners time to talk about the pictures and the importance of using pictures and words to understand a story.

END OF STORY REFLECTION
Wasn't that a great story? Let's think together about the illustrations. Which ones were your favorites and why? Which illustrations helped you understand the story a little better?

Think together. Which illustrations helped you? Which ones did you like?

SHARE THE LEARNING
Focus on Using Pictures to Support Comprehension

Tip for Share the Reading

Cover the image with a sticky note and read "Scared" expressively to the children. Guide a conversation about the visual images they get when they read this poem. If they were to create an illustration to go with this text, what would they put in the picture? Have children work with a partner to create an illustration that would support this poem and then share their creation explaining how it supports the reading.

Scared?
By Linda Hoyt

The round, round face
The beady eyes
A pumpkin turned to a scary disguise
Should I scare . . .
Should I dare . . .
Should I feel I should beware?

The smile is big
And full of glee
I think that eye just winked at me!

But wait . . .
The mouth is turning down
The eyes are rolling round and round
Should I scare . . .
Should I dare . . .
Should I feel I should beware?

Tip for Readers Theater Script

Guide the children in noticing how the picture supports the text and deepens their understanding before beginning to interpret the selection orally. Read "Designed for Survival" to the students and make sure each section is clear to them. Then divide the group into three teams and rehearse to perform the script as Readers Theater.

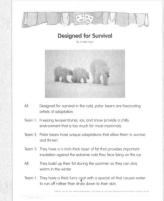

Designed for Survival
By Linda Hoyt

All: Designed for survival in the cold, polar bears are fascinating artists of adaptation.

Team 1: Freezing temperatures, ice, and snow provide a chilly environment that is too much for most mammals.

Team 2: Polar bears have unique adaptations that allow them to survive and thrive!

Team 3: They have a 4-inch-thick layer of fat that provides important insulation against the extreme cold they face living on the ice.

All: They build up their fat during the summer so they can stay warm in the winter.

Team 1: They have a thick furry coat with a special oil that causes water to run off rather than drain down to their skin.

EXTEND THE LEARNING

☆ Have the students create wordless books in which their illustrations need to convey the meaning. Provide opportunities to look at *The Snowman* by Raymond Briggs or *Good Dog, Carl* by Alexandra Day to help them understand that pictures can tell a story.

☆ After a read-aloud, have children evaluate which illustrations best supported their understanding.

☆ In a science selection, cover the text and use the pictures only to try to determine the meaning. Then, read the text and talk about how the words and illustrations worked together to help us understand.

☆ During writers workshop, ask writers to explain how their illustrations support their writings.

ASSESS THE LEARNING

> Listen in as partners interpret the illustrations to determine their success in using pictures to create meaning.

> During small group instruction, read and discuss the illustrations and assess the children's ability to predict words they expect to see in print.

> Confer with individuals during independent reading to assess their ability to independently use pictures to support comprehension.

INFUSION OF FORMAL LANGUAGE
Test-style language

Which line *best* tells how the boy felt about going to get milk?

  A. How dark it was!

  B. The night is so dark.

  C. I dreaded to go.

  D. There's nothing to fear.

"I dreaded to go." *Dreaded* means

  A. feared.

  B. liked.

  C. hoped.

  D. None of the above.

Scared?

By Linda Hoyt

The round, round face
The beady eyes
A pumpkin turned to a scary disguise
Should I scare . . .
Should I dare . . .
Should I feel I should beware?

The smile is big
And full of glee
I think that eye just winked at me!

But wait . . .
The mouth is turning down
The eyes are rolling round and round
Should I scare . . .
Should I dare . . .
Should I feel I should beware?

Designed for Survival

By Linda Hoyt

All: Designed for survival in the cold, polar bears are fascinating artists of adaptation.

Team 1: Freezing temperatures, ice, and snow provide a chilly environment that is too much for most mammals.

Team 2: Polar bears have unique adaptations that allow them to survive and thrive!

Team 3: They have a 4-inch-thick layer of fat that provides important insulation against the extreme cold they face living on the ice.

All: They build up their fat during the summer so they can stay warm in the winter.

Team 1: They have a thick furry coat with a special oil that causes water to run off rather than drain down to their skin.

Team 2: The hairs on the top layer are stiff and oily,

Team 3: while the undercoat is softer and very dense to trap body heat and keep the bears warm.

All: Notice how small the ears are . . .

Team 1: Small ears help prevent heat loss from the body.

All: Notice their nose . . .

Team 2: They have an amazing sense of smell that helps them find food even in the dark.

All: Notice the big feet and curved claws . . .

Team 3: Their curved claws help them dig into slippery ice, while the thick rough pads on the bottom of their feet act like warm, nonstick slippers!

All: Polar bears . . . designed for survival!

Hansel and Gretel

Retold by Rika Lesser

FOCUS THE LEARNING

Introduction: We summarize all the time. When you get home from school and someone asks "How was your day?" you summarize and tell the most interesting parts of the day. When someone asks you about a movie you saw, you can summarize the movie and tell what it was about. Let's practice.

Think about getting up and getting ready for school today. You don't have to tell everything, just the most important parts. Think together! Tell each other about your morning.

As I read *Hansel and Gretel* by Rika Lesser, your job is to think about the story and the important parts you want to include in a summary at the end.

INTERACTIVE READ-ALOUD
Model and Guide Practice

Story Map
Title _____ Author_____
Setting   Characters
The Problem: Events • • • • • •
Solution

READ THE FIRST TWO PAGES OF THE STORY. Our story map reminds me that I need to think about the setting, the characters, and the problem. Listen to me summarize what I know so far. "A mother and father are so poor that they can't feed their children so they are going to leave the children in the forest."

Thinking partners, put your heads together. How was my summary? Is there anything else you would have added?

READ TO WHERE HANSEL GATHERS THE WHITE PEBBLES. I am going to pause for a moment and look at the story map. Listen to my summary now. "A mother and father are so poor that they can't feed their children so the mother suggests they leave the children in the forest. The children hear them talking about their plan and Hansel, who is very smart, gathers white pebbles so he can find his way home."

READ TO WHERE HANSEL AND GRETEL USE THE PEBBLES TO FIND THEIR WAY HOME.

Let's look at the story map. Put your heads together. Summarize the story to this point.

CONTINUE TO THE END. Pause occasionally to direct attention to the story map and have partners add to their summaries. Be sure to fill out the story map as the story unfolds.

END OF STORY REFLECTION

We are going to use a "cumulative retell" (Hoyt, 1999) to summarize our story. Ready?

(Have one person come forward and tell the first event. That person stays at the front. Ask for a volunteer to tell what happened next. When the second person walks to the front, the first person tells his or her part again before the second event is described. As each event is added, keep starting from the beginning so the summary is cumulative.)

SHARE THE LEARNING
Focus on Summarizing

Tip for Share the Reading

Invite the students to look at the illustrations. Then read in unison. Explain that their job is to work with a partner to plan a summary of the content. This time there isn't a problem and solution. They need to consider the information in the passage and decide what is important enough to include in a summary.

Big Muscle

To build a big building, machines are needed to move rocks and soil. These big machines clear the building site, scooping up rocks and dirt that are dumped into dump trucks. The dump trucks then carry the load away from the building site so there is room to begin construction of the new building.

Tip for Readers Theater Script

For emergent readers, enjoy "Hansel and Gretel" as an echo poem: teacher reads and children echo. For developing readers, you might want to enjoy the script as a three-team experience. For fluent readers, small groups of three can read the script together, rehearsing for fluency and expression.

Hansel and Gretel
Readers Theater Adaptation by Linda Hoyt

Narrator 1:	Once upon a time, a poor family had nothing to eat.
Narrator 2:	The mother decided the children should be left in the woods alone.
Narrator 3:	But Hansel was smart and dropped white pebbles in the path.
All:	He and his sister found their way home by following the trail of pebbles.
Narrator 2:	Once again the children were taken into the woods and left alone.
Narrator 1:	This time Hansel had no pebbles,
Narrator 3:	and they were hopelessly lost.
All:	They came across a little house made of bread and candy.
Narrator 1:	The children were so hungry they started eating the house.
Narrator 3:	The witch who owned the house locked Hansel in a cage
Narrator 2:	and made Gretel do all of her work.
Narrator 1:	For four long weeks, the children were trapped.
Narrator 1:	One day, Gretel locked the witch in the oven.
All:	The children found their way home.
Narrator 1:	Their father was thrilled to see them.
Narrators 2 and 3:	And they lived happily ever after.

EXTEND THE LEARNING

☆ Summarize a variety of selections including fiction, nonfiction, magazine articles, and poetry.

☆ Build summaries into read-alouds with midstream as well as end-of-story retells.

☆ Use the Cumulative Retell in various settings to encourage well-developed summaries.

☆ Teach learners to draw several small illustrations to help them remember key points in a summary before beginning an oral or written retell.

☆ Have children read a selection and plan a summary. Then provide an opportunity to meet with members of another classroom so the listeners provide an authentic audience for the summary.

☆ Encourage parents to ask their children to summarize bedtime stories or events such as going for pizza or visiting a relative.

ASSESS THE LEARNING

➤ Listen in as partners summarize to assess their proficiency.

➤ During small group instruction, assess children's summaries of guided selections.

➤ Confer with individuals during independent reading to assess their ability to read and summarize independently.

INFUSION OF FORMAL LANGUAGE
Test-style language

What *unexpected* event happened in the story?
   A. The children were lost.
   B. The father and mother left them in the forest.
   C. The witch had a lot of food.
   D. Gretel pushed the witch into the oven.

Hansel gathered white pebbles and used a bone to make the witch think he was thin. There is enough evidence to suggest that Hansel is
   A. clever.
   B. a good problem solver.
   C. smart.
   D. All of the above.

Big Muscle

To build a big building, machines are needed to move rocks and soil. These big machines clear the building site, scooping up rocks and dirt that are dumped into dump trucks. The dump trucks then carry the load away from the building site so there is room to begin construction of the new building.

Hansel and Gretel

Readers Theater Adaptation by Linda Hoyt

Narrator 1:	Once upon a time, a poor family had nothing to eat.
Narrator 2:	The mother decided the children should be left in the woods alone.
Narrator 3:	But Hansel was smart and dropped white pebbles in the path.
All:	He and his sister found their way home by following the trail of pebbles.
Narrator 2:	Once again the children were taken into the woods and left alone.
Narrator 1:	This time Hansel had no pebbles,
Narrator 3:	and they were hopelessly lost.
All:	They came across a little house made of bread and candy.
Narrator 1:	The children were so hungry they started eating the house.
Narrator 3:	The witch who owned the house locked Hansel in a cage
Narrator 2:	and made Gretel do all of her work.
Narrator 3:	For four long weeks, the children were trapped.
Narrator 1:	One day, Gretel locked the witch in the oven.
All:	The children found their way home.
Narrator 1:	Their father was thrilled to see them.
Narrators 2 and 3:	And they lived happily ever after.

DISTINGUISH REAL FROM MAKE-BELIEVE

Stellaluna
Janell Cannon

FOCUS THE LEARNING

Introduction: Writers of fiction books often use a combination of things they make up and things that are true as they create their stories. As we read *Stellaluna* by Janell Cannon, you will find a wonderful mix of things that real bats do and things that are just make-believe. I am going to make a chart to help us record our thinking about Things That Are Real and Things That Are Make-Believe in this book. I am going to add a third column because we may find some things we aren't sure about and want to check in a book about bats after we are done with this story.

Things That Are Real	Things That Are Make-Believe	Things We Want to Know

---

INTERACTIVE READ-ALOUD
Model and Guide Practice

READ PAGE 1. I found a place where the author used make-believe. She said, "Mother Bat crooned to her baby and said, 'I'll name you Stellaluna.'" We know a mother bat can't talk. This is make-believe. I am going to add it to the chart.

READ THE SECOND PAGE. I know that owls feed at night, and since bats also fly at night, I think this is something real. I am going to write "owl attacks bat" on the chart under things that are real.

READ TO WHERE STELLALUNA LANDS IN THE NEST.

Think together. Think about real and make-believe. What do you notice about this page? What might we write on the chart?

READ TO WHERE STELLALUNA PROMISES TO OBEY THE RULES.

Think together. What is real? What is make-believe? What should we write on our chart?

CONTINUE TO THE END. Stop frequently to talk about real, make-believe, and things we need to research because we aren't absolutely sure.

END OF STORY REFLECTION
Let's look at our chart. Partners, think together. What was make-believe in the story? Please share your thinking. Partners, let's think again. If you were going to tell someone about the real and make-believe mixed together in this story, what would you say?

SHARE THE LEARNING
Focus on Distinguishing Real from Make-Believe

Tip for Share the Reading

Explain to the children that there are two passages: one that is based on truth and one make-believe. They have the same title. The children's job is to listen to the two passages and then talk with their partner. Which one is which, and what are the clues? After they have heard the passages and discussed them, invite the children to join you in chorally reading the two selections.

Adam

Adam is a monkey who lives in a zoo with his mother. The animal keepers bring him food and make sure his house is clean and safe. He loves to eat bananas, apples, and all kinds of vegetables. For a special treat, he gets to eat a bit of pineapple, which is one of his favorite foods. When Adam is fully grown, he will be about four feet tall and weigh 45 pounds.

Adam

Adam looked over at his mom and squawked, "Mom, look out! There is a crack in the branch you are sitting on." His mother jumped off of the branch just as it split and tumbled to the ground far below.

"Adam, you saved me!" his thankful mother called. Adam felt really proud.

Tip for Readers Theater Script

Guide the children in examining the photographs of the bat wing and the baby bat. Divide students into two teams and read the script as a call-and-response experience. As they gain confidence, have students read the entire selection with a partner, focusing on reading with expression and fluency.

EXTEND THE LEARNING

☆ Keep a two-column chart labeled Fact and Fiction. After each read-aloud, write the title of the book under the category that best describes it.

☆ Have partners interview each other to find out who likes fiction books and who likes factual books.

☆ Read nonfiction selections on bats and then read *Stellaluna* again. Did the additional information help make the story easier to understand? Did the information make it clearer which parts were fact and which were fiction?

☆ Create "Fact" or "Fib" statements by having students fold 3 x 5 cards in half. On the front they write statements such as "Bats are blind." The 3 x 5 card can then be opened to reveal the answer. "That is a fib! Bats are not blind." (From *Revisit, Reflect, Retell*, Hoyt: Heinemann. 1999.)

ASSESS THE LEARNING

> During small group instruction, have children sort books into fact/fiction categories to assess their understanding.

> Confer with readers during independent reading to see if they are able to identify elements of truth and make-believe independently.

INFUSION OF FORMAL LANGUAGE
Test-style language

When something is make-believe, that means it
- A. doesn't happen in real life.
- B. is pretend.
- C. is something the author made up.
- D. All of the above.

Pip, Flitter, and Flap landed gracefully on a branch. *Gracefully* means
- A. hard.
- B. fast.
- C. smoothly.
- D. awkwardly.

Adam

Adam is a monkey who lives in a zoo with his mother. The animal keepers bring him food and make sure his house is clean and safe. He loves to eat bananas, apples, and all kinds of vegetables. For a special treat, he gets to eat a bit of pineapple, which is one of his favorite foods. When Adam is fully grown, he will be about four feet tall and weigh 45 pounds.

Adam

Adam looked over at his mom and squawked, "Mom, look out! There is a crack in the branch you are sitting on."

His mother jumped off of the branch just as it split and tumbled to the ground far below.

"Adam, you saved me!" his thankful mother called. Adam felt really proud.

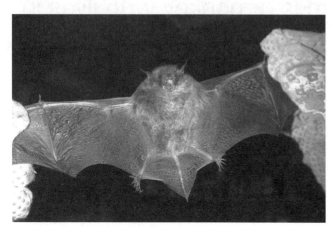

Group 1	Group 2
Bats lay eggs.	That's not true.
Bat babies are born alive.	That's a fact.
The babies are put in a nursery so they can learn to play.	That's make-believe.
Babies are in a nursery so their mothers can hunt for food.	That's a fact.
Bats have feathers.	No Way!
Bats have skin on their wings.	That's a fact.
Bat wings are a lot like a human hand.	Are you sure?
There are long "fingers" that hold the wings out and a "thumb" that looks like a claw at the top of the wing.	What an interesting fact!
Bats talk to their babies.	That's make-believe.
Bats give their babies names.	That belongs in a story!
Bats are blind.	Not true!
Bats don't see very well.	That's better.
Bats use echo-location to find their way around.	That's a fact.
Bats get stuck in people's hair.	No way.
We should be afraid of bats.	That's make-believe.
Bats are mammals that can fly.	Now, that's a fact!

Story Elements

The story elements strand includes identifying events in a plot sequence, discerning the author's purpose, tracking character development, developing a statement of theme for a text, and so on. There is also support for examining structural elements such as climax, setting, problem/solution, and the role of the narrator.

DISTINGUISH FICTION/NONFICTION

The Man Who Walked Between the Towers
Mordicai Gerstein

FOCUS THE LEARNING

Introduction: Biographies are nonfiction books about real people who actually lived. In a biography we hear the story of things a real person did and learn about what was important to that person. Everything in a biography needs to be true or it isn't a biography. It is fiction. Today we are going to read a biography, *The Man Who Walked Between the Towers* by Mordicai Gerstein. This book won the Caldecott medal for best art in 2004. It is important before we start to remember what we know about the Twin Towers in New York. These two huge buildings were the tallest buildings in America. They were destroyed when airplanes flew into them on September 11, 2001. The buildings aren't there anymore but this story lives on.

INTERACTIVE READ-ALOUD
Model and Guide Practice

READ TO "HE WANTED TO WALK BETWEEN THE TWO TOWERS."
I am thinking about how hard it would be to walk and dance on a rope up in the air. Think about how hard it would be to balance and not fall off! I can imagine someone walking on a rope just a little way above the ground, but to walk on a rope between two buildings?

Think together. What do you think of that?

READ TO "MAYBE IF I DRESSED AS A CONSTRUCTION WORKER."
I am remembering that this is a true story. Since it is a biography, I know everything in this book really happened. I can understand why the police wouldn't want him to do it. It is dangerous.

Talk to your thinking partner. What are you thinking about this biography? The title is The Man Who Walked Between the Towers. *We know he did it. What are you wondering?*

READ TO "THE WIRE WAS ⅞ OF AN INCH THICK." (Help the children visualize the size of the wire by showing ⅞ of an inch on a yardstick.) This is amazing. He carried a 440-lb. spool of wire up 180 stairs and crawled down the side of the building to get the arrow.

What are you thinking now?

CONTINUE TO THE END. Pause to show the two fold-out pages where he is crossing between the towers. Pause occasionally to give partners time to talk about this nonfiction selection.

END OF STORY REFLECTION

Wasn't that an amazing biography? We know that what Philippe Pettit did was very dangerous and that he was lucky to be alive afterward. I am so glad you wouldn't try anything like that. You are smart and you know how to stay safe. Let's think about biography. That means that you are telling about a person. You don't have to tell about the person's whole life. You can just focus on an important part. For example, if we were going to do a biography about me, I would want the biography to be about my work as a teacher. We wouldn't need to tell the year I was born and every little thing about me—just focus on my teaching and why it is important. If someone was to write a biography about you, what would you want to have in it?

Thinking partners, tell each other what experience you would want included in a biography about you.

Tip for Share the Reading

Read "No Wooden Teeth" to the children, making sure that they understand this is a biography. Everything really happened; nothing is make-believe. Bring their attention to the fact that this biography focuses on Washington's teeth, not his entire life. Have the children join in reading chorally as they are ready, and then have them create illustrations to support the meaning of this biography.

No Wooden Teeth
By Linda Hoyt

People like to say that George Washington had wooden teeth. But that isn't true! He did, however, have a lot of trouble with his mouth.

While he led our country's fight for freedom, George Washington was in constant pain from his teeth. He fought through the pain and led his men through the war. Very few people knew how much he was hurting. During this time, his teeth kept falling out and many had to be pulled.

When George Washington was elected President, he had only two teeth remaining. He learned to speak with his lips close together and tried hard not to smile so people wouldn't know about his teeth.

He finally had false teeth specially carved from the ivory of a hippopotamus. Although these teeth were painful for him to wear, they allowed him to smile. He had many sets of false teeth after that, but none of them were wood.

Tip for Readers Theater Script

For emergent readers, enjoy "The Man Who Walked Between the Towers" as an echo poem: teacher reads and children echo. Then have them create an illustration about this biography. For developing readers, enjoy the script as a two-team experience. With increased proficiency, partners can read the poem together for fluency and expression.

The Man Who Walked Between the Towers
Readers Theater Adaptation by Linda Hoyt

Team 1: There once was a man who loved tightropes.
Team 2: He walked and danced on a wire.
Team 1: He dreamed of spanning the Twin Towers
Team 2: And believed he could make it work.
Team 1: He thought and planned how to do it,
Team 2: And he got himself up to the roof.
Team 1: A wire was strung between the buildings.
Team 2: At dawn he stepped out on the wire.
Team 1: New York lay far down below him . . .
Team 2: Winds blew and whirled from beneath.
Team 1: Below, people gasped, amazed—
Team 2: They couldn't believe what they'd seen!
Team 1: He held out his hands for policemen . . .
Team 2: He knew what he did was unlawful.
Team 1: The judge banged his gavel and told him
Team 2: To perform for the kids in the park.

EXTEND THE LEARNING

☆ Read an array of biographies. Heinemann Classroom, National Geographic, Rigby, the Wright Group, and other publishers offer highly appealing biographies for young children.

☆ Have children create a biography of a classmate or a parent. Use a supportive structure such as *The Important Book* by Margaret Wise Brown: "The important thing about _____ is that _____." This structure focuses the writer on a "single-idea biography."

☆ After reading nonfiction selections, have children create illustrations and write about what was learned. Use nonfiction text features such as labels, captions, close-ups, and headings. Encourage the children to talk about their nonfiction writing and how it is different than fiction.

☆ After an art project or science experience, engage the children in an interactive write focused on procedure. Create a materials list and list each step in the process to model the format and language of procedural nonfiction text.

ASSESS THE LEARNING

> Confer with individuals and interview them about fiction and nonfiction to determine their levels of understanding.

> During small group instruction, read and write in many nonfiction forms such as procedure, biography, and description. Assess students' ability to identify and navigate these forms.

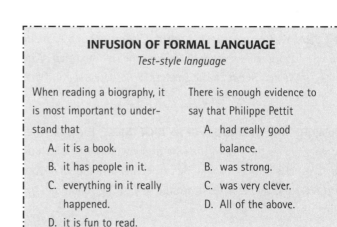

INFUSION OF FORMAL LANGUAGE
Test-style language

When reading a biography, it is most important to understand that
  A. it is a book.
  B. it has people in it.
  C. everything in it really happened.
  D. it is fun to read.

There is enough evidence to say that Philippe Petit
  A. had really good balance.
  B. was strong.
  C. was very clever.
  D. All of the above.

No Wooden Teeth

By Linda Hoyt

People like to say that George Washington had wooden teeth. But that isn't true! He did, however, have a lot of trouble with his mouth.

While he led our country's fight for freedom, George Washington was in constant pain from his teeth. He fought through the pain and led his men through the war. Very few people knew how much he was hurting. During this time, his teeth kept falling out and many had to be pulled.

When George Washington was elected President, he had only two teeth remaining. He learned to speak with his lips close together and tried hard not to smile so people wouldn't know about his teeth.

He finally had false teeth specially carved from the ivory of a hippopotamus. Although these teeth were painful for him to wear, they allowed him to smile. He had many sets of false teeth after that, but none of them were wood.

The Man Who Walked Between the Towers

Readers Theater Adaptation by Linda Hoyt

Team 1:   There once was a man who loved tightropes.

Team 2:   He walked and danced on a wire.

Team 1:   He dreamed of spanning the Twin Towers

Team 2:   And believed he could make it work.

Team 1:   He thought and planned how to do it,

Team 2:   And he got himself up to the roof.

Team 1:   A wire was strung between the buildings.

Team 2:   At dawn he stepped out on the wire.

Team 1:   New York lay far down below him . . .

Team 2:   Winds blew and whirled from beneath.

Team 1:   Below, people gasped, amazed—

Team 2:   They couldn't believe what they'd seen!

Team 1:   He held out his hands for policemen . . .

Team 2:   He knew what he did was unlawful.

Team 1:   The judge banged his gavel and told him

Team 2:   To perform for the kids in the park.

SEQUENCE OF EVENTS/PLOT

Goggles!
Ezra Jack Keats

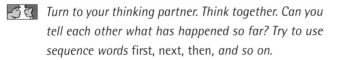

FOCUS THE LEARNING

(Prepare cards on which you have written *first, second, third, then, next, now,* and *finally*.)

Introduction: One of the things we do as readers is keep track of the order in which things happen. We think about what happened first, second, third, and so on. These are called sequence words. Let's practice by thinking about our day so far. First (hold up the card that says *first*), we came in and hung up our coats. Then (hold up the card), we had independent reading time. Next, we worked on math, and now we are having our read-aloud time. Did I cover it all?

Turn to your partner. Tell what happened after you left school yesterday. Tell what happened first, second, and third.

This is the kind of thinking we will do as we read *Goggles!* by Ezra Jack Keats. We will think about the order in which things happen.

INTERACTIVE READ-ALOUD
Model and Guide Practice

READ PAGE 1. I am going to stop reading and think for a minute. I think that Peter is the boy in the red shirt holding up the goggles because it says Peter is the one who found the goggles. That means that Archie must be the boy in the blue shirt. So here is what I know so far. The first (hold up the card that says *first*) thing that happened is that Peter found some motorcycle goggles and he told his friend, Archie, about the goggles.

READ PAGES 2–3. I am going to stop reading and think about what has happened so far. I am going to start at the beginning. (Use the cards.) First, Peter found some goggles and told his friend Archie. Next, they went into their hideout, and now they are going to go to Archie's house.

 Turn to your thinking partner. Think together. Can you tell each other what has happened so far? Try to use sequence words first, next, then, *and so on.*

READ TO WHERE PETER GETS KNOCKED DOWN.

 Turn to your thinking partner. Think together. Start at the beginning and tell what has happened so far.

CONTINUE TO THE END. Pause occasionally to give partners time to retell the sequence of events. Keep reminding the children to use sequence words as they talk to each other.

END OF STORY REFLECTION

Wow! That story was exciting. Let's use our sequence words and try to put the events in the correct order. First, . . . (Call on someone to stand up and hold the card and tell what happened first.) Second, . . . who would like to hold the card and tell what happened second? (When the second child comes forward, start over. Have the person holding the *first* card say their part again. As each event is added, keep going back to the beginning so the children hear the sequence of events over and over as they build toward the end. This is called a "cumulative retell" [Hoyt, 1999].)

SHARE THE LEARNING
Focus on Sequence of Events

Tip for Share the Reading

Read the directions slowly, asking the children to visualize the sequence of steps as you read. Then have them join in reading with you. Finally, invite them to follow the steps to create their own snowflakes.

How to Make a Paper Snowflake
By Linda Hoyt

First, cut a piece of paper into a square.

Next, fold the square into a triangle.

Fold the triangle in half one more time to make a smaller triangle.

Then, fold it once again to make an even smaller triangle.

Cut interesting shapes along the fold lines.

Finally, open the paper and enjoy your beautiful snowflake.

Tip for Readers Theater Script

Remind students of the sequence of events in *Goldilocks and the Three Bears*. Remind them that new variations on old favorites are often a bit different from the original. Work with the students to present "Goldilocks and the Cops" with enthusiasm and an emphasis on sequence of events.

EXTEND THE LEARNING

☆ Use the sequence cards frequently to retell classroom events and stories. Encourage the children to use the words in daily communication.

☆ Use the sequence cards to explain steps in art projects, science experiments, and so on.

☆ Have children create four-part sketches that reflect a sequence of events. Label the sketches *first, second, third*, and *fourth*. Add text to the sketches.

ASSESS THE LEARNING

➤ Confer with readers during guided and independent reading to monitor their ability to correctly sequence story events.

➤ Listen as partners retell events to see if they are correctly using sequence words.

INFUSION OF FORMAL LANGUAGE
Test-style language

In the final scene of the story, the boys were
A. running from the big kids.
B. sitting on Archie's front porch.
C. still really scared.
D. playing with Willie.

The first event in the story was when
A. Peter found the goggles.
B. Willy climbed into the tube.
C. the boys were in their hideout.
D. they were talking through the tube.

How to Make a Paper Snowflake

By Linda Hoyt

First, cut a piece of paper into a square.

Next, fold the square into a triangle.

Fold the triangle in half one more time to make a smaller triangle.

Then, fold it once again to make an even smaller triangle.

Cut interesting shapes along the fold lines.

Finally, open the paper and enjoy your beautiful snowflake.

Goldilocks and the Cops

Readers Theater Adaptation by Linda Hoyt

Teacher:	**In the beginning . . .**
Baby Bear:	Hey, Mom! I'm starving. Let's eat!
Momma Bear:	Bad news, honey. The porridge is too hot. Let's go for a walk while it cools.
Teacher:	**Meanwhile . . .**
Goldilocks:	Hey, Mom… I'm headed out for a while. I'm taking my bike on a spin through the woods. Be back later . . .
Goldilock's Mother:	Be home by ten. You have swimming today!
Teacher:	**Then . . .**
Goldilocks:	Hey, check out this cool little house! I'm going to take a look.
Narrator 1:	As you know, Goldilocks wasn't a very nice little girl. She marched right into the house of the bears and started eating their breakfast!
Narrator 2:	Then she sat in their chairs and broke the baby bear's chair all to bits!
Teacher:	**Next . . .**
Narrator 3:	The crazy girl went upstairs and, after trying all the beds, went to sleep in the bed of the baby bear.
Teacher:	**Is that all?**

Narrator 1:	Oh, no. Then the bears came home.
Baby Bear and Momma Bear:	It doesn't smell right in here. Something's wrong.
Narrator 2:	Was it ever! Baby Bear and Momma Bear found the empty porridge bowl and the broken chair, and then . . .
Teacher:	**Is this the end?**
Narrator 1:	Momma Bear called the police!
Narrator 2:	When the police arrived, they handcuffed that naughty Goldilocks and marched her up to her front door. *(Make a knocking sound.)*
Goldilock's Mother:	Hello, officers. *(Looks shocked.)* Goldilocks! What is happening here? Why is my beautiful little girl in handcuffs?
Narrator 1:	Then Mom got an earful about how her daughter deserved to be in jail for
Narrator 2:	Breaking and entering.
Narrator 3:	Vandalism.
All:	General uncontrolled behavior!
Teacher:	**How did it end?**
Narrator 1:	The bears put their house back together.
Narrator 2:	Goldilocks was grounded for a whole year.
Narrator 3:	And everyone lived happily ever after!

INITIATING EVENT AND CONCLUSION

Cheyenne Again
Eve Bunting

FOCUS THE LEARNING:

Introduction: The initiating event in a story is like a springboard into the action. This is where you realize what the problem may be and feel a connection to the characters and the situation. The conclusion is where everything comes together and you get a clear sense that the story is ending. In the conclusion you often see that a problem has been solved. In *Cheyenne Again* by Eve Bunting we will watch for these two important story elements.

INTERACTIVE READ-ALOUD
Model and Guide Practice

READ PAGES 5 AND 7. We have the initiating event. The police-man is trying to take this young boy from his family.

 An initiating event often leaves you with a lot of questions. It draws you into the story. What do you think of this opening? Is this a powerful initiating event?

READ TO PAGE 11. I am watching for a conclusion. I can tell this isn't it because it doesn't feel like an ending yet. It is causing me to ask more questions and wonder what will happen.

READ TO PAGE 13. This makes me so sad. Who would want to trade soft leather for scratchy wool clothes? And braids are honorable in Indian culture. Getting his hair cut must have been terrible for him. They are taking away everything he knows and understands.

 Talk to your thinking partner. Would this be a good conclusion to the story? Why or why not?

CONTINUE TO THE END. Pause occasionally to give partners time to talk.

 Talk to your thinking partner. This is clearly the end. What did you think of the conclusion? Was this a good ending for the story? Why or why not?

END OF STORY REFLECTION

Let's consider the initiating event and the conclusion in this story. What can we learn from the way Eve Bunting wrote the beginning and the ending? How might her initiating event and conclusion help us as writers? Partners, get your ideas ready. I am going to write down everyone's thinking.

(Make a chart to collect these ideas.)

 **SHARE THE LEARNING**

Focus on Initiating Event and Conclusion

Tip for Share the Reading

Engage the students in reading the passage together. Then ask them to think with a partner: Would this be more likely to be an initiating event or a conclusion? What are the clues? If they were to create a conclusion for this passage, what would make sense? What would bring this situation to a satisfying conclusion?

> Scrape! Skid... Screech! The skateboards skidded across the sidewalk and through the door of the grocery store. Splat! Down went three laughing kids. As they rolled on the floor, giggling hysterically, they realized they were right at the feet of the furious store owner.
>
> "You crazy kids! I told you if you ever rode your skateboards into my store again, I would call your parents," roared the grocer.
>
> "Stand still and don't move. This is only the beginning of your troubles." He stomped to the phone and started to dial.

Tip for Readers Theater Script

Have the students read "The Trial of Jack . . . and the Beanstalk" and then discuss: The judge challenged everyone to describe the conclusion and determine if it ended fairly. Have partners put their heads together. How might they describe the conclusion? Is there another ending that might have been more fair? Does the conclusion leave the reader feeling satisfied? How should the judge settle the case? You might challenge students to write a conclusion for the Readers Theater script.

EXTEND THE LEARNING

☆ Read a variety of fiction books and have the students identify the initiating event and conclusion in each.

☆ Have the students plan a piece of fiction writing, taking time to map out an initiating event and conclusion before they begin drafting.

☆ Find the initiating event and conclusion in a movie.

☆ Locate the initiating event and conclusion in a situation at school (doing a research project, conducting a science experiment, and so on).

☆ Compare the initiating events and conclusions in several stories. Decide which ones are best and why.

ASSESS THE LEARNING

➤ Listen in as partners discuss initiating events and conclusions to determine their levels of understanding.

➤ During small group instruction, identify initiating events and conclusions.

➤ Have students reread fiction writing selections they have created and attempt to strengthen the initiating event and conclusion.

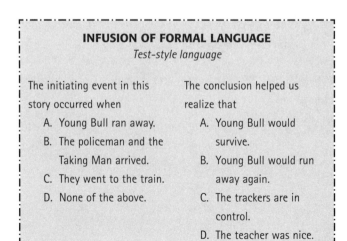

Scrape! Skid… Screech! The skateboards skidded across the sidewalk and through the door of the grocery store. Splat! Down went three laughing kids. As they rolled on the floor, giggling hysterically, they realized they were right at the feet of the furious store owner.

"You crazy kids! I told you if you ever rode your skateboards into my store again, I would call your parents," roared the grocer.

"Stand still and don't move. This is only the beginning of your troubles." He stomped to the phone and started to dial.

The Trial of Jack . . . and the Beanstalk

By Linda Hoyt

Characters:	Jack, Judge, Baliff, Mother, Giant
Baliff:	Har ye, har ye. All stand for the Honorable Judge _____.
Mother (sniffling):	I am so worried about Jack. He can be very foolish, but he should never have taken those things from the Giant.
Baliff:	Jack, you have been charged with entering the home of the Giant and stealing his prized possessions. How do you plead?
Jack:	Not guilty, sir. I was thirsty and hungry and Mrs. Giant told me to come in and hide.
Judge:	I find it difficult to believe that you just stumbled into a castle in the clouds because you were hungry. I think we need to go back and start at the beginning, young man. Tell me, what was the *initiating event*? How did this craziness get started?
Mother:	I can help with that. It all started when I sent Jack to sell our cow so we would have money for food. The foolish boy traded our valuable cow for some stupid beans! I was so furious I threw the beans out the window, and overnight they sprouted into a beanstalk. That is what initiated everything . . . that stupid beanstalk!

Judge: So the problem was the beanstalk?

Mother: That was part of the problem. The real problem began when Jack climbed the beanstalk and walked right into the Giant's house. Foolish boy never would listen to me!

Jack: You see, sir, it really wasn't my fault. My mom threw the beans into the garden, and I just had to see where that beanstalk went. It was hard work climbing that tall stalk and by the time I got to the castle, I was starving and really thirsty. That's why I went inside.

Giant: Fee, fi, fo fiddly! You make up stories like a little kiddly. You came into my house because you wanted my harp, my goose that laid the golden egg, and my money! You are a thief!

Judge: It appears that we have identified the *initiating event* to this story. Now, all of you need to find a way to describe the *conclusion*. How did this end? And did it end fairly? Our job in this court is to reach a conclusion. We are now going to call for a recess while you work out the details of the conclusion. I will call you back together shortly to hear your versions of the conclusion to this sorry tale.

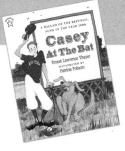

CLIMAX AND FALLING ACTION

Casey at the Bat
Ernest Lawrence Thayer

FOCUS THE LEARNING

Introduction: The climax in a story is the point of highest interest. Sometimes a climax can be exciting. When you are at the climax of a story, you might feel like holding your breath or you might be worried about the character and what will happen. After the climax, we have "falling action." This is the time when the author finishes the story and gives it a closing. Let's think about *Goldilocks and the Three Bears*. The climax in that story was when the bears walked in and found Goldilocks asleep on their bed. That was a pretty exciting part because we didn't know what would happen to Goldilocks.

Thinking partners, put your heads together. What happened after the climax in Goldilocks and the Three Bears?

We are going to read *Casey at the Bat* by Ernest Lawrence Thayer. While we enjoy the story, we are going to be thinking about the climax and then noticing the falling action as the story ends.

INTERACTIVE READ-ALOUD
Model and Guide Practice

(You will need a felt pen and a copy of the story map drawn on a chart or placed on the overhead projector.)

READ THE FIRST TWO PAGES. I am going to use a story map to help us think about the way the story builds to a climax. We know that Casey is the main character. He is a baseball player. We know he thinks he is the best player, so I am going to write "confident Casey." The first event is, he is late for the game. On the first line, I will write "late."

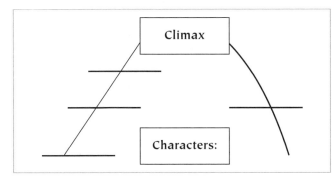

READ TO WHERE IT SAYS JIMMY WAS SAFE AT SECOND.

Think together. I want to use the next line to show that Jimmy and Flynn are on base. How should I say that?

READ TO WHERE CASEY LETS THE FIRST BALL PASS BY. I am

going to use the third line on the map to write, "Casey is at bat." This isn't the climax yet, but I think it is coming soon.

READ TO WHERE CASEY LETS THE SECOND BALL GO BY.

Thinking partners, he has two strikes. If he gets three, he is out. What do you think will happen?

READ TO WHERE "THE AIR IS SHATTERED BY THE FORCE OF HIS BLOW."

Put your heads together. Do you think this is it? Is this the climax? Are you wondering what will happen? Are you just a little worried?

CONTINUE TO THE END. Pause to write the climax on the top of the chart, point out the falling action as they walk home, and be sure the children notice that the umpire is Casey's dad!

END OF STORY REFLECTION

Let's act out the climax. Who wants to be Casey? We will also need an umpire, a pitcher, and two people on base. Remember, the climax was the most exciting part. We aren't going to act out the whole story, just the climax.

(Afterwards, have children act out the falling action to bring closure to the story.)

SHARE THE LEARNING
Focus on Climax

Tip for Share the Reading

Share the reading (the climax) by reading in unison and emphasizing the natural tension of the first two stanzas. Help readers understand that they can add drama and interest by reading the last two lines slowly and sadly. These are the beginning of the falling action which follows the climax.

They saw his face grow stern and cold,
They saw his muscles strain.
They knew that Casey wouldn't let that ball go by again.

The sneer is gone from Casey's lip,
His teeth are clenched in hate;
And now the pitcher holds the ball,
And now he lets it fly.

He swings . . .
He misses.
. . . There is no joy in Mudville.
Mighty Casey has struck out.

Tip for Readers Theater Script

For emergent readers, enjoy "Casey at the Bat" as an echo poem: teacher reads and children echo. For developing and fluent readers, enjoy the script as a four-team experience. With increased proficiency, small groups of four could read the poem together for fluency, expression, and dramatic interpretation.

Casey at the Bat
Readers Theater Adaptation by Linda Hoyt

Team #2:	There were two outs
Team #1:	And two men on.
Team #4:	The crowd was in a roar.
Team #3:	They really needed Casey to
All:	Hit the ball and score.
Team #2:	The ball came screaming at him
Team #4:	But Casey let it go.
Team #3:	The crowd was in an uproar.
Team #1:	The Umpire had to go,
All:	"Strike One!"
Team #3:	Once again the pitcher threw . . .
Team #2:	The ball screamed past the plate.
Team #1:	Casey still just stood there.
Team #4:	The Umpire yelled,
All:	"Strike Two."

EXTEND THE LEARNING

☆ Use the story map for this selection with a variety of read-aloud selections to help children identify the climax and falling action.

☆ Conduct a contest for "best climax in a story." Have children read and search to find books with tension and well-developed climax. Read the selections aloud and vote to see which one they think has the best climax.

☆ Watch a movie together and stop the viewing at the point of the climax. After the children discuss the climax, have them watch the falling action and see how the movie uses the same technique as books.

☆ In interactive writing, use the story map shown in this lesson to plan a story with a climax. Then work together to create a draft.

☆ Pause in a read-aloud to create an illustration of just the climax. Model how you can focus on a single element in a story with an illustration. Enhance your illustration with labels.

ASSESS THE LEARNING

> Listen in as partners discuss climax and falling action to assess their understanding.

> During small group instruction, read selections with a climax and assess learner ability to identify the element.

> Have students draw and write about the climax in a story. Then assess their illustration and writing to see if they identified the correct portion of the story.

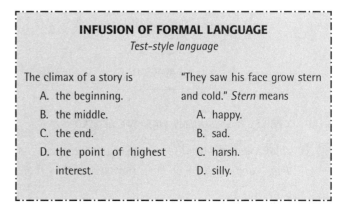

INFUSION OF FORMAL LANGUAGE
Test-style language

The climax of a story is
  A. the beginning.
  B. the middle.
  C. the end.
  D. the point of highest interest.

"They saw his face grow stern and cold." *Stern* means
  A. happy.
  B. sad.
  C. harsh.
  D. silly.

They saw his face grow stern and cold,
They saw his muscles strain.
They knew that Casey wouldn't let that ball go by again.

The sneer is gone from Casey's lip,
His teeth are clenched in hate;
And now the pitcher holds the ball,
And now he lets it fly.

He swings . . .
He misses.
. . . There is no joy in Mudville.
Mighty Casey has struck out.

Casey at the Bat

Readers Theater Adaptation by Linda Hoyt

Team #2:   There were two outs

Team #1:   And two men on.

Team #4:   The crowd was in a roar.

Team #3:   They really needed Casey to

All: Hit the ball and score.

Team #2:   The ball came screaming at him

Team #4:   But Casey let it go.

Team #3:   The crowd was in an uproar.

Team #1:   The Umpire had to go,

All: "Strike One!"

Team #3:   Once again the pitcher threw . . .

Team #2:   The ball screamed past the plate.

Team #1:   Casey still just stood there.

Team #4:   The Umpire yelled,

All: "Strike Two."

Team #1:   His face grew stern,

Team #2:   His muscles strained.

Team #3:   This was the ball to watch.

Team #4:   The pitcher let it go again.

Teams #2 and #4:   The ball screamed toward

home plate.

Teams #1 and #3:   They turned and watched for

Casey . . .

Teams #2 and #4:   What a home run he would make!

Teams #1 and #3:   But Casey missed the ball again.

All: Strike three and he was out!

Snowflake Bentley
Jacqueline Briggs Martin

FOCUS THE LEARNING

Introduction: Let's play a game. I am going to ask you questions and your job is to answer with the main idea. Here are some examples: Why do we go to school? You could say, "The main idea is to learn!" Why do we brush our teeth? You could say, "The main idea is to keep them clean so we don't get cavities." Let's try another one. Why do you look both ways before you cross the street?

Turn to your partner. "The main idea is _____."

Here is another example: Our playground is a fun place to play but we have rules that need to be followed so we can all be safe. We have a rule that says there is no jumping off the top of the climbing bars. We have another rule that says only one person can be on a swing at a time. These rules help to keep us safe when we are on the playground.

Turn to your partner. "The main idea is _____."

Today we are going to read *Snowflake Bentley* by Jacqueline Briggs Martin. This is a true story, a biography, about a man who lived a long time ago in Vermont. While I read this to you, your job is to be thinking about the main idea: Why did the author write the book? What did she want us to understand? (Note: The sidenotes are fascinating but might be better read during a second experience with the book.)

INTERACTIVE READ-ALOUD
Model and Guide Practice

READ TO WHERE SNOWFLAKE BENTLEY WAS TRYING TO DRAW SNOWFLAKES. I am thinking about the main idea, about the reason Jacqueline Martin wrote this book. So far, everything we have learned suggests that Willie loved snow more than anything. I am going to keep reading and see if I still think that could be the main idea.

READ TO THE PAGE THAT SHOWS A HORSE PULLING A SLEIGH. I am going to stop reading and think about the main idea again. I am thinking that the main idea is still that Willie loved snow more than anything, but I also want to say how patient he was and how he never gave up. Let me try to put all that together: "The main idea is that a very patient man named Willie loved snow more than anything and wanted to learn about it so badly that he never gave up." How did I do? Did you notice that I am not telling what happened in the story? I am not trying to list the events. I am thinking about the main idea . . .

CONTINUE TO THE END.

Think together: The main idea is _____.

END OF STORY REFLECTION

Let's practice some more main ideas. We can find main ideas for a whole story, and we can find main ideas for parts of books. Let's try it with some parts of the book. Willie's mom and dad used their savings to buy him a very expensive camera that cost more than ten cows. What is the main idea? Why did they do it?

The main idea of that part is _____.

After Willie died, a monument was built for him in the center of town so everyone would remember the man who studied snow. What is the main idea? Why did the people of the town build it?

The main idea of that part is _____.

SHARE THE LEARNING
Focus on Main Idea

Tip for Share the Thinking

Working on the overhead or chart paper, guide the students in thinking with you about how to complete these lines about the book. Notice that the first and last sentences are the same, which reinforces the main idea and gives a strong poetic feeling to the writing.

The important thing about Snowflake Bentley is

_____

_____. It is true that

he _____ and

_____. He even

_____

But, the important thing about Snowflake

Bentley is _____

_____

(Format based on *The Important Book* by Margaret Wise Brown, 1949.)

Tip for Readers Theater Script

For emergent readers, read "Snakes" to the students and talk with them about the main idea of the passage. As they are ready, they may want to chime in chorally, reading and dramatizing familiar lines, or create illustrations for the script. For developing and fluent readers, read the selection to model fluent, expressive reading. Then divide them into two teams to present the script. As students gain proficiency, have them read the passage in partners for fluency practice.

EXTEND THE LEARNING

☆ Have children determine main ideas in guided reading selections or in poems.

☆ Have children illustrate the main idea from a read-aloud and then share their thinking with partners.

☆ Engage writers in drawing and thinking about their main idea before they start writing words. Encourage them to share their main ideas with a partner before they begin to draft.

☆ Utilize the paragraph frame from Share the Thinking with many topics.

ASSESS THE LEARNING

> Review children's drawings of main ideas.

> Confer with readers during independent reading to see if they can identify main ideas when reading independently.

> Assess student writing to see if the writing is held together by a main idea.

INFUSION OF FORMAL LANGUAGE
Test-style language

The main idea of this book is
  A. Snowflake Bentley was a farmer-scientist who studied snow.
  B. lots of people live in the snow.
  C. Snowflake Bentley took pictures.
  D. a museum was built in Vermont.

Which of the following is *not* true?
  A. Snowflake Bentley lived in Vermont.
  B. He liked to go hiking.
  C. He studied snow.
  D. He loved the shapes of snow crystals.

The important thing about Snowflake Bentley is

_____

_____. It is true that

he _____ and

_____. He even

_____.

But, the important thing about Snowflake

Bentley is _____

_____.

(Format based on The Important Book by Margaret Wise Brown, 1948.)

Snakes

By Linda Hoyt

Team 1

Snakes are cold-blooded animals.

When it is cold outside, the snake is cold.

Snakes are always looking for ways to make themselves more comfortable.

On a cold day, they love to lie in the sun . . .

The main idea is snakes are cold-blooded animals.

Team 2

They cannot control their own body heat.

When it is hot outside, the snake is hot.

On a sunny day, they like to lie in the shade where it is cool.

or on a warm rock to gather heat from the sun.

The main idea is snakes are cold-blooded animals.

Owl Moon
Jane Yolen

INTERACTIVE READ-ALOUD
Model and Guide Practice

READ PAGE 1. THEN PAUSE TO THINK ALOUD. I am trying to get a picture in my mind, and Jane Yolen, the author, is really helping me. I can visualize that it's night but that it is bright outside because of the snow. I can visualize the bare trees with no leaves.

READ PAGE 2. I think it must have gotten really noisy when the dogs started barking at the train, but then it got really quiet. The author said, "It was as quiet as a dream." I can visualize everything is really quiet so I would want to whisper if I were there. I am learning a lot about the setting.

READ PAGES 3 AND 4.

Turn to your thinking partner. What did you learn about the setting on these pages? What are you visualizing as you try to make a picture in your mind?

READ TO "YOU HAVE TO BE QUIET AND MAKE YOUR OWN HEAT." I am going to stop reading for a minute and think about what has been happening.

Turn to your thinking partner. Think together. What do you know about the setting now? What are you visualizing in your mind?

Did you notice the way Jane Yolen helped us to *feel* the cold on this page? She used some amazing details to help us understand: "feel the cold as if someone's icy hand was palm-down on my back" and "the tops of my cheeks felt cold and hot at the same time."

CONTINUE TO THE END. Pause frequently to encourage partners to talk about the setting.

END OF STORY REFLECTION

I feel as if the setting in this story really came alive for me. The combination of the pictures and the words really helped me to visualize the setting. Let's make a list to show what we learned about the setting in *Owl Moon*. You provide the words, and I will write them down to help us think about the setting.

SHARE THE LEARNING
Focus on Setting

Tip for Share the Reading

Place the text on the overhead projector and read it aloud with expression. You might read this as a poem or trade off reading every other line to emphasize the language patterns. Invite students to describe what they learned about the setting from this passage. Which words and phrases gave them the most information? What did Jane Yolen do that helped them to visualize the setting?

> I could feel the cold,
> As if someone's icy hand
> Was palm-down on my back.
> And my nose
> And the tops of my cheeks
> Felt cold and hot
> At the same time.
> But I never said a word.
> If you go owling
> You have to be quiet
> And make your own heat.

Tip for Readers Theater Script

For emergent readers, read "Hiding" to the children, stopping periodically to make comments about the setting. Ask the children to think together about the setting and the images they are visualizing as the script unfolds. Children may enjoy creating an illustration for the setting or acting out the script as it is read aloud. For developing readers, engage them in reading chorally after they have heard the script once. Encourage them to emphasize the words that make the setting clear. For fluent readers, try narration teams or small groups for additional readings.

Hiding
By Linda Hoyt

Narrator 1: The ground shakes as each huge foot hits the ground.

Narrator 2: Leaves tremble on the trees.

Narrator 3: Birds and small animals screech and dart away.

Narrator 4: Hiding in a deep thicket of branches and greenery,

Narrator 2: I listen in fear as the thundering footsteps draw closer.

Narrator 3: What can it be?

Narrator 1: I tuck myself into a tiny ball under the branch of a tree,

Narrator 4: Waiting.

EXTEND THE LEARNING

☆ Use the words and phrases listed in the End of Story Reflection to create a list poem. Write it on chart paper and read it again and again to savor the richness of the setting in *Owl Moon*.

☆ Model a piece of writing highlighting a setting you know well. Think out loud for the students about words and phrases that could make the setting come alive for a reader. Take time to create an illustration to go with your writing and think aloud about how illustrations help readers understand important elements of the setting.

☆ Guide the students in creating illustrations and writing about a setting they know. Encourage the use of descriptive words and phrases and help them focus on details.

☆ Have the children look through their independent reading books for well-described settings.

ASSESS THE LEARNING

> Confer with writers as they plan a piece of writing to assess their understanding of the importance of setting and strategies for making setting come alive for their readers.

> Confer with readers during independent reading to see if they understand and recognize various settings and the author's strategies for highlighting setting.

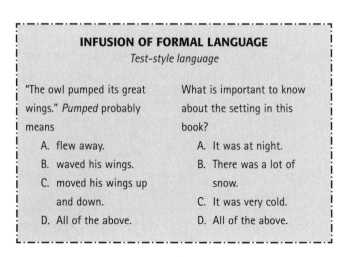

INFUSION OF FORMAL LANGUAGE
Test-style language

"The owl pumped its great wings." *Pumped* probably means

   A. flew away.
   B. waved his wings.
   C. moved his wings up and down.
   D. All of the above.

What is important to know about the setting in this book?

   A. It was at night.
   B. There was a lot of snow.
   C. It was very cold.
   D. All of the above.

I could feel the cold,

As if someone's icy hand

Was palm-down on my back.

And my nose

And the tops of my cheeks

Felt cold and hot

At the same time.

But I never said a word.

If you go owling

You have to be quiet

And make your own heat.

Hiding

By Linda Hoyt

Narrator 1: The ground shakes as each huge foot hits the ground.

Narrator 2: Leaves tremble on the trees.

Narrator 3: Birds and small animals screech and dart away.

Narrator 4: Hiding in a deep thicket of branches and greenery,

Narrator 2: I listen in fear as the thundering footsteps draw closer.

Narrator 3: What can it be?

Narrator 1: I tuck myself into a tiny ball under the branch of a tree,

Narrator 4: Waiting,

Narrator 2: Peering through the dense brush.

Narrator 3: Treetops are swaying wildly.

Narrator 1: A trumpeting sound splits the air.

Narrator 4: I'm so frightened!

Narrator 2: A long gray arm snakes out and

Narrator 3: Rips away the leafy branch hanging over my head.

Narrator 1: I'm so glad elephants don't eat

Everyone: people!

CHARACTER DEVELOPMENT

Mufaro's Beautiful Daughters
John Steptoe

FOCUS THE LEARNING

Introduction: In a good story we learn about the people and animals in a story. We notice the way characters act, the choices they make, and the kind of people they are. When characters are interesting and we understand what makes them unique, that means that the author has used "characterization" and done a good job of making the characters come to life.

Today we are going to read a wonderful book, *Mufaro's Beautiful Daughters* by John Steptoe. It will be our job to pay special attention to the characters and think of words we can use to describe them. As I read to you, we will be stopping often to write words that help us understand the characters. As you listen, notice the characterization in this story.

INTERACTIVE READ-ALOUD
Model and Guide Practice
(Create a chart and add words as you share them with the students.)

READ THE FIRST THREE PAGES. THEN PAUSE TO THINK ALOUD. I am going to write *Manyara* and *Nyasha* on our chart. I am already getting the idea that Manyara is grumpy so I am going to write "grumpy" under her name. I also think she is mean. Manyara is not being nice when she talks to her sister. I am going to write "mean" under her name. Please be thinking about words to describe the characters as I read on.

READ TO WHERE NYASHA MEETS THE SNAKE AND SINGS TO HIM. I am thinking of Nyasha now. No matter how mean her sister is, Nyasha smiles and sings and is even nice to snakes. I know I want to write "nice" under Nyasha's name.

 Turn to your thinking partner. What words can you think of to describe Nyasha? Think together.

(After learners talk, add a word or two.)

READ TO WHERE MANYARA RUNS THROUGH THE NIGHT TO THE CITY.

 Turn to your thinking partner. We know so much more now. What words can you use to describe Manyara now? What should we add to our chart?

READ TO WHERE MANYARA TELLS NYASHA NOT TO GO INTO THE CITY BECAUSE OF THE GREAT MONSTER.

 Turn to your thinking partner. What can you say about the sisters now?

CONTINUE TO THE END. Pause occasionally to give partners time to talk and suggest descriptors to add to the chart. Encourage them to add words to describe Mufaro and the King, too.

END OF STORY REFLECTION
(Review the descriptors on the chart and show children how you can link several descriptive words to create a statement.)

Nyasha was "generous" to share her food and "brave" when she went in to see the great monster. How am I doing? Am I describing the character the way you would?

 Turn and talk to your partner. Select words from the chart that you can use to describe a character in the book. You can use one word or several words from the chart to tell about a character.

SHARE THE LEARNING
Focus on Characterization

Tip for Share the Reading	Tip for Readers Theater Script

Place the text on the overhead projector and read it aloud with great expression, making your voice shift clearly from speaker to narration. Explain to the children that their job is to show characterization in their reading. Read the passage again, asking a group of students to be Manyara and act out her part. Go back to the chart and encourage children to add describing words for each character.

> In her hurry, Manyara almost stumbled over a small boy who suddenly appeared, standing in her path.
>
> "Please," said the boy. "I am hungry. Will you give me something to eat?"
>
> "I have brought only enough for myself," Manyara replied.
>
> "But, please!" said the boy. "I am so *very* hungry."
>
> "Out of my way boy! Tomorrow I will become your queen. How dare you stand in my path!"

Focus attention on the illustration for "Finding Courage" and consider what can be learned about the characters just from the illustration. Read the script to the children, acting out each of the parts. Emphasize characterization through voice change, mannerism, and expressive interpretation of the two characters in the script. Invite the children to join in chorally, and then read the script in teams or partners.

> **Finding Courage**
> By Linda Hoyt
>
> **Character 1**
> You can do this.
> Come on now. Be brave.
> It will only take a minute.
> Here we go.
> Yes, you can. Be brave.
>
> **Character 2**
> No. No. No. Don't make me!
> No, No, No!
> I can't!
> I can't! I can't! I can't!
> I'm scared!

EXTEND THE LEARNING

☆ Have students work with partners to revisit familiar books and write sticky-note reviews to describe the main characters. These can be familiar Big Books, books from read-alouds, or from independent reading. Give students opportunities to share their observations. Emergent readers can name the character and draw a face to reflect their analysis.

☆ Encourage children to visit this kid-friendly website for information on the people, land, and culture of Zimbabwe. URL: *www.afroam.org/children/discover/zimbabwe/zimbabwe.html*

☆ The names of the characters in this folktale are from the Shona language. Mufaro (moo-FAR-oh) means "happy man," Nyasha (ne-AH-sha) means "mercy," Manyara (mahn-YAR-ah) means "ashamed," and Myoka (mee-YO-kah) means "snake." Talk with the children about why the author chose these names.

ASSESS THE LEARNING

➤ Circulate and listen closely as partners attempt to describe characters in various books.

➤ Analyze their sticky-note reviews and their conversations for evidence of understanding of character.

➤ As you confer with individuals reading fiction, assess their understanding of character development in their reading selections.

INFUSION OF FORMAL LANGUAGE
Test-style language

Mufaro proclaimed that he was the _____ father in the world.
   A. biggest
   B. strongest
   C. happiest
   D. kindest

Manyara was *most* frightened when
   A. her sister sang to the snake.
   B. the old woman told her not to laugh.
   C. she saw the small boy.
   D. she saw the monster.

In her hurry, Manyara almost stumbled over a small boy who suddenly appeared, standing in her path.

"Please," said the boy. "I am hungry. Will you give me something to eat?"

"I have brought only enough for myself," Manyara replied.

"But, please!" said the boy. "I am so *very* hungry."

"Out of my way boy! Tomorrow I will become your queen. How dare you stand in my path!"

Finding Courage

By Linda Hoyt

Character 1

You can do this.

Come on now. Be brave.

It will only take a minute.

Here we go.

Yes, you can. Be brave.

Character 2

No. No. No. Don't make me!

No, No, No!

I can't!

I can't! I can't! I can't!

I'm scared!

NARRATION AND DIALOGUE

When Sophie Gets Angry—Really, Really Angry…
Molly Bang

FOCUS THE LEARNING

Introduction: I am going to read *When Sophie Gets Angry—Really, Really Angry…* by Molly Bang. As I read, we are going to focus on the role of the narrator as well as "dialogue."

🗨️ *Think together about what you already know. What does the narrator do in a story?*

INTERACTIVE READ-ALOUD
Model and Guide Practice
(You will need sticky notes and a fine-tip felt pen.)

READ THE FIRST TWO PAGES. This is definitely the narrator talking. The narrator is describing what Sophie and her sister did. Sophie and her sister are not talking. The narrator is telling the story for us.

READ THE NEXT TWO PAGES. Let's experience these pages a second time. I need two people to help me. One person needs to be Sophie. (All Sophie has to say is "NO.") One person needs to be the mother, and I will be the narrator. Sophie and the mother are going to act this out. I am the narrator. Listen to the way I hold the story together with my narration.

🗨️ *Thinking partners, think together about this. Can you name one thing the narrator said? Can you name one thing the mother said?*

READ TO "ROARS A BIG RED ROAR." Let's think for a minute. Who is talking? Is it the narrator, or is it Sophie? How do you know?

🗨️ *Think together.*

It is the narrator talking, but I am wondering what Sophie would have had to say. I am going to use my sticky notes and add dialogue, words that Sophie might have wanted to say. I am going to start on the page with Sophie's face. I think she would have said, "I am so mad! This isn't fair." I will write that on a sticky note and put the new dialogue right on the page. This isn't the narrator talking now; it is Sophie.

SHOW THE PAGE WHERE SHE "KICKS AND SCREAMS."
I am thinking about the cat. What dialogue could we add for the cat? What would the cat want to say?

🗨️ *Think together. What dialogue can we create for the cat? We'll use a sticky note to add our ideas for dialogue right into the book.*

CONTINUE TO THE END. Pause occasionally to give partners time to consider dialogue that can be added. Point out that the narrator is telling most of the story. Be sure to add dialogue for Sophie's mom and dad at the end.

END OF STORY REFLECTION
We know this story was mostly told by the narrator, but we added quite a bit of dialogue for the characters. We are going to read the whole thing again. I will be the narrator, but I will need your help to make the dialogue sound interesting.

🗨️ *Think together. What should Sophie sound like? How about her mom? Her dad? The cat? Think about how to make the voices sound different.*

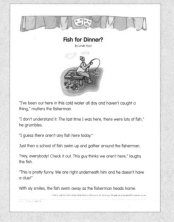

SHARE THE LEARNING
Focus on Narration and Dialogue

Tip for Share the Reading

Read the passage to the children using different voices for the narrator, Sophie, and the cat. Show them how the quotation marks help you to know when you are reading dialogue so you can use a special voice for the character. Engage the children in a shared reading of the text.
As they are ready, divide into groups with one group reading Sophie's part, one group reading the cat's part, and one group doing the narration.

> Sophie is really angry because her sister has the gorilla.
>
> "I am so mad. This just isn't fair," yells Sophie.
>
> She kicks and screams and yells.
>
> "Sophie is acting really crazy. I will go and hide!" squeals the cat.
>
> Sophie runs out the front door and takes a walk.
>
> "I am going to climb my favorite tree and just sit there a while," Sophie whispers. "Maybe that will make me feel better."

Tip for Readers Theater Script

Show the children the quotation marks in "Fish for Dinner?" and help them notice the places where dialogue and narration are positioned on the page. Invite the students to represent the dialogue and narration with different voices, deliberately emphasizing the attitudes represented by the fish and the fisherman.

> **Fish for Dinner?**
> By Linda Hoyt
>
> "I've been out here in this cold water all day and haven't caught a thing," mutters the fisherman.
>
> "I don't understand it. The last time I was here, there were lots of fish," he grumbles.
>
> "I guess there aren't any fish here today."
>
> Just then a school of fish swim up and gather around the fisherman.
>
> "Hey, everybody! Check it out. This guy thinks we aren't here," laughs the fish.
>
> "This is pretty funny. We are right underneath him and he doesn't have a clue!"
>
> With sly smiles, the fish swim away as the fisherman heads home.

EXTEND THE LEARNING

☆ During small group instruction, provide opportunities to read stories with dialogue. Discuss shifts in oral reading voice when reading narration and dialogue.

☆ Do a modeled write showing how to include dialogue and quotation marks in your writing.

☆ Use sticky notes to add dialogue to books read during small group instruction.

☆ Make tape recordings of the children doing dramatic readings and retellings of books with dialogue and narration.

☆ Have children create illustrations about stories from read-aloud selections and then add dialogue as speech bubbles in their illustrations.

ASSESS THE LEARNING

➤ Listen in as partners discuss dialogue and narration to assess their understanding.

➤ During small group instruction, assess students' ability to differentiate between dialogue and narration.

➤ Confer with readers during independent reading to see if they can identify narration and dialogue independently.

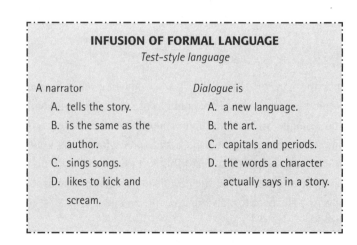

INFUSION OF FORMAL LANGUAGE
Test-style language

A narrator
  A. tells the story.
  B. is the same as the author.
  C. sings songs.
  D. likes to kick and scream.

Dialogue is
  A. a new language.
  B. the art.
  C. capitals and periods.
  D. the words a character actually says in a story.

Sophie is really angry because her sister has the gorilla.

"I am so mad. This just isn't fair," yells Sophie.

She kicks and screams and yells.

"Sophie is acting really crazy. I will go and hide!" squeals the cat.

Sophie runs out the front door and takes a walk.

"I am going to climb my favorite tree and just sit there a while," Sophie whispers. "Maybe that will make me feel better."

Fish for Dinner?

By Linda Hoyt

"I've been out here in this cold water all day and haven't caught a thing," mutters the fisherman.

"I don't understand it. The last time I was here, there were lots of fish," he grumbles.

"I guess there aren't any fish here today."

Just then a school of fish swim up and gather around the fisherman.

"Hey, everybody! Check it out. This guy thinks we aren't here," laughs the fish.

"This is pretty funny. We are right underneath him and he doesn't have a clue!"

With sly smiles, the fish swim away as the fisherman heads home.

THEME AND AUTHOR'S PURPOSE

The Ugly Duckling
Lorinda Bryan Cauley

FOCUS THE LEARNING

Introduction: We know that good writers have a purpose for their writing. Our job as readers is to try to understand what the author had in mind. We need to wonder if there is a theme or a message to the story and try to determine the author's purpose. Today we are going to read *The Ugly Duckling* retold by Lorinda Bryan Cauley.

Think together. Do you remember hearing this story before? If so, what do you remember?

INTERACTIVE READ-ALOUD
Model and Guide Practice

LOOK AT THE COVER. Let's start by looking at the cover of the book. Look at the faces of the animals. What do you think is happening?

Think together. What do you think? What seems important?

READ TO WHERE THE UGLY DUCKLING HATCHES AND GOES FOR A SWIM. It sure is a good thing the mother duck took care of the big egg so it could hatch like the others. I am wondering if the author's message is to remind us to take good care of everyone.

READ TO WHERE THE DUCKLINGS ARE IN THE BARNYARD AND ALL THE ANIMALS ARE PICKING ON THE UGLY DUCKLING.

Talk to your thinking partner. Think together. What do you think of this? Is it okay to treat someone badly just because they don't look the way you think they should? What are your ideas about the author's message?

READ TO WHERE THE HUNTERS FRIGHTEN HIM AND HE TRIES TO LIVE WITH THE FARM ANIMALS.

Isn't this interesting? Each animal thinks the Ugly Duckling should be just like they are. What are your thoughts about the author's message now?

CONTINUE TO THE END. Pause occasionally to give partners time to talk about the author's message or purpose.

END OF STORY REFLECTION

We have a lot of ideas about the author and her message or purpose for writing this book. Partners, get your ideas ready. I am going to write down everyone's thinking about the author's purpose and the message or theme in this book. (Make a chart to collect their thinking and then begin narrowing the list of options until you can create a statement that sounds like a theme.)

SHARE THE LEARNING
Focus on Theme and Author's Purpose

Tip for Share the Reading

Read the passage fluently with expression. Then ask the students to join you in a shared reading. Guide a conversation about this passage and the author's message that you have already discussed. Read it again as a celebration of the story and its important message.

He looked down and saw himself in the water. He was no longer a large, clumsy duckling. He was . . . a swan! The big swans swam around him and stroked him with their beaks.

Children came running to the pond and called, "Look, there is a new one. He is the most beautiful of all!"

The old swans bowed their heads before him. He was so happy. No one would make fun of him now.

Tip for Readers Theater Script

Enjoy "The Ugly Duckling" as a three-team experience, emphasizing the portions where everyone reads with extra volume and feeling. Transition to three-person teams for additional readings.

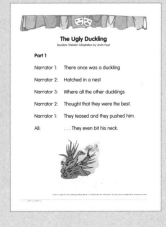

The Ugly Duckling
Readers Theater Adaptation by Linda Hoyt

Part 1

Narrator 1:	There once was a duckling
Narrator 2:	Hatched in a nest
Narrator 3:	Where all the other ducklings
Narrator 2:	Thought that they were the best.
Narrator 1:	They teased and they pushed him.
All:	. . . They even bit his neck.

EXTEND THE LEARNING

☆ Read many stories and poems to support discussion of theme and author's purpose.

☆ Read nonfiction selections and consider the author's purpose and message.

☆ Write a letter to a published author explaining the theme the class identified for one of the author's books. Ask the author to respond to the children so they will know if they were correct about the theme.

☆ Look at recipe books, brochures, and a wide array of nonfiction texts and talk about the author's purpose for each.

ASSESS THE LEARNING

> Have children create illustrations to show the author's message or theme and then have them explain their thinking.

> During small group instruction, discuss theme and author's purpose.

INFUSION OF FORMAL LANGUAGE
Test-style language

Which idea is part of the theme of this story?
  A. No one was nice to the duckling.
  B. The duckling needed someone to love him just as he was.
  C. No one knows what they will look like when they grow up.
  D. All of the above.

Why did the duckling end up frozen in the pond?
  A. He was running away from the house full of children.
  B. He was looking for food.
  C. He was hoping to find a mother.
  D. He likes ice.

He looked down and saw himself in the water. He was no longer a large, clumsy duckling. He was . . . a swan! The big swans swam around him and stroked him with their beaks.

Children came running to the pond and called, "Look, there is a new one. He is the most beautiful of all!"

The old swans bowed their heads before him. He was so happy. No one would make fun of him now.

The Ugly Duckling

Readers Theater Adaptation by Linda Hoyt

Part 1

Narrator 1:   There once was a duckling

Narrator 2:   Hatched in a nest

Narrator 3:   Where all the other ducklings

Narrator 2:   Thought that they were the best.

Narrator 1:   They teased and they pushed him.

All: . . . They even bit his neck.

Part II

Narrator 3:   The winter was awful

Narrator 2:   But he did survive.

Narrator 1:   When spring came around

Narrator 3:   He was glad to be alive.

Narrator 2:   He looked in the water

Narrator 3:   And saw that he had grown—

Narrator 1:   He was a swan on a lake

All: Peaceful and serene.

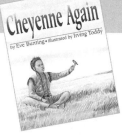

Cheyenne Again

Eve Bunting

FOCUS THE LEARNING

Introduction: In *Cheyenne Again* by Eve Bunting, a young boy is taken away from his parents, from his tribe, and from the ways he was raised. He is placed in a school where the goal is to make him an "American." As we read this book, your job is to think about what it would be like to lose everything that is familiar to you and to be forced to speak a new language, wear clothes that feel strange, and act in ways that are really different from the ways of your family.

INTERACTIVE READ-ALOUD
Model and Guide Practice

READ PAGES 5 AND 7. I am thinking about Young Bull. He lives in a teepee and wears moccasins and soft-leather clothing. He wears his hair in braids just like his parents. These are all part of his culture. How frightened he must be: he has been told he must go and learn "the White Man's ways."

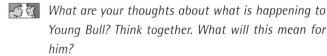 *What are your thoughts about what is happening to Young Bull? Think together. What will this mean for him?*

READ TO PAGE 11. I am thinking about culture and the changes he is experiencing. I am thinking about the sleeping room and the train. How different these are from the way he grew up.

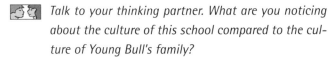 *Talk to your thinking partner. What are you noticing about the culture of this school compared to the culture of Young Bull's family?*

READ TO PAGE 13. This makes me so sad. Who would want to trade soft leather for scratchy wool clothes? And braids are honorable in Indian culture. Getting his hair cut must have been terrible for him. They are taking away everything he knows and understands.

 Talk to your thinking partner. What do you think of this? Is it okay to treat him like this?

READ TO PAGE 21. I am thinking again about culture. The idea of this school was to teach him the "White Man's ways." But is this school really like the culture of the United States? Are they really helping him?

 Think together. How would you interpret this? What else could they have done to teach him about American culture?

CONTINUE TO THE END. Pause occasionally to give partners time to make connections to Young Bull's experience and to offer opinions about what happened.

END OF STORY REFLECTION

Every country in the world has its own culture. How might we help individuals to learn a new culture without giving up everything they know and love about their own culture? Do you know someone who has moved here from another country? How did they learn English? Did they change the way they dressed and the kind of home they lived in so they would fit in here? Did they learn to eat new foods?

 Think together.

(After thinking partners talk, invite them to share ideas with the group.)

SHARE THE LEARNING
Focus on Culture in Literature

Tip for Share the Reading

Ask the children to make connections to Young Bull's culture through this passage. What does this passage teach us about his culture? What was important to Young Bull? Practice reading the passage slowly and dramatically.

> "This is the Sleeping Room," they say.
> So bare a place.
>
> . . .
>
> No huddle of my brothers, warm around.
> No smell of smoke.
> No robe spread on the ground.
>
> . . .
>
> They take away my buckskins and my shirt.
> The deerskin moccasins my mother made.
> They cut my braids,
> give me a uniform of scratchy wool
> the color of an ashen sky.
>
> . . .
>
> "No more Cheyenne," they say.

Tip for Readers Theater Script

Have the children engage in an oral retell of the story line before reading "Young Bull." Read the poem to them emphasizing expressive interpretation. Invite the students to join you in a choral reading. Then shift to partner reading and eventually to individual interpretation of the poem. Students may enjoy adding illustrations. A dramatic interpretation can be created by playing soft background music while the students present the script.

Young Bull
Readers Theater Adaptation by Linda Hoyt

Taken by a policeman
To a place that they called school,
His braids were cut
His buckskins gone
His language taken away.
He marched and drilled and cried at night
Until he ran away.

An understanding teacher,
Who cared and gave him strength,
Encouraged him to draw and dream
To hold his memories tight.
So with pencil and with paper
He brought his dreams to life.
He rode with pride and majesty
Cheyenne—
From dawn til night.

EXTEND THE LEARNING

☆ If you have students, staff members, or community members who have immigrated from another country, invite them to share their experiences in learning a new language and culture.

☆ Help children compare foods from several cultures. If possible, provide experience tasting multicultural recipes.

☆ Read *Crow Boy* by Taro Yashima. Crow Boy's life was very different from his schoolmates'. He spoke the same language and lived in the same country but lived a very different culture than the other children at school.

☆ Engage students in writing about family traditions and family routines that are part of the culture of each family.

☆ Think with the students about the culture of your classroom. What routines and ways of doing things are unique to your classroom and different from other classes in the school?

☆ Engage students in comparing the culture of school with the culture of their homes. How are they alike and different?

ASSESS THE LEARNING

> Listen in as partners interpret the story to determine their levels of understanding.

> During small group instruction, read and discuss selections in which culture plays a role.

> Have students write about the benefits and challenges of being bicultural. They may draw on their reading or personal experience.

INFUSION OF FORMAL LANGUAGE
Test-style language

Which of the following was important in Young Bull's culture?

A. Sleeping in a teepee with his family huddled around

B. Wearing deerskin moccasins made by his mother

C. Speaking Cheyenne

D. All of the above.

The author's purpose was *mainly* to

A. explain about Indian schools a long time ago.

B. teach about Indian clothing.

C. convince us to learn a new language.

D. describe Indian teepees.

"This is the Sleeping Room," they say.

So bare a place.

. . .

No huddle of my brothers, warm around.

No smell of smoke.

No robe spread on the ground.

. . .

They take away my buckskins and my shirt.

The deerskin moccasins my mother made.

They cut my braids,

give me a uniform of scratchy wool

the color of an ashen sky.

. . .

"No more Cheyenne," they say.

Young Bull

Readers Theater Adaptation by Linda Hoyt

Taken by a policeman

To a place that they called school,

His braids were cut

His buckskins gone

His language taken away.

He marched and drilled and cried at night

Until he ran away.

An understanding teacher,

Who cared and gave him strength,

Encouraged him to draw and dream

To hold his memories tight.

So with pencil and with paper

He brought his dreams to life.

He rode with pride and majesty

Cheyenne—

From dawn til night.

Puss In Boots

Malcolm Arthur

FOCUS THE LEARNING

Introduction: One strategy that writers often use is to focus the story on a problem and then design interesting ways to solve the problem. Today we are going to read *Puss In Boots* by Malcolm Arthur. It will be our job to pay special attention to the problem and how it is solved.

INTERACTIVE READ-ALOUD
Model and Guide Practice

(Begin a chart labeled Problem + Steps Toward Solving the Problem + Solution.)

READ THE FIRST TWO PAGES. I am thinking that the youngest son has a problem. He only has a cat, and he doesn't know how he will make money.

READ THE NEXT PAGE. I am looking for a solution to the youngest son's problem, and I am not sure how giving a cat a pair of boots will help the young man have money.

 Turn to your thinking partner. What do you think? Any ideas about how the problem will be solved?

READ TO WHERE PUSS HAS BEEN BRINGING GAME TO THE KING FOR TWO OR THREE MONTHS.

 This seems to be a pretty smart cat. Talk with your partner and think together about why Puss brought food to the King instead of feeding the young man. Do you think this will solve the problem?

READ TO WHERE THE KING'S GUARDS PULL THE YOUNG MAN OUT OF THE RIVER AND PUSS SAYS HIS CLOTHING WAS STOLEN.

 What do you think the cat is up to? How will this solve the young man's problem?

READ TO WHERE PUSS CHALLENGES THE OGRE TO TURN INTO A SMALL ANIMAL. (But don't read the line that tells what Puss does with the mouse.)

 Why do you suppose Puss wants the Ogre to be a small animal? How will that solve the problem?

READ THE CONCLUSION.

END OF STORY REFLECTION

Let's review our chart and the steps Puss followed to solve the problem.

 Turn and talk to your partner. If you were to select just one solution for the problem that you think is most important to the story, which one would it be? Why?

Problem:
Steps Toward Solving the Problem:
Solution:

SHARE THE LEARNING
Focus on Problem/Solution

Tip for Share the Reading

Remind children of the problem in the story and explain that they are going to reread the solution. Place the text on the overhead projector and read it aloud with expression and fluency.

> Puss said, "I hear you can turn yourself into small animals, too, a rat or a mouse, for instance. That seems impossible."
>
> "It seems impossible, does it?" said the Ogre.
>
> A second later the Ogre was gone and a mouse was scurrying across the floor. Puss pounced and caught him and gobbled him up.

Tip for Readers Theater Script

Read "Puss In Boots," emphasizing fluency and expression. Encourage a postreading discussion about the story line. What do the students think of tricking the King and causing the King to believe things that were not true? Have partners meet to identify the problem and solution in the script.

Puss In Boots
Readers Theater Adaptation by Linda Hoyt

Teacher: Once there was a young man who had no money and didn't know what to do.

Students: He had a problem.

Teacher: His cat said he could help if the young man would get him a sack and a pair of boots.

Students: He still had a problem.

Teacher: One day the King took his daughter for a ride near the river. While the young man was swimming, Puss pretended the young man was drowning and needed to be saved. The King gave the young man fine clothes to wear and invited him to ride in the carriage because he thought he was rich and powerful.

Students: Puss is working on a solution.

EXTEND THE LEARNING

☆ Use the terms "problem" and "solution" for situations in the classroom. For example: I noticed we have a *problem* at the sink. The paints have spilled and the paint brushes are in the way so we can't wash our hands. How should we *solve* our problem?"

☆ Have the children write and draw using the stems: The problem in this story was _____. The problem was solved when _____.

☆ Stretch children's thinking with a stem such as: Describe the steps Puss followed to solve the problem and tell which step you thought was most important.

☆ Look for problems and solutions in other read-aloud selections. Start a class chart to monitor the problems and solutions you find in various read-alouds.

☆ Engage learners in retells focused on telling the problem and the solution.

ASSESS THE LEARNING

> Watch and listen closely as students contribute ideas about problems and solutions in read-alouds.

> Analyze their drawing and writing to see if there is evidence of understanding the problem/solution structure.

> Confer with individuals and ask them to identify problems and solutions in the classroom and in familiar books.

> Encourage students to identify problems they have faced and the strategies they used to solve their problems.

INFUSION OF FORMAL LANGUAGE
Test-style language

The problem in this story was resolved when

   A. the young man went for a swim.

   B. Puss ate the mouse.

   C. the King liked the meat.

   D. Puss got his boots.

Which of the following is *not* true?

   A. Puss was a smart cat.

   B. The young man didn't know how to make money.

   C. The princess helped the young man.

   D. Puss was a good hunter.

Puss said, "I hear you can turn yourself into small animals, too, a rat or a mouse, for instance. That seems impossible."

"It seems impossible, does it?" said the Ogre.

A second later the Ogre was gone and a mouse was scurrying across the floor. Puss pounced and caught him and gobbled him up.

Puss In Boots

Readers Theater Adaptation by Linda Hoyt

Teacher: Once there was a young man who had no money and didn't know what to do.

Students: He had a problem.

Teacher: His cat said he could help if the young man would get him a sack and a pair of boots.

Students: He still had a problem.

Teacher: One day the King took his daughter for a ride near the river. While the young man was swimming, Puss pretended the young man was drowning and needed to be saved. The King gave the young man fine clothes to wear and invited him to ride in the carriage because he thought he was rich and powerful.

Students: Puss is working on a solution.

Teacher: Puss got the peasants to say their fields belonged to the young man.

Students: Puss is working on a solution.

Teacher: Then Puss tricked the Ogre so the young man could entertain the King in the Ogre's castle, making the King think the castle belonged to the young man.

Students: Puss is working on a solution.

Teacher: The King was so impressed by the beautiful castle and wonderful food that he let the young man marry his daughter right away.

Students: Puss found a solution!

Teacher: Puss, the young man, and the princess lived happily ever after. Puss became a great lord and even gave up chasing mice.

ALL: The End.

Vocabulary/
Literary Language

Standards in this strand encourage learners to observe the power of precise vocabulary; to identify and appreciate rhythm, rhyme, onomatopoeia, alliteration, and literary language; and to discern the meanings of unfamiliar words through context clues. Transition words and words with multiple meanings are also highlighted in this strand.

Sylvester and the Magic Pebble
William Steig

INTERACTIVE READ-ALOUD
Model and Guide Practice

READ THE FIRST SEVERAL PAGES. I just have to stop for a moment. There have been so many wonderful words I want to stop and think about them! On the first page, it said that Sylvester collected pebbles of unusual shape and color. I am going to write "unusual" on this chart. This is such a great word. It helps me know that the pebbles aren't like the pebbles we see every day. "Unusual" means these are different! I wonder if these pebbles are in some really interesting colors and shapes . . .

I also notice that the author said that Sylvester began to "shiver" . . . I am thinking what it is like to shiver. Can you shiver? What does it mean to shiver?

Turn to your partner and talk about "shiver." What might it mean? Can you shiver? What would cause you to shiver? Show your partner what you would look like if you were shivering in the rain.

Aren't these words great! I am going to write "shiver" on our chart, too, so we will remember to use these words in lots of ways.

READ TO WHERE SYLVESTER IS IN THE RAIN AND WISHING FOR IT TO STOP. Were there any interesting words you noticed in this section of the story?

Which interesting words did you notice? Talk to your partner and think together about words we might add to our chart.
(Examples: "ceased," "disappeared," "shooting")

CONTINUE TO WHERE SYLVESTER MEETS THE LION. I am going to read this part again. It says that Sylvester was "startled" to see a mean, hungry lion looking right at him. Wow! This is another great word. "Startled . . ."

Show your partner what you would look like if you were startled.

CONTINUE TO THE END. Pause occasionally to savor wonderful words and add them to the chart.

END OF STORY REFLECTION

What a relief that Sylvester and his parents are together again! The great words in this story really helped me to understand what was happening. We are going to challenge ourselves to use some of these wonderful words this week. Whenever I can, I am going to try to use these words when I am talking with you so I get used to using them. Great words are so much fun that using them makes me want to shiver! Did you notice? I just used "shiver" from our list. Hooray for me!

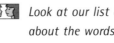 *Look at our list of words. Turn and tell your partner about the words you like the best. Try to use one of the words in a sentence.*

SHARE THE LEARNING
Focus on Vocabulary

Tip for Share the Reading

Place Passage 1 on the overhead projector and read it aloud. Ask students to try to visualize what is happening. Talk about words that would make sense in the blanks. Write the student-selected words in the blanks. Show William Steig's text (Passage 2). Have students read it with you, inviting them to compare their words and the words from the book.

> **Passage 1:** To his great surprise the rain stopped. It didn't stop _____ as rains usually do. It ceased. The drops _____ on the way down, the clouds disappeared, everything was dry, and the sun was shining as if the rain had never _____.
>
> **Passage 2:** To his great surprise the rain stopped. It didn't stop gradually as rains usually do. It CEASED. The drops vanished on the way down, the clouds disappeared, everything was dry, and the sun was shining as if the rain had never existed.

Tip for Readers Theater Script

For emergent readers, act out "A Celebration of Words". Explain that we could write "He went to the park," but it is much more interesting to use lively words like these. For developing and fluent readers, divide into three teams to read the script, expressing meaning with your voices. Then turn the children loose to write their own list poems.

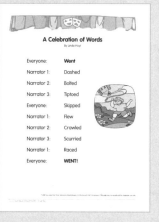

A Celebration of Words
By Linda Hoyt

Everyone:	**Went**
Narrator 1:	Dashed
Narrator 2:	Bolted
Narrator 3:	Tiptoed
Everyone:	Skipped
Narrator 1:	Flew
Narrator 2:	Crawled
Narrator 3:	Scurried
Narrator 1:	Raced
Everyone:	**WENT!**

EXTEND THE LEARNING

☆ Make a conscious effort to use words from the chart when talking to the children. Bring attention to your use of the words.

☆ Dramatize words from the story.

☆ Have children place a tally mark next to a word if they use it when talking to a partner during the day.

☆ Celebrate if students can use some of the target words in their writing or as labels for drawings.

☆ Continue to build excitement about words by pointing out interesting words in other books.

☆ Encourage children to bring attention to interesting words they find in independent reading.

ASSESS THE LEARNING

➤ As partners talk, listen for active use of the vocabulary.

➤ Analyze students' drawing and writing to see if there is use and understanding of vocabulary.

➤ Monitor the vocabulary chart to see which words are being used and which need more instruction. You may also be able to determine who is using the words and who needs more support to use them.

INFUSION OF FORMAL LANGUAGE
Test-style language

They tried their best to be happy, to go about their usual ways. But they were miserable. Life had no meaning for them anymore.

In this passage, the word *miserable* probably means

    A. bored.

    B. very unhappy.

    C. cheap.

    D. unlucky.

The word *startled* means the same as

    A. surprised.

    B. unaware.

    C. not sure.

    D. staring at stars.

Passage 1: To his great surprise the rain stopped.

It didn't stop _____ as rains usually do.

It ceased. The drops _____ on the way

down, the clouds disappeared, everything was dry,

and the sun was shining as if the rain had never

_____.

Passage 2: To his great surprise the rain stopped.

It didn't stop gradually as rains usually do. It

CEASED. The drops vanished on the way down, the

clouds disappeared, everything was dry, and the

sun was shining as if the rain had never existed.

A Celebration of Words

By Linda Hoyt

Everyone: **Went**

Narrator 1:   Dashed

Narrator 2:   Bolted

Narrator 3:   Tiptoed

Everyone: Skipped

Narrator 1:   Flew

Narrator 2:   Crawled

Narrator 3:   Scurried

Narrator 1:   Raced

Everyone: **WENT!**

Mufaro's Beautiful Daughters
John Steptoe

FOCUS THE LEARNING

Introduction: As we read *Mufaro's Beautiful Daughters* by John Steptoe today, we will be watching for interesting words and then thinking together about how the illustrations and the meaning of the passage can be used as tools for understanding. This is really important because the words themselves can mean different things. Look at these examples. (Write "read," "bow," and "minute" on the chalkboard.)

Think together. What do these words say? Could they say anything else? How do you determine the meaning?

Let's try using context from the story. "Her cry rent the air."

Think together. What is the meaning of "rent" in that sentence?

INTERACTIVE READ-ALOUD
Model and Guide Practice

READ TO WHERE IT SAYS THAT NYASHA IGNORED HER SISTER'S WORDS. I am thinking about the word "ignored." I am looking in the context for clues to the meaning. I see that it says she went about her chores, singing, working in her vegetables. I think "ignored" means she didn't pay attention, that she disregarded her sister's unkind words.

Think together. What clues did you notice for the meaning of "ignored?"

READ TO WHERE MUFARO HAS HIS ARMS AROUND THE GIRLS. It said that Nyasha was too "considerate" to complain.

Turn to your thinking partner. What context clues can you think of for the word "considerate"?

CONTINUE TO THE END. Pause occasionally to point out interesting words and give partners time to discuss context clues that support the meaning. Words to watch for: *worthy, painful, stole* (walked softly), *greed, stumbled, silhouette, clearing, foretold, grove, acknowledge, chant, brightly plumed, uppermost, transfixed, descended, rent* (split), *proclaimed.*

END OF STORY REFLECTION

Good readers use context as one of their tools for determining word meaning.

What should a good reader do when using context clues?

Guide the students in a conversation about context clues and what good readers should do. Write their thoughts on a chart and then add to it over time as they read and think about additional stories. Review the chart frequently to ensure that it is growing and is in active use during reading.

 **SHARE THE LEARNING**
Focus on Using Context Clues

Tip for Share the Reading

Place the cloze passage on the overhead projector and read it aloud with expression. Guide conversations about the missing words and the way context supports our understanding. Have students generate synonyms which can be tested in the sentence to ensure that the passage makes sense.

Mars is a planet that has attracted the interest of scientists over time. There is some _____ to suggest that microscopic life may have existed on Mars more than three billion years ago. But, there is no life there today that can be detected by our instruments.

Mars is far too _____ for human life as we know it. The air pressure there is so low that your blood would boil if you _____ on the surface without a space suit. The temperature is frigid. You would _____ almost instantly if you tried to walk around without the protection of a very _____ space suit.

Tip for Readers Theater Script

For emergent readers, read "Approaching the City" to them and share a conversation about vocabulary words that may be unfamiliar. Encourage them to use context to unravel meaning whenever possible. English language learners may benefit from acting out some of the vocabulary words. For developing and fluent readers, after modeling the reading, read the script chorally, focusing on expressive reading. As students gain confidence with the vocabulary, have them read the narrator parts and focus on smooth, fluent interpretation of the script.

Approaching the City
Readers Theater Adaptation by Linda Hoyt

Narrator 1: Nyasha ran ahead and topped the rise before the others could catch up.

Narrator 2: She stood transfixed at her first sight of the beautiful city.

Narrator 3: Arm in arm, Nyasha and her father descended the hill, crossed the river, and approached the gate.

All: How happy they were to have finally arrived!

Narrator 1: Suddenly, the air was split by piercing cries.

Narrator 2: Manyara ran wildly out of the city, falling on her knees and sobbing.

Narrator 3: She had seen a frightening sight and was running in terror.

Narrator 1: She warned her sister not to proceed.

EXTEND THE LEARNING

☆ Pause frequently during small group instruction to guide conversations on context clues.

☆ Read aloud from books with wonderful, rich language and words that are well supported by context clues. Books by William Steig are especially good for this.

☆ Encourage students to assess context clues in their own writing by rereading sentences to ensure they support interesting words and reconsidering illustrations to see if word meaning is supported.

☆ Provide practice using context clues in nonfiction selections.

☆ Provide cloze experiences with texts for science, social studies, and math as well as literature to encourage the active use of context clues.

☆ Have partners create cloze experiences for each other by covering words with sticky notes and then trading books.

ASSESS THE LEARNING

➤ Circulate and listen closely as partners discuss context clues and word meaning.

➤ During small group instruction, interview students about context clues to assess understanding.

➤ During independent reading, confer with individuals to assess ability to use context clues.

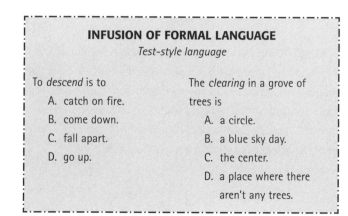

INFUSION OF FORMAL LANGUAGE
Test-style language

To *descend* is to

A. catch on fire.

B. come down.

C. fall apart.

D. go up.

The *clearing* in a grove of trees is

A. a circle.

B. a blue sky day.

C. the center.

D. a place where there aren't any trees.

Mars is a planet that has attracted the interest of scientists over time. There is some _____ to suggest that microscopic life may have existed on Mars more than three billion years ago. But, there is no life there today that can be detected by our instruments.

Mars is far too _____ for human life as we know it. The air pressure there is so low that your blood would boil if you _____ on the surface without a space suit. The temperature is frigid. You would _____ almost instantly if you tried to walk around without the protection of a very _____ space suit.

Approaching the City
Readers Theater Adaptation by Linda Hoyt

Narrator 1: Nyasha ran ahead and topped the rise before the others could catch up.

Narrator 2: She stood transfixed at her first sight of the beautiful city.

Narrator 3: Arm in arm, Nyasha and her father descended the hill, crossed the river, and approached the gate.

All: How happy they were to have finally arrived!

Narrator 1: Suddenly, the air was split by piercing cries.

Narrator 2: Manyara ran wildly out of the city, falling on her knees and sobbing.

Narrator 3: She had seen a frightening sight and was running in terror.

Narrator 1: She warned her sister not to proceed.

Narrator 2: But Nyasha went into the city anyway.

Narrator 3: What a happy surprise when Nyasha found her friend, the small snake,

Narrator 1: sitting on the throne.

All: He greeted her warmly and showed himself as king.

Narrator 2: The king chose a wife with a good heart and kind spirit.

Narrator 3: He could not select a woman who was unkind and selfish.

All: Nyasha would be queen.

Narrator 1: Mufaro proclaimed that he was the happiest father in the world.

LITERARY/FIGURATIVE LANGUAGE LEADS

Mirandy and Brother Wind by Patric McKissack, *Frederick* by Leo Lionni, *Stellaluna,* and *Shrek!* by William Steig

---

FOCUS THE LEARNING

(Prepare a chart with heads "Author's Words" and "Information".)

Introduction: I brought several of my favorite books to share. As we look at these books today, we are going to think about the words authors use when they start a story. I am going to use this chart to write ideas for great ways to start a story. This will help us to think about good beginnings or "leads," when we write our own stories.

 Think together about some of our favorite stories. Think about Cinderella, Little Red Riding Hood, *and* The Three Little Pigs. *What do you remember about the way they start? Can you remember the way you started your last piece of writing?*

INTERACTIVE READ-ALOUD
Model and Guide Practice

BEGIN WITH *MIRANDY AND BROTHER WIND* (PATRICIA MCKISSACK). Listen carefully. I am only going to read the first page. "Swish! Swish! It was spring, and Brother Wind was back." Isn't this interesting? Patricia McKissack started her story by helping us think about the setting. If I was going to write a story about what we are doing right now, I could say, "Early one winter day at _____ (name of school)."

 Think together. I am going to read that page one more time. Listen to the words the author used to start a story. How does her opening help us get ready to read the story?

READ THE FIRST LINE FROM *FREDERICK* (LEO LIONNI). This starts, "All along the meadow…" and then it tells us about the setting. Isn't this interesting? Two of our authors have started with information about the setting. I could use what I am learning about starting a story and say, "Early one winter day at _____ (name of school), the students were gathered close together sharing some favorite stories."

Author's Words	Information
Swish! Swish! It was spring.	Time of year.
All along the meadow where the cows grazed	Where.

READ THE FIRST LINES FROM *STELLALUNA* (JANELL CANON).

 Think together. What did you notice about the beginning of this story? What should we add to our chart? What are you noticing about these leads?

READ THE OPENING TO *SHREK!* (WILLIAM STEIG). Guide the children to compare a lead that describes a character and add that information to the chart.

END OF STORY REFLECTION

We learned a lot about starting stories.

 Think together for a moment. If you were going to write a story about going out for pizza, how would you want your story to start? Look at our chart and think about the books we have been looking at. How would you start?

(Do a modeled write using an interesting lead that includes time, place and something interesting to hook the reader. A helpful tip is to open with a "sound word" as in *Mirandy and Brother Wind*. Think out loud as you draft so the children can see you looking at the chart or at one of the books and thinking about your lead as you write.)

 **SHARE THE LEARNING**

Focus on Literary/Figurative Language Leads

Tip for Share the Reading

Read the passage fluently with expression. Then, guide students in a conversation about the words this author used. Is this a lead that makes them want to read more? What made them feel like that? If they were to add this story to the chart, what would they say about the opening? Did they like the addition of "sound words"? Could they use sound words in a story of their own?

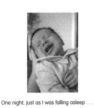

One night, just as I was falling asleep . . . Waaaaaaa! The baby started to cry. I covered my ears. I pulled my pillow over my head. I even put my stuffed bunny on my head. But nothing worked. Waaaaa! That baby was really upset.

Tip for Readers Theater Script

Explain that "Leads" captures some of the things we should think about to create a great opening to a piece of writing. Read the poem to the students and have them talk about it. What do they notice? Do they agree? What does the ending mean? Engage the children in reading chorally and then in teams. Help students create a poem about endings, descriptions, powerful verbs, or other dimensions of literary language.

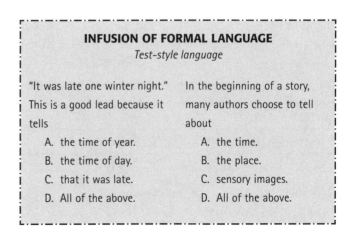

Leads
By Linda Hoyt

Narrator 1: Open a window into the story

Narrator 2: Help the reader visualize what is happening

Narrator 3: Pull the reader in

Narrator 1: Make them want to stay and read more

Narrator 2: Tease the reader with sounds and senses

Narrator 3: Offer a little humor

Narrator 1: Grab the reader and . . .

Narrators 2 and 3: **They will read on.**

EXTEND THE LEARNING

☆ During small group instruction, compare the words authors use in their leads.

☆ During read-alouds, continue comparing the words authors use to start their stories.

☆ During writers workshop, confer in small groups to talk about interesting words the students might use to begin their writing.

☆ Guide an interactive writing group to create an opening for a story. Begin by looking at the chart about story openings. Then craft a piece of writing together.

☆ Meet with individuals to revise story openings.

☆ Have children create illustrations based on just the first page of a story. See how much detail they are able to include.

ASSESS THE LEARNING

> During small group instruction, have children point out the beginning of the selection and share thinking about the way the author chose to begin.

> Confer with readers about the beginnings of books they are reading for independent reading.

> Confer with writers to assess their ability to use varied openings to their writing.

INFUSION OF FORMAL LANGUAGE
Test-style language

"It was late one winter night." This is a good lead because it tells

    A. the time of year.
    B. the time of day.
    C. that it was late.
    D. All of the above.

In the beginning of a story, many authors choose to tell about

    A. the time.
    B. the place.
    C. sensory images.
    D. All of the above.

One night, just as I was falling asleep . . .

Waaaaaaa! The baby started to cry.

I covered my ears. I pulled my pillow over

my head. I even put my stuffed bunny on

my head. But nothing worked. Waaaaa!

That baby was really upset.

Leads

By Linda Hoyt

Narrator 1: Open a window into the story

Narrator 2: Help the reader visualize what is happening

Narrator 3: Pull the reader in

Narrator 1: Make them want to stay and read more

Narrator 2: Tease the reader with sounds and senses

Narrator 3: Offer a little humor

Narrator 1: Grab the reader and . . .

Narrators 2 and 3: **They will read on.**

A Chocolate Moose for Dinner
Fred Gwynne

FOCUS THE LEARNING

(If you are working with English language learners, you may want to gather photographs and realia to help explain some of the concepts in this lesson. Dramatizing will also offer support to language learners.)

Introduction: Yesterday I played with a bat and a ball. Then I watched a nature show that showed a bat flying. Isn't it interesting that one word can mean such different things? In one sentence, a bat is a tool you use to hit a ball. In the other, a bat is an animal. "Bat" is a multiple-meaning word—it has more than one meaning. To understand the meaning, we need to think about the other words in the sentence. You wouldn't use a flying mammal to hit a ball, but you would see that flying mammal in a zoo. Today our book is *A Chocolate Moose for Dinner* by Fred Gwynne. As we read it, we will think about multiple-meaning words.

INTERACTIVE READ-ALOUD
Model and Guide Practice

SHOW THE COVER. The cover is funny! The word m-o-o-s-e sounds a lot like the word m-o-u-s-s-e. I am going to write the words on the board so you can see what they look like. Mousse is a yummy dessert. Can you imagine having a chocolate moose—the animal—over for dinner? Let's read on to find out what other funny ways this author used words with multiple meanings.

READ TO THE PAGE WITH DADDY IN A TOASTER.

 Thinking partners, talk about the words. "Toast" is a multiple-meaning word. What happens when you toast a person? What meaning of "toast" do you see here?

STOP AT THE PAGE WITH THE CAR POOLS.
This is another funny picture the author was able to make with multiple-meaning words.

 What is another meaning for "car pool?" What meaning does "car pool" have on these pages?

CONTINUE TO THE END. Pause to talk about multiple-meaning words. You may have to explain some meanings. For example, students may not know that Dali is a painter, that "the pen" is a slang term for jail, or that a scull is a watercraft. Allow students time to talk with thinking partners about the multiple-meaning words. What other meanings do they know these words have? How are the words used in the text? Children will enjoy the humorous illustrations—you'll want to allow time for those "Oh, I get it!" moments.

END OF STORY REFLECTION
Fred Gwynne found very funny ways to use multiple-meaning words. When something drives me up the wall, I'll picture a car really driving up the wall!

 Thinking partners, pick your favorite page. Talk about the words. What are the meanings shown in the picture? What are the other meanings of the words?

SHARE THE LEARNING
Focus on Multiple-Meaning Words

Tip for Share the Reading

 Put the story on an overhead. Invite children to read the text aloud after listening to you read. Have partners consider the meanings of the underlined words in the text. What strategies are they using to determine word meanings? Provide a list of multiple-meaning words and encourage partners to orally create sentences that reflect their various meanings.

Our Field Trip to the Zoo

It seemed like we had waited forever for the day to arrive when our class took a trip to the zoo. Excited and eager, we surged through the gates, ready to explore. The first thing we noticed was that there were more <u>kinds</u> of animals than we had imagined! The variety was incredible. It was also clear that the zoo keepers and volunteers working with the animals had a <u>kind</u> and gentle way with the animals in their care. As we walked around we had a good laugh when we heard hyenas <u>barking</u> in the African exhibit. Curious about the noise they were making, we raced over and noticed that they were scratching themselves on the <u>bark</u> of a tree in the exhibit. They were so funny!

Tip for Readers Theater Script

Read "Have You Ever Seen?" together to be sure that students understand the jokes. For ELL students, you can use visuals, realia, and dramatization to help them understand the concepts. All students may enjoy creating visuals to show multiple interpretations of each two-line pairing.

Have You Ever Seen?
By Lynnette Brent

Reader 1:	Have you ever seen a horsefly?
All:	No, I have never seen a horse fly!
Reader 2:	Have you ever seen a housefly?
All:	No, I have never seen a house fly!
Reader 3:	Have you ever seen a rubberband?
All:	No, I have never seen a rubber band!
Reader 4:	Have you ever seen a barndance?
All:	No, I have never seen a barn dance!
Reader 5:	Have you ever seen a butterfly?
All:	No, I have never seen butter fly!

EXTEND THE LEARNING

☆ Invite students to create a bulletin board display of multiple-meaning words. Students can write or draw pictures to illustrate the different meanings of the words.

☆ Return to a piece of writing you created with children. Talk with students about multiple-meaning words and the power of choosing the best word for a piece. Invite students to look for places to add more specific words to their writing.

☆ Students may enjoy choosing a page from *A Chocolate Moose for Dinner* and illustrating it the "right" way with the meaning of the word that makes sense in the text.

☆ Encourage students to watch for multiple-meaning words in independent reading. Record each word and the strategies they used to determine its meaning in that particular context.

ASSESS THE LEARNING

> Listen in as partners discuss the multiple-meaning words. Students should be able to tell which meaning is being used and how the context helps them figure it out.

> Conference with students, looking over individual pieces of writing. Invite students to choose places they can strengthen by adding context for multiple-meaning words.

INFUSION OF FORMAL LANGUAGE
Test-style language

Which answer has the same meaning as the underlined word?

The <u>pen</u> dripped ink on my desk.

   A. Pigs live in a pen.

   B. Please pen the dog if you leave the house.

   C. May I borrow a pen to write a letter?

   D. The writer will pen a new book this year.

Let's <u>run</u> around the block for exercise.

   A. My mom decided to run for mayor.

   B. How long does it take you to run a mile?

   C. The baseball player knocked in a run.

   D. I had a run of good luck last week.

Our Field Trip to the Zoo

It seemed like we had waited forever for the day to arrive when our class took a trip to the zoo. Excited and eager, we surged through the gates, ready to explore. The first thing we noticed was that there were more <u>kinds</u> of animals than we had imagined! The variety was incredible. It was also clear that the zoo keepers and volunteers working with the animals had a <u>kind</u> and gentle way with the animals in their care. As we walked around we had a good laugh when we heard hyenas <u>barking</u> in the African exhibit. Curious about the noise they were making, we raced over and noticed that they were scratching themselves on the <u>bark</u> of a tree in the exhibit. They were so funny!

Have You Ever Seen?

By Lynnette Brent

Reader 1:   Have you ever seen a horsefly?

All: No, I have never seen a horse fly!

Reader 2:   Have you ever seen a housefly?

All: No, I have never seen a house fly!

Reader 3:   Have you ever seen a rubberband?

All: No, I have never seen a rubber band!

Reader 4:   Have you ever seen a barn dance?

All: No, I have never seen a barn dance!

Reader 5:   Have you ever seen a butterfly?

All: No, I have never seen butter fly!

Reader 6:   Have you ever seen a catfish?

All: No, I have never seen a cat fish!

Reader 7:   Have you ever seen a banana split?

All: No, I have never seen a banana split!

Reader 8:   Have you ever seen a cowhide?

All: No, I have never seen a cow hide!

Reader 9:   Have you ever seen a fishbowl?

All: No, I have never seen a fish bowl!

Reader 10:   Have you ever seen a boardwalk?

All: No, I have never seen a board walk!

Some Smug Slug
Pamela Duncan Edwards

FOCUS THE LEARNING

Introduction: I know a tongue twister that's hard to say ten times fast! "Peter Piper picked a peck of pickled peppers." What do you notice about it? Listen to all those "p" sounds! Many tongue twisters use a device called alliteration. *Alliteration* is repeating a consonant sound at the beginning of words. Alliteration is fun to say, and it's fun to hear, too. Writers use alliteration to call attention to words. You probably do that without even knowing it! If you tell someone you're "down in the dumps," you're using alliteration.

INTERACTIVE READ-ALOUD
Model and Guide Practice

SHOW THE COVER. Let's read the title. Can you hear the alliteration? I'm wondering why the slug is smug.

READ TO THE END OF PAGE 7. This story is fun to read out loud. Listen to these great "s" words. "Slowly." "Slug." "Stringing." "Sparkling." "Silk." When I hear those words, it almost sounds like what I imagine it would sound like when a slug moves.

 Thinking partners, what do you like about the way that the author uses alliteration?

STOP AT PAGE 14. The author not only uses alliteration, she uses some delicious words to describe how the animals talk— "screamed," "shrieked," "sighed," and "snickered."

 Put your heads together and talk about the words. What are the advantages of alliteration?

STOP AT PAGE 22. It's amazing that the author could think of so many wonderful words that all begin with the letter "s"!

 Think together. What are your favorite words for describing the slug? String them together with alliteration and get ready to share.

END OF STORY REFLECTION

Alliteration is a great way to enrich our writing. Let's use alliteration to describe a snake.

 Thinking partners, put your heads together. Think of ways to use alliteration to describe a snake.

SHARE THE LEARNING
Focus on Alliteration

Tip for Share the Reading

Share the poem on the overhead. Ask students to talk with partners about alliteration in the poem. How does alliteration add to the message? Play quiet music in the background and have the students perform the poem with expressive fluency.

> At the game
> My coach cries loudly,
> "Now or never!
> Do or die!
> Sink or swim!"
> Back at home,
> My mother murmurs,
> "Safe and sound,"
> And turns out the light.
> Darkness dimming, dreams begin
> Of running the bases again.

Tip for Readers Theater Script

"Interview with a Slug and a Snail" includes facts that you might find in a nonfiction text about slugs. Read through the script together, asking students to identify facts. Divide students into teams so that all students can participate. Students might enjoy rewriting parts of the script to include alliteration.

Interview with a Slug and . . . a Snail
By Lynnette Brent

Reporter #1: We're here today to interview a slug. How are you doing today, Mr. Slug?

Snail: Actually, I am a snail. Don't you notice the shell coiled on my back? The slug is over there. He doesn't have a shell. Other than that, we're pretty much the same.

Reporter #2: We're sorry! Oh, I think I see Mr. Slug over there.

Slug: It's not that hard to find me. On a wet day, you can find me nibbling lettuce in a garden.

Reporter #1: Where else do you like to go?

Slug: I like rain. So if it's dry outside, I hide under rocks or twigs.

Reporter #2: I don't see any feet. How do you move across those leaves?

Slug: I have one big foot.

EXTEND THE LEARNING

☆ Read aloud the information about the author and illustrator of *Some Smug Slug*. Invite students to write about themselves using alliteration. Encourage them to use the first letter of their first names for their initial consonant.

☆ Return to a piece of writing you created with the children. Talk with students about alliteration and the power it has to draw attention to an idea. Alliteration also adds a unique sound. Encourage students to add alliteration to the piece of writing.

☆ Create alliteration poems such as:

Eagle

Powerful, plunging, predator

Searching, soaring, seeking

(See *Revisit, Reflect, Retell.* Hoyt, 1999.)

ASSESS THE LEARNING

> Listen in as students discuss alliteration, making sure they can identify initial consonant sounds in words. As students become adept at identifying alliteration, encourage them to explain the effects of the alliteration in what they read.

> Confer with children about alliteration in their own writing. As you conference with students, find places where alliteration will make their writing memorable. Ask students to point out instances where alliteration might detract from rather than enhance their writing.

INFUSION OF FORMAL LANGUAGE
Test-style language

Alliteration is

A. the order the events happen in a story.

B. repeating a vowel sound at the beginning of words.

C. repeating a consonant sound at the beginning of words.

D. the way an author describes a character.

All of the following are true *except:*

A. The slug strolled on Sunday.

B. A sparrow warned the slug.

C. A squirrel scolded the slug.

D. A skunk ate the slug.

At the game

My coach cries loudly,

"Now or never!

Do or die!

Sink or swim!"

Back at home,

My mother murmurs,

"Safe and sound,"

And turns out the light.

Darkness dimming, dreams begin

Of running the bases again.

Interview with a Slug and . . . a Snail

By Lynnette Brent

Reporter #1:	We're here today to interview a slug. How are you doing today, Mr. Slug?
Snail:	Actually, I am a snail. Don't you notice the shell coiled on my back? The slug is over there. He doesn't have a shell. Other than that, we're pretty much the same.
Reporter #2:	We're sorry! Oh, I think I see Mr. Slug over there.
Slug:	It's not that hard to find me. On a wet day, you can find me nibbling lettuce in a garden.
Reporter #1:	Where else do you like to go?
Slug:	I like rain. So if it's dry outside, I hide under rocks or twigs.
Reporter #2:	I don't see any feet. How do you move across those leaves?
Slug:	I have one big foot.

Reporter #1:   Is it hard to walk with one big foot?

Slug: Have you ever stretched out on your back and inched across the living room floor by curving and straightening your back?

Reporter #2:   I remember doing that once.

Slug: Well, that's the same thing I do with my one big foot. I move by curving and straightening my foot.

Reporter #1:   Are you slimy?

Snail: I can answer that question.
We aren't slimy.
But we can do something that slugs do, too.
We make a slimy, silvery trail of mucous on a dry surface. The mucous gives us a trail to glide along.

Reporter #2:   What else does the mucous do?

Slug: It lets us slide over sharp objects and not get cut. We can even slide over razor blades!
And if a toad tries to eat me, I can clog his mouth with gooey, sticky slime.

Reporter #1:   I guess I won't try to eat you for dinner, then!

Reporter #2:   Thank you for your time today. And that ends our interview with a slug.

Snail: And a snail!

Kitten's First Full Moon
Kevin Henkes

FOCUS THE LEARNING

Introduction: "Kerplink, kerplunk, kerplink" . . . Do you notice how that sounds like something is dropping into a tin can? How about "clip, clop, clip, clop?" What could make a sound like that? Let's try "swoosh." What would make that kind of sound? These words all have onomatopoeia. That means the words imitate real sounds. Can you make the sound of a cow? A sheep? A horse? These words all have onomatopoeia, too.

Think together. What sound does a bee make? What sound does popcorn make when it is popping?

As we enjoy *Kitten's First Full Moon,* our job is to think of sounds that Kitten's actions may make. I am going to use sticky notes and add your onomatopoeia words right into the book.

INTERACTIVE READ-ALOUD
Model and Guide Practice

READ TO WHERE KITTEN GETS A BUG ON HER TONGUE. I am thinking about the sounds that might go with each of these pages. On the second page, Kitten opened her mouth and "licked." I am going to write "mmmm" on a sticky note and put it on this page. On the next page, Kitten got a bug on her tongue! I am going to use a sticky note and write "Aahhh!" to show she is sticking out her tongue to get rid of the bug.

Think together. Can you think of any other words that might help us understand the sounds we might hear?

READ TO WHERE KITTEN FALLS OFF THE STEPS. On this first page, where Kitten is starting to leap, I am going to write "boing!" since Kitten is leaping so high she is like a spring. On the page where she has fallen, I am going to write "bump, bump, thump!" so we can think about what we would hear if we listened to her falling down the stairs.

READ TO WHERE KITTEN IS AT THE TOP OF THE TREE AND LOOKING SCARED. Let's think about Kitten climbing. She is digging her nails into the tree bark to hold on.

Talk to your thinking partner. Can you make the noise we might hear if we listened to Kitten as she climbed? I think Kitten is really frightened up at the top of the tree. What kind of noise might she be making?

READ TO WHERE KITTEN LEAPS INTO THE POND. What kind of sound might she make when she jumps? When she runs through the grass?

Think together.

CONTINUE TO THE END. Pause occasionally to give partners time to generate onomatopoeia words.

END OF STORY REFLECTION

We added lots of great onomatopoeia words to this story.

Think together. What were your favorite onomatopoeia words?

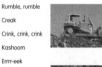 **SHARE THE LEARNING**
Focus on Onomatopoeia

Tip for Share the Reading

 Have the students think about the noises that might be made by a bulldozer and a big dump truck. Read the poem with expression and ask students to talk with partners about what each line might mean. What is happening? How do the onomatopoeia words help us understand the action? Children may enjoy dramatizing as they reread for fluency.

Rumble, rumble
Creak
Crink, crink, crink
Kashoom
Errrr-eek
Swoosh
Scrape
Thud
Rumble, rumble

Tip for Readers Theater Script

For emergent readers and ELL students, read "The Three Billy Goats" to the students, taking special care to interpret the onomatopoeia words so they imitate real sounds. Provide copies of the script and have children follow along as you read it again, this time stopping on each line of onomatopoeia and asking students to decide how to best represent each set of sound words. For developing and fluent readers, turn the script into a performance by having the students stand for each of their lines. As they gain confidence, students may want to read in partners with one partner taking on the role of the "teacher."

The Three Billy Goats
by Linda Hoyt

Teacher: Once upon a time, there were three Billy Goats who wanted to cross the bridge to eat the sweet grass on the other side of the river. They were so hungry, their stomachs were growling.

Students: **Gurgle, gurgle, gurgle.**

Teacher: Little Billy Goat was the first to cross and get to the sweet green grass.

Students: **Trip, trap, trip, trap, trip, trap. Yum!**

Teacher: Middle Billy Goat started across the bridge next. He was much heavier and the bridge swayed under his weight.

Students: **Creak..., crack..., creak..., crack...**

Teacher: Middle Billy Goat was worried that the bridge couldn't hold him so he ran the rest of the way across the bridge to get to the sweet green grass.

EXTEND THE LEARNING

☆ Read *Blueberries for Sal* by Robert McCluskey to savor the onomatopoeia words the author used. Then use sticky notes and add more.

☆ Whisper-read *The Little Engine That Could* by Watty Piper to discover the onomatopoeia in the phrase "I think I can, I think I can."

☆ Read *Farmer Duck* by Helen Oxenbury or *Hattie and the Fox* by Mem Fox to insert onomatopoeia words through the stories.

☆ Guide the students in thinking of onomatopoeia words to describe classroom sounds (scraping chairs, scratching pencils, splashing water, tapping pencils, moving feet, etc.).

☆ Have students take existing pieces of writing and try to insert onomatopoeia words into the illustration and even the text. Have conversations about how onomatopoeia livens up their writing.

ASSESS THE LEARNING

> Listen in as partners think together about onomatopoeia words that describe sounds in stories.

> During small group instruction, have students add onomatopoeia words to the illustrations and text.

> Assess their ability to insert onomatopoeia words into their own illustrations and writing.

INFUSION OF FORMAL LANGUAGE
Test-style language

Which of the following is the best onomatopoeia for when Kitten leaped into the pond?
A. Plip
B. Ticktock
C. Splash!
D. Drip

Onomatopoeia words are those which
A. imitate sounds in the real world.
B. are funny.
C. are hard to say.
D. can make us laugh.

Rumble, rumble

Creak

Crink, crink, crink

Kashoom

Errrr-eek

Swoosh

Scrape

Thud

Rumble, rumble

The Three Billy Goats

By Linda Hoyt

Teacher: Once upon a time, there were three Billy Goats who wanted to cross the bridge to eat the sweet grass on the other side of the river. They were so hungry, their stomachs were growling.

Students: **Gurgle, gurgle, gurgle.**

Teacher: Little Billy Goat was the first to cross and get to the sweet green grass.

Students: **Trip, trap, trip, trap, trip, trap. Yum!**

Teacher: Middle Billy Goat started across the bridge next. He was much heavier and the bridge swayed under his weight.

Students: **Creak..., crack..., creak..., crack...**

Teacher: Middle Billy Goat was worried that the bridge couldn't hold him so he ran the rest of the way across the bridge to get to the sweet green grass.

Students: **Trip, trap, trip, trap, trip, trap. Yum!**

Teacher: Great Big Billy Goat put one foot then another onto the bridge to test its strength . . .

Students: **Creak, crack . . . creak, crack . . .**

Teacher: Great Big Billy Goat decided to start running!

Students: **Trip, trap, trip, trap!**

CRUNCH . . . BOOM . . . SPLASH!

Goldilocks and the Three Bears

James Marshall

FOCUS THE LEARNING

(Post a chart with transition words listed on it. You might want to include: *before, after, now, first, then, finally, next, after, but, soon, once, now, right before, whenever, one day, so suddenly, because, when, now, just then*.)

Introduction: Transition words are words that help us connect one thing to another as we tell a story. Some transition words you are used to seeing are on this chart. These words and phrases help a story to move along faster, and they link events together. Here is an example: "Yesterday *while* you were getting ready to go home, I jotted down some notes of things I wanted to do today. *Then*, I gathered the books that I needed for today's read-aloud. *Meanwhile*, I noticed that you had done a terrific job of gathering your things, organizing our room, and *finally* lining up."

INTERACTIVE READ-ALOUD
Model and Guide Practice

READ PAGES 1–2. I have already noticed several transition words. On page 1, I found "once." On page 2, I found "one morning" and "but."

READ TO THE PLACE WHERE GOLDILOCKS IS READY TO EAT PORRIDGE.

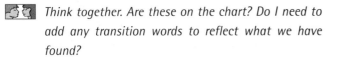 *Turn to your thinking partner. What transition words did you notice?*

(Direct their attention to "meanwhile," "so," and "a few minutes later.")

READ TO WHERE GOLDILOCKS SAT IN THE BIGGEST CHAIR. I found "but," "in fact," and "right away." These are different from some of the others.

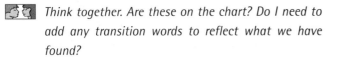 *Think together. Are these on the chart? Do I need to add any transition words to reflect what we have found?*

CONTINUE TO THE END. Pause occasionally to give partners time to talk about transition words and add new words to the chart. Be sure to notice some of the subtle transitions, such as "In the parlor."

END OF STORY REFLECTION

There were lots of transition words in that story. Your challenge now is to work with a partner to retell the story using transition words to help your retell to sound interesting, have the correct sequence, and make sense. Please write the transition words you are planning to use on 3 x 5 cards so you can hold them up when you use a transition during your retell.

SHARE THE LEARNING
Focus on Transition Words

Tip for Share the Reading

Read the shared reading passage with an emphasis on the transition words. Have the students chorally read it with you emphasizing fluent, expressive interpretation.

A few minutes later Goldilocks arrived at the bears' house. She walked right in without even bothering to knock. On the dining room table were three inviting bowls of porridge.

In the parlor there were three chairs. The big chair was much too hard so *next* she moved to the medium-size chair. *Then* she sat in the little chair. It was just right, but it fell all to pieces.

Now that she was all worn out, Goldilocks took a little nap.

Meanwhile, in came . . .

Tip for Readers Theater Script

Before reading "On the Beach" guide the students in a conversation about sea turtles, thinking about their habitat and size. Explain that nonfiction texts also use transition words. Then read the script straight through to model fluency and expression. Read the script a second time chorally with the students joining in unison. Guide a discussion about speed for reading a text like this. Should it be fast or slow? Finally, break the group into teams and present the script as a Readers Theater with an emphasis on fluency and expression. You may want to add soft music in the background for additional drama and expression.

On the Beach
By Linda Hoyt

All:	A female sea turtle digs a deep hole in the sand.
Teacher:	*Next,* she lowers her great body over the hole
Team 1:	and lays more than a hundred eggs.
Teacher:	*While* the eggs settle together,
All:	the mother turtle gently spoons sand over the nest.
Teacher:	*Then,* she levels and smooths the sand
Team 2:	so no one can tell the eggs are there.
Teacher:	*Without a backward glance,*

EXTEND THE LEARNING

☆ During read-alouds, keep the list of transition words at hand to help students note the frequency of transitions and to add new words as they are encountered.

☆ Have children work in pairs to read and find transition words in independent reading selections.

☆ Challenge writers to include transition words in their writing. Have them count and monitor their own use of transitions.

☆ Have students look at newspapers for transition words.

☆ Have students watch a newscast and listen for transition words during the broadcast.

ASSESS THE LEARNING

> Confer with independent readers to assess their ability to identify transition words.

> Confer with writers to assess their writing folders for evidence of transition words.

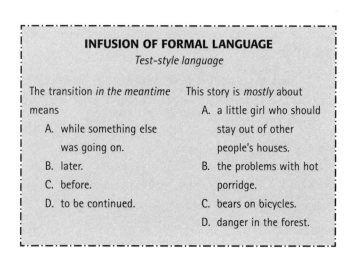

INFUSION OF FORMAL LANGUAGE
Test-style language

The transition *in the meantime* means

  A. while something else was going on.

  B. later.

  C. before.

  D. to be continued.

This story is *mostly* about

  A. a little girl who should stay out of other people's houses.

  B. the problems with hot porridge.

  C. bears on bicycles.

  D. danger in the forest.

A few minutes later Goldilocks arrived at the bears' house.
She walked right in without even bothering to knock. On
the dining room table were three inviting bowls of porridge.

In the parlor there were three chairs. The big chair was
much too hard *so next* she moved to the medium-size
chair. *Then* she sat in the little chair. It was just right, but it
fell all to pieces.

Now that she was all worn out, Goldilocks took a little nap.

Meanwhile, in came . . .

On the Beach

By Linda Hoyt

All: A female sea turtle digs a deep hole in the sand.

Teacher: *Next,* she lowers her great body over the hole

Team 1: and lays more than a hundred eggs.

Teacher: *While* the eggs settle together,

All: the mother turtle gently spoons sand over the nest.

Teacher: *Then,* she levels and smooths the sand

Team 2: so no one can tell the eggs are there.

Teacher: *Without a backward glance,*

Team 1:   she moves into the ocean.

Teacher: *Meanwhile,*

Team 2:   the tiny turtles in the eggs continue to grow.

Teacher: *Soon,*

Team 1:   they chip their way out of the shell,

Team 2:   dig their way to the surface,

Teacher: and, *finally,*

All: begin a dangerous journey to the sea

Teacher: with no one to guide them.

Literary Elements and Devices

Literary elements and devices, such as point of view, foreshadowing, repetition, and exaggeration, get at the heart of the way an author structures a text to effectively tell a story. Standards in this strand involve readers in more complex story structures and more sophisticated language devices such as simile/metaphor and allusion.

The True Story of the Three Little Pigs

Jon Scieszka

FOCUS THE LEARNING

Introduction: The way a story sounds is greatly affected by the person who is telling the story and that person's point of view. Imagine hearing *Jack and the Beanstalk* told by the giant. I think the giant would be really mad that a boy came into his house and stole things! We know that isn't the way people should act. What do you think the giant would have to say about Jack?

 Think about Goldilocks and the Three Bears. *What would the story sound like if the bears were telling the story? What would the bears have to say?*

We are going to focus on point of view as we read *The True Story of the Three Little Pigs* by Jon Scieszka

---

INTERACTIVE READ-ALOUD
Model and Guide Practice

LOOK AT THE COVER. This looks like a newspaper article. It says it is written by A. Wolf. It's called *The True Story of the Three Little Pigs.* I wonder who thinks this is the true story. I wonder if the cover looks like a newspaper to make us think that, like a newspaper, this is reporting the "truth."

Talk to your thinking partner. What can you figure out about the point of view? Who do you think is telling this story?

READ TO WHERE THE WOLF RUNS OUT OF SUGAR. I noticed that this story has the words "I" and "me." Who is the "I" in the story? That tells you the point of view.

Who is telling this story? How is his point of view different from the story you know about three little pigs?

READ TO "THINK OF IT AS A BIG CHEESEBURGER JUST LYING THERE." This story is certainly different when the wolf tells it!

Thinking partners, what is the wolf's point of view? When you hear the story told from this point of view, how do your feelings about the wolf change?

READ TO THE END. What does it mean to be "framed"? I think it means that the wolf really didn't do anything wrong but he was blamed for it.

Thinking partners, talk about the end of the story. Do you think that the wolf really was framed? Do you believe his point of view? Talk about why or why not.

END OF STORY REFLECTION

The wolf thinks he's innocent. He ruined the houses accidentally; he ate the pigs because he was hungry. This is a different point of view from *The Three Little Pigs* I know!

What do you think about the wolf's point of view? Do you think that this is the real story? What makes his story easy to believe? Hard to believe?

TURN TO WHERE THE WOLF DESCRIBES THE POLICE COMING TO THE PIG'S HOUSE. The wolf is telling the story, using the word "I." The whole story is from the wolf's point of view!

Think together. When we hear the original story of The Three Little Pigs, *the wolf says, "I'll huff, and I'll puff, and I'll blow the house down." How is the version we read today different from the story you know?*

SHARE THE LEARNING
Focus on Point of View

Tip for Share the Reading

 Read "On the Scene" aloud to model fluency. Ask children to join in as you read it a second time. Discuss point of view. What clues help children figure out the point of view? Encourage students to read the piece again as if they are delivering the evening news. Emphasize smooth and fluent interpretation.

On the Scene

My dispatcher sent me out on an emergency run. I had a story to write, but it had to wait. I leaped into the news van and raced to the scene. There was a huge, shaggy wolf stomping around outside a brick house. He was yelling and making all kinds of noise. Man, that wolf was upset! He yelled that the pig had said bad things about his granny. The wolf was huffing and puffing and looked like he was trying to blow the house down! Even though everyone knows you can't blow down a house made of bricks, it was pretty scary to watch.

That wolf had already eaten two pigs. He was definitely dangerous, and I knew I was not going near him. Before he had a chance to wolf down another ham dinner, I called 911 so they could take him to jail and lock him up.

Tip for Readers Theater Script

Read "Wolves and Pigs." Ask children to identify the two points of view. Then divide into teams: wolves and pigs. Work with children to help them understand which lines are nonfiction. Then celebrate this script for two voices by having each team rehearse their part before bringing everyone together for a performance.

Wolves and Pigs
By Lynnette Brent

Wolves	Pigs
We are different colors: gray, black, red, or white.	We are different colors: gray, pink, black, white, or spotted.
We have sharp teeth. We eat mainly meat.	We eat plants and meat.
We have an amazing sense of smell.	We have an amazing sense of smell.
We live in the woods.	Some of us live on farms. Some of us live in the wild.
We have lost a lot of our habitat.	We live on continents all over the world.
We can run 30 miles an hour!	We don't run very quickly.
We are smart.	We are very smart.
We are in many stories.	We are in many stories.
Sometimes in stories we're bad, but those stories are just made up!	Charlotte's Web is our favorite!
It's great being A WOLF!	It's great being A PIG!

EXTEND THE LEARNING

☆ Work with children to create a Venn diagram, comparing and contrasting Jon Scieszka's version of the story with the traditional telling of *The Three Little Pigs.*

☆ Ask children to dramatize a trial for the wolf. They will need a judge, attorneys, pigs, and observers to testify for and against the wolf. In each case, dramatize and illustrate the point of view of the speaker.

☆ Ask children to take the point of view of a real animal, telling about a day in "their" life from the alternative point of view. What would a day be like from a dog's point of view?

☆ Read *Diary of a Spider* or *Diary of a Worm* by Doreen Cronin.

☆ Think together about events in the school and consider them from multiple points of view. For example, talk about the cafeteria from the students' point of view. Then have children interview the cook and talk about the lunch experience from her point of view.

ASSESS THE LEARNING

> Listen in as thinking partners talk about point of view. They should link point of view with the character's feelings and tell how point of view affects the story.

> Choose another text children have read. Ask them to identify the point of view and to explain how it affects their understanding of the characters.

> As children approach a new piece of writing, whether fiction or nonfiction, ask them to consider point of view. What point of view will they choose? Why? How will readers know who is telling the story?

INFUSION OF FORMAL LANGUAGE
Test-style language

Point of view describes
- A. where the story takes place.
- B. who is telling the story.
- C. when the story takes place.
- D. the most exciting part of the story.

This story was told mostly from the point of view of
- A. the wolf.
- B. the first little pig.
- C. the third little pig.
- D. the wolf's grandmother.

On the Scene

My dispatcher sent me out on an emergency run. I had a story to write, but it had to wait. I leaped into the news van and raced to the scene. There was a huge, shaggy wolf stomping around outside a brick house. He was yelling and making all kinds of noise. Man, that wolf was upset! He yelled that the pig had said bad things about his granny. The wolf was huffing and puffing and looked like he was trying to blow the house down! Even though everyone knows you can't blow down a house made of bricks, it was pretty scary to watch.

That wolf had already eaten two pigs. He was definitely dangerous, and I knew I was not going near him. Before he had a chance to wolf down another ham dinner, I called 911 so they could take him to jail and lock him up.

Wolves and Pigs

By Lynnette Brent

Wolves

We are different colors: gray, black, red, or white.

We have sharp teeth.
We eat mainly meat.

We have an amazing sense of smell.

We live in the woods.

We have lost a lot of our habitat.

We can run 30 miles an hour!

We are smart.

We are in many stories.

Sometimes in stories we're bad, but those stories are just made up!

It's great being A WOLF!

Pigs

We are different colors: gray, pink, black, white, or spotted.

We eat plants and meat.

We have an amazing sense of smell.

Some of us live on farms.
Some of us live in the wild.

We live on continents all over the world.

We don't run very quickly.

We are very smart.

We are in many stories.

Charlotte's Web is our favorite!

It's great being A PIG!

Little Bear's Visit
Else Holmelund Minarik

FOCUS THE LEARNING

Introduction: Writers have many ways of helping us understand their messages. One way is called *personification*. That means that the author of the book has animals acting like people instead of animals. For example, would a real bear at the zoo wear a hat and sit at a table? No! Look at the cover of *Little Bear's Visit* by Else Holmelund Minarik. We can tell right away that this author has used personification because even the cover has bears doing things that real bears could never do.

INTERACTIVE READ-ALOUD
Model and Guide Practice

READ PAGES 9–13. I am going to stop reading for a minute and think about examples of personification I have found so far. I am going to write them on a chart so we can remember what we find. First, I noticed that Grandmother and Grandfather Bear live in a house. Real bears don't have houses. That is personification for sure. I also notice that the grandparents are wearing clothes. I will add that to my list, too.

 Turn to your thinking partner. What examples of personification can you add?

READ PAGES 14–19. I am going to stop reading for a minute, think about what has been happening, and add some examples of personification to our list.

 Turn to your thinking partner. Think together about examples of personification I should be sure to add.

READ TO PAGE 23.

You know what to do. Turn to your thinking partner. Think together. Help me think of examples of personification we can add to our chart.

CONTINUE TO THE END. Pause occasionally to give partners time to talk and appreciate the humor as well as the sequence of this story.

END OF STORY REFLECTION:

Look at all of these examples of personification. This author really used a lot of personification.

 Turn and talk to your partner. What was your favorite example of personification in this story?

SHARE THE LEARNING
Focus on Personification

Tip for Share the Reading

Explain that sometimes personification is clear, as it is in the story of *Little Bear's Visit*. Other times, personification is more subtle, giving human qualities to forces of nature. Read "Wind" to the children and ask them to talk with a partner about personification. What evidence of personification can they find? Read the poem again chorally, emphasizing dramatic interpretation.

Wind
By Linda Hoyt and Wendy Murray

Once a kiss upon my cheek
Then a push upon my back
Lifting kites and spinning mills
Blowing curtains upon windowsills

Wind—sometimes a sunny lullaby
Sometimes a howling scream across the sky

Tip for Readers Theater Script

Guide children in a conversation about the illustration. What evidence of personification do they see in the picture? Read each "Sun" poem to the children and guide comments about personification within the poem. Then compare and contrast. What traits are being attributed to the sun in each poem? If the sun were a person, what would we notice about the sun's personality just by reading the poems? Invite the children to join you in reading the poems chorally. Then move to partner and individual reading as children are ready. Some learners may enjoy writing personification poems in which they give human characteristics to nonhuman things.

Sun
By Linda Hoyt

Glowing
Watching
Smiling down on us

Bringing us light
Helping things grow
Friendly face in a bright blue sky

Sun
By Linda Hoyt

Hot
Burning
Punisher

Drying the ground
Hurting our skin
Why are you angry?

EXTEND THE LEARNING

☆ Have the children look through their independent reading books for examples of personification and give them a chance to share with partners.

☆ Have students select books in which animals talk. Then let them work with a partner to read a small portion aloud, applying their knowledge of how people act to the words of the animals in the book.

☆ Have the children select a passage in which animals show personification and practice it to read at home. Have them plan how they will explain personification to their parents.

☆ Look for and share poetry that personifies nonhuman things.

☆ Model a piece of writing that personifies something familiar in the classroom or in the environment.

ASSESS THE LEARNING

> Listen in as partners converse about examples of personification.

> Confer with readers during independent reading to see if they understand and recognize personification.

INFUSION OF FORMAL LANGUAGE
Test-style language

In this story, personification was used when
  A. the bears lived in a house.
  B. the bears ate at a table.
  C. the bears wore clothes.
  D. All of the above.

All of the following are true *except:*
  A. Little Bear loved visiting his grandparents.
  B. He liked his grandmother's cooking.
  C. He went fishing.
  D. Grandma and Grandpa Bear told him stories.

Wind

By Linda Hoyt and Wendy Murray

Once a kiss upon my cheek

Then a push upon my back

Lifting kites and spinning mills

Blowing curtains upon windowsills

Wind—sometimes a sunny lullaby

Sometimes a howling scream across the sky

Sun

By Linda Hoyt

Glowing
Watching
Smiling down on us

Bringing us light
Helping things grow
Friendly face in a bright blue sky

Sun

By Linda Hoyt

Hot
Burning
Punisher

Drying the ground
Hurting our skin
Why are you angry?

Strega Nona
Tomie dePaola

FOCUS THE LEARNING

Introduction: Imagine you look out the window and see dark clouds moving toward you. When you open the window, you feel a cold wind. You can tell there is likely to be a storm. The clues—the clouds and the wind—foreshadow what is coming and give you a warning. Sometimes writers put clues in a story, like those storm clouds. They foreshadow coming events and give you a warning. Foreshadowing is a powerful tool as it can make a story more suspenseful, create a feeling that something is about to happen—and make you want to read on! As we read *Strega Nona* by Tomie dePaola look for *foreshadowing*—clues that give you a hint about what is coming later.

INTERACTIVE READ-ALOUD
Model and Guide Practice

(Show the cover and talk with students about what kind of story this might be. Students will probably conclude that this story is not realistic but more like a folktale or fairy tale.)

READ TO "'OH, SI, YES,' SAID BIG ANTHONY."

Thinking partners, talk about the story. What does Strega Nona ask Anthony to do? Think about other stories you have read with warnings like this. What might this foreshadow?

READ TO "...BECAUSE HE DIDN'T SEE STREGA NONA BLOW THREE KISSES TO THE MAGIC PASTA POT."

Thinking partners, why is blowing kisses to the magic pasta pot so important? The author is foreshadowing here. What problem might the author be warning us about?

READ TO "BUT, ALAS, HE DID NOT BLOW THE THREE KISSES!"

Thinking partners, do you see some foreshadowing here? What do you know about the three kisses? What do you think is going to happen?

CONTINUE TO THE END. Pause periodically to encourage the children to anticipate events based on clues. Remind them that foreshadowing isn't "guessing"—it's based on clues in the story.

END OF STORY REFLECTION

Big Anthony certainly learned a lesson! Tomie dePaola warned us with his foreshadowing that something was going to happen...

Talk together about foreshadowing. What were the clues the author used to warn you of coming events?

SHARE THE LEARNING
Focus on Foreshadowing

Tip for Share the Reading

🖱 Read "What's Going On?" aloud to the students or have them join you in chorally interpreting the selection. Ask partners to consider what the events in the story might foreshadow.

What's Going On?

The phone rang—again! This time it was Aunt Sue. Aunt Sue hardly ever called, and she was the third relative to call tonight. Amelia handed the phone to her mom and asked why all these relatives were calling. Her mom just smiled.

Later, Amelia went to get her coat out of the closet.

"Don't open that door," her mom squeaked, alarmed.

"Why not?" asked Amelia.

"Um, because your coat is already hanging on the peg by the front door," her mom stammered.

Amelia grabbed her coat, then shrugged and went outside. Her mom sure was acting weird!

The mail carrier was just walking up to the front porch with three boxes. Two boxes were from her favorite toy store and one was from the florist.

"Hey, Mom!" called Amelia. "There are boxes here from the toy store and the florist. What's going on?"

Tip for Readers Theater Script

💿 Gather the foreshadowing clues in "What Should We Make?" Emerging readers can read the "All" lines as a group. Developing and independent readers can have fun reading with expression and gusto!

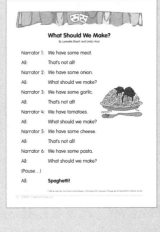

What Should We Make?
By Lynnette Brent and Linda Hoyt

Narrator 1:	We have some meat.
All:	That's not all!
Narrator 2:	We have some onion.
All:	What should we make?
Narrator 3:	We have some garlic.
All:	That's not all!
Narrator 4:	We have some tomatoes.
All:	What should we make?
Narrator 5:	We have some cheese.
All:	That's not all!
Narrator 6:	We have some pasta.
All:	What should we make?
(Pause...)	
All:	**Spaghetti!**

EXTEND THE LEARNING

☆ Work with students to create a list of other stories they have read and movies they have seen that include foreshadowing. What hints did they see in the text or movie? How did those hints tell them what would happen next?

☆ Watch for foreshadowing as you read aloud from other books.

☆ Read *Dandelion* by Don Freeman and *Rosie's Walk* by Pat Hutchins to discuss additional examples of foreshadowing.

☆ Encourage students to include foreshadowing in their own writing, using phrases such as "trouble wasn't far behind," "he had no idea what a mistake he had made," and so on.

☆ Read *Sylvester and the Magic Pebble* by William Steig, *The Cat in the Hat* by Dr. Seuss, *The Biggest Bear* by Lynd Ward, and *Encounter* by Jane Yolen to look for examples of foreshadowing.

ASSESS THE LEARNING

➤ Listen in as thinking partners discuss foreshadowing. Be sure that students don't make guesses. Foreshadowing involves identifying clues in the text.

➤ As you conference with students about stories they have written, ask them to point out the foreshadowing they included. Ask: What clues did you put in your story? How do you think those clues will tell your readers what happens next?

INFUSION OF FORMAL LANGUAGE
Test-style language

Foreshadowing is
A. the most important event in a story.
B. a hint or clue of something that will happen.
C. a scene that tells something that happened before.
D. the event that happens at the end of a story.

The townspeople laugh at Big Anthony because
A. the magic pot is overflowing.
B. they see Anthony blowing kisses to a pot.
C. no one believes the magic pot will work.
D. Strega Nona makes him eat until he is full.

What's Going On?

The phone rang—again! This time it was Aunt Sue. Aunt Sue hardly ever called, and she was the third relative to call tonight. Amelia handed the phone to her mom and asked why all these relatives were calling. Her mom just smiled.

Later, Amelia went to get her coat out of the closet.

"Don't open that door," her mom squeaked, alarmed.

"Why not?" asked Amelia.

"Um, because your coat is already hanging on the peg by the front door," her mom stammered.

Amelia grabbed her coat, then shrugged and went outside. Her mom sure was acting weird!

The mail carrier was just walking up to the front porch with three boxes. Two boxes were from her favorite toy store and one was from the florist.

"Hey, Mom!" called Amelia. "There are boxes here from the toy store and the florist. What's going on?"

What Should We Make?

By Lynnette Brent and Linda Hoyt

Narrator 1:   We have some meat.

All: That's not all!

Narrator 2:   We have some onion.

All: What should we make?

Narrator 3:   We have some garlic.

All: That's not all!

Narrator 4:   We have tomatoes.

All: What should we make?

Narrator 5:   We have some cheese.

All: That's not all!

Narrator 6:   We have some pasta.

All: What should we make?

(Pause…)

All: **Spaghetti!**

The True Story of the Three Little Pigs
Jon Scieszka

> ### FOCUS THE LEARNING
> Introduction: Sometimes when we are reading a story, the author pauses to tell us something that happened before the story started. This is called *flashback*. As readers, we can flash back to something that will give us important information and help us understand the story better. *The True Story of the Three Little Pigs* has a flashback in it. Let's read to see if we can find it.

INTERACTIVE READ-ALOUD
Model and Guide Practice

READ PAGE 1. This part of the story takes place now. Someone is telling us the story—he uses the word "I." It must be the wolf.

READ THE NEXT FOUR PAGES. On these pages, the story takes place now, in the present. The wolf is telling us that he's not really big and bad, that people don't understand the real story. Since this is happening now, I know it isn't the flashback. When we get to the flashback, it will tell about something that already happened.

READ TO WHERE THE WOLF BEGINS TO TELL THE STORY OF MAKING THE BIRTHDAY CAKE. Here it is! The flashback is starting! There are clues on this page that tell me that this part of the story took place in a different time.

> *Thinking partners, pick out some clues on this page that show you this part of the story is a flashback. Remember that in a flashback, the story pauses to "rewind" to tell something that already happened.*

READ THE REST OF THE STORY. Pause periodically to ask children how the flashback is helping them understand the events of the rest of the story.

> *At the beginning of the story, the wolf says that he is not really a big bad wolf. What do you learn about the wolf in the flashback?*

END OF STORY REFLECTION
At the end of the story, the wolf says that the news reporters wanted to make the story more exciting so they added details to the story of the three little pigs.

> *Talk with your partner. What does the flashback help you understand about the story? How would this story be different without the flashback? Would you understand as well?*

SHARE THE LEARNING
Focus on Flashback

Tip for Share the Reading

Place the text on the overhead and read it straight through with the students. Ask partners to think together to identify the flashback and discuss ways the flashback improved our understanding. What clues does the author provide to signal the beginning of the flashback? How can you tell when the main story picks up again?

Renee didn't know how she ended up being the coach, but she was. She needed to do volunteer work for school. When her teacher matched each student with a job, Renee hoped that she would plant flowers, read to younger kids, or even bring dogs to visit hospital patients. But coach a softball team for young kids? Renee was terrified!

Her players greeted her with excitement—all except one. Dominick was shy, and he didn't like the game. When it was his turn, he came to home plate but he barely lifted the bat. Renee had started to like coaching, but she was upset that Dominick wouldn't try.

As she watched him, Renee thought back to when she was in third grade and on a team herself. She remembered being afraid to play kickball, and she remembered being afraid to try to connect with the ball. But Coach Dale was kind to her. He came up to the plate and showed her how to kick. He cheered for her from the sidelines. He helped her find the courage and do her best.

With renewed confidence, Renee looked at Dominick and smiled. She hoped her smile would make him feel better. If Coach Dale could work with her, she could work with Dominick. Coaching might not be so bad after all!

Tip for Readers Theater Script

Have children identify the flashback in "The Trial." You might have two separate "casts"—one to read the information that takes place in the present and one to read the flashbacks. Prompt a discussion about the information that is added by the flashbacks. Because this script is a "trial," be sure to discuss with children the voice and tone they would use as they "testify."

The Trial
By Lynnette Brent

In the Courtroom

Reporter: We are here today at the trial of the Big Bad Wolf.

Wolf: I am not big and bad!

Reporter: No interruptions, Wolf! As I was saying, we're here at the trial of the Big Bad Wolf. Let's listen in as the trial begins.

Judge: Jury, today you will hear from the wolf and from the third little pig. Listen carefully to their stories. You will have to decide whether the wolf is guilty of destroying property and eating pigs without an invitation.

Please come to the stand, Mr. Third Little Pig.

Bailiff: Will you tell the truth, the whole truth, and nothing but the truth?

Pig: *(staring fiercely at the wolf)* I will.

Judge: Tell the jury what happened at your house.

Pig: It happened like this.

The Flashback

Wolf: Little pig, little pig, let me in.

Pig: Please leave me alone, Wolf. I am shaving the hairs on my chinny chin chin.

EXTEND THE LEARNING

☆ Demonstrate by telling a story about a personal experience and inserting a flashback in the retelling. Children can use your model to tell their own stories with flashbacks.

☆ Read aloud another book that contains flashbacks. In *Miss Rumphius* by Barbara Cooney, for example, the main character recalls advice that her grandfather gave her when she was a child.

☆ Children can create comic strips that contain a flashback. One frame in the middle, for example, can recall an event in the past. Thinking partners can identify the flashbacks and the information that those flashbacks provide.

☆ Have children read a variety of books with flashbacks such as *The Dinosaurs of Waterhouse Hawkins* by Barbara Kerley, *Home Place* by Crescent Dragonwagon, *The Keeping Quilt* by Patricia Polacco, and *Roxaboxen* by Alice McLerran. In each, have students identify the flashback and talk about the way it influenced their comprehension.

ASSESS THE LEARNING

> Listen in as thinking partners discuss flashback in *The True Story of the Three Little Pigs*. Can they pinpoint clues that signal flashback? Can they identify information that the flashback provides?

> As children retell stories, ask them to identify places at which flashbacks could be inserted to provide more information.

INFUSION OF FORMAL LANGUAGE
Test-style language

The flashback in this story begins when

  A. the wolf starts baking the cake.

  B. the wolf eats the First Little Pig.

  C. the police come to the pigs' house.

  D. the reporters write about the wolf.

The wolf says that the reporters *jazzed up* the story. This means that the reporters

  A. told only the facts.

  B. wrote music to go with the story.

  C. added details to make the story more exciting.

  D. wrote a story that no one would want to read.

Renee didn't know how she ended up being the coach, but she was. She needed to do volunteer work for school. When her teacher matched each student with a job, Renee hoped that she would plant flowers, read to younger kids, or even bring dogs to visit hospital patients. But coach a softball team for young kids? Renee was terrified!

Her players greeted her with excitement—all except one. Dominick was shy, and he didn't like the game. When it was his turn, he came to home plate but he barely lifted the bat. Renee had started to like coaching, but she was upset that Dominick wouldn't try.

As she watched him, Renee thought back to when she was in third grade and on a team herself. She remembered being afraid to play kickball, and she remembered being afraid to try to connect to the ball. But Coach Dale was kind to her. He came up to the plate and showed her how to kick. He cheered for her from the sidelines. He helped her find the courage and do her best.

With renewed confidence, Renee looked at Dominick and smiled. She hoped her smile would make him feel better. If Coach Dale could work with her, she could work with Dominick. Coaching might not be so bad after all!

The Trial

By Lynnette Brent

In the Courtroom

Reporter: We are here today at the trial of the Big Bad Wolf.

Wolf: I am not big and bad!

Reporter: No interruptions, Wolf! As I was saying, we're here at the trial of the Big Bad Wolf. Let's listen in as the trial begins.

Judge: Jury, today you will hear from the wolf and from the third little pig. Listen carefully to their stories. You will have to decide whether the wolf is guilty of destroying property and eating pigs without an invitation.

Please come to the stand, Mr. Third Little Pig.

Bailiff: Will you tell the truth, the whole truth, and nothing but the truth?

Pig: *(staring fiercely at the wolf)* I will.

Judge: Tell the jury what happened at your house.

Pig: It happened like this.

The Flashback

Wolf: Little pig, little pig, let me in.

Pig: Please leave me alone, Wolf. I am shaving the hairs on my chinny chin chin.

Wolf: If you won't let me in, I'll huff and I'll puff, and I'll blow your house in.

Pig: I wouldn't do that, Mr. Wolf!

Wolf: Why not, little pig? Let me in!

Pig: I am going to call the police if you don't go away. I don't want to be rude, but I'm busy right now.

Wolf: I'm huffing and puffing!

Pig: Then I'm sorry, Mr. Wolf, but I am calling the police. I tried to warn you.

Back in the Courtroom

Judge: So you were polite and warned the wolf to leave you alone?

Pig: Of course, your honor. I was just busy. The wolf said he would blow down my house. I had to call the police.

Judge: Thank you, Mr. Third Little Pig. You may go back to your seat.

Mr. Wolf, will you please come to the stand?

Bailiff: Will you tell the truth, the whole truth, and nothing but the truth?

Wolf: *(staring fiercely at the pig)* I will.

Judge: Tell the jury what happened at the pig's house.

Wolf: It happened like this.

The Flashback

Wolf: Good morning, little pig! I am baking a cake for my granny's birthday. Would you please lend me a cup of sugar?

Pig: Go away, Wolf! I am busy right now. I won't lend you the sugar!

Wolf: I am sorry to bother you, but I need to bake this cake and I've been searching for sugar all day. Can you please lend me the sugar?

Pig: Your granny can go sit on a pin! Go away! Leave me alone!

Wolf: *(coughing, wheezing, and sneezing)* Please don't say such bad things about my dear old granny.

Pig: Are you trying to blow down my house?

Wolf: *(huffing and puffing and sneezing)* I am sneezing. I have a cold!

Pig: Help! Police! A wolf is blowing down my house!

Back in the Courtroom

Judge: So you were polite and asked the pig for sugar?

Pig: Of course, your honor. I wanted to make a nice cake for my granny. The pig was rude to me.

Judge: Thank you, Mr. Wolf. You may go back to your seat.

Jury, you have heard both sides of the story. Which is the *real* story of the sneeze, the sugar, and the third little pig?

Seven Blind Mice
Ed Young

FOCUS THE LEARNING

Introduction: Similes help us compare things. By adding the words "like," "as," or "than," we can help ourselves visualize and understand more deeply. Here are some examples: She is as mad as a hornet! Her eyes are like chocolate pudding. Tommy is wilder than the wind. These are all similes. I am going to write the signal words "like," "as," and "than" on the board to help us remember them. Let's practice a bit more. We could say, (Name a child)_____'s hair is as dark as midnight. (Name a child) _____'s eyes are as blue as the sky. (Name a child)_____ is as speedy as a race car. We walk down the hall like a train of ants.

 Think together. I want to say, "_____ is more gentle than a lamb." Partners, whose name should I use? Who is really gentle?

Today we will read *Seven Blind Mice* by Ed Young and practice using similes to compare things.

INTERACTIVE READ-ALOUD
Model and Guide Practice

READ THE BOOK STRAIGHT THROUGH. What a great story! Let's go back to the beginning and think about similes. Let's start with the mouse who thought the elephant's leg was a pillar. I can turn that into a simile. I am going to try it with each of our signal words: It's as sturdy as a pillar. It is round like a pillar. It is taller than a pillar.

Think together. Which simile do you think best describes the elephant's leg?

Let's think together about the elephant's trunk. What similes can we come up with to describe the trunk? Remember the mouse said it is like a snake.

Think together. Create a simile about the trunk.

CONTINUE REREADING. Pause periodically to have partners create similes using each of the signal words to describe parts of the elephant.

END OF STORY REFLECTION

We have used so many similes! Let's write some of them down. Similes are great ways to describe things.

SHARE THE LEARNING
Focus on Simile

Tip for Share the Reading

Work with the students to read each line and come up with ideas for completing the simile. After the similes are complete, read the poem for fluency and expression.

I'm as small as a _____.
I'm as strong as _____.
I'm as quiet as _____.
I'm as loud as _____.
I'm as wiggly as _____.
I'm as slow as catsup coming out of a new bottle.
I'm as fast as _____.
I'm more patient than _____.
I'm more _____ than _____.
I'm more _____ than _____.
I'm _____ like a _____.
I'm perfect just like I am.

Tip for Readers Theater Script

Read "This Classroom" to the children as they follow along. Next, have them retell the similes. Provide repeated experiences with the similes, having children read in unison and in partners to support fluency and expression.

This Classroom
By Linda Hoyt

This classroom is as loud as a rock concert.
It's as quiet as a church.
This classroom is bigger than a bedroom.
It's smaller than a gymnasium.
This classroom hums like a well-oiled machine.
It can be crazier than a day at the zoo.
This classroom is a special place . . .
Where we learn like scholars,
Work like bees,
Think like inventors,
Are as creative as our teacher,
And have a wonderful time being the best we can be.

EXTEND THE LEARNING

☆ Read *Quick as a Cricket* by Audrey Wood.

☆ Use similes throughout the classroom day. "You need to be quick as a cricket while you wash your hands for lunch!" "Let's be quiet as mice while we walk down the hall."

☆ Model a piece of writing using a simile in the writing.

☆ During interactive writing, help the children generate and write similes.

☆ Read *Owl Moon* by Jane Yolen and search for similes.

☆ Create similes for favorite characters in stories. "Goldilocks was as scared as a mouse when she ran out the door after the bears came home." "Cinderella was as fast as a deer when she ran out of the ball at midnight."

☆ Read *Tar Beach* by Faith Ringgold and look for similes and metaphors.

ASSESS THE LEARNING

➤ As partners think together, listen in to determine their ability to generate and understand simile.

➤ Ask students to add similes to a piece of writing. Then assess their writing.

➤ After a read-aloud, help the children create similes about characters and setting. Assess their ability to show relationships and make comparisons through simile.

INFUSION OF FORMAL LANGUAGE
Test-style language

Finish the simile: The school bus creeps along like a _____.

A bird
B. dog
C. snail
D. deer

Which of the following is a simile?

A. You are fast.
B. You are really fast.
C. You run really fast.
D. You're as fast as a cheetah!

I'm as small as a _____.

I'm as strong as _____.

I'm as quiet as _____.

I'm as loud as _____.

I'm as wiggly as _____.

I'm as slow as catsup coming out of a new bottle.

I'm as fast as _____.

I'm more patient than _____.

I'm more _____ than _____.

I'm more _____ than _____.

I'm _____ like a _____.

I'm perfect just like I am.

This Classroom

By Linda Hoyt

This classroom is as loud as a rock concert.

It's as quiet as a church.

This classroom is bigger than a bedroom.

It's smaller than a gymnasium.

This classroom hums like a well-oiled machine.

It can be crazier than a day at the zoo.

This classroom is a special place . . .

Where we learn like scholars,

Work like bees,

Think like inventors,

Are as creative as our teacher,

And have a wonderful time being the best we can be.

Sleeping Ugly
Jane Yolen

FOCUS THE LEARNING

Introduction: Allusion is a literary device that authors often use to add humor and interest to stories. To do this, an author makes references to another story and hopes that you will notice. I am going to tell a story. Listen for reminders of another story you know. "My family and I went for a walk while we waited for our dinner to cool off."

What was the allusion? What story did that remind you of?

Today we are going to read *Sleeping Ugly* by Jane Yolen. The title is an allusion to *Sleeping Beauty*. What do you remember about *Sleeping Beauty*? What might we predict about a story entitled *Sleeping Ugly*?

INTERACTIVE READ-ALOUD
Model and Guide Practice

READ THROUGH PAGE 15. This has surprised me a bit. I expected allusion to *Sleeping Beauty*, but the author has made allusions to several fairy tales. I noticed, for example, the framed picture at the beginning, which reminded me of the mirror in *Sleeping Beauty*. I noticed that the princess is named Miserella. That is an allusion to Cinderella, but the two aren't very much alike, are they?

Thinking partners, how would you compare Miserella and Cinderella?

READ PAGE 16. Here is another allusion. Remember Rip Van Winkle? He was the man who fell asleep under a tree and slept for a really long time.

READ TO PAGE 21.

Partners, do you notice the wand? This is another allusion to Cinderella. What do you remember about the wand in Cinderella?

CONTINUE TO THE END. Pause to discuss allusions. (Jane, for example, receives three wishes. When Miserella is cross, the fairy punishes her. Her foot turns to stone like in *King Midas*. The prince kisses the fairy and Miserella to wake them up and so on.)

Thinking partners, talk about the prince in Sleeping Ugly. *How is the prince an allusion? What story characters does he remind you of? How is he different from the princes in other stories?*

END OF STORY REFLECTION

The allusions make this story fun to read. I expected to read something familiar, but the allusions sometimes turn out differently! In *Snow White*, for example, the prince kisses Snow White because she is beautiful. But in this story, the prince decides to kiss the fairy and the plain girl first.

(Begin a chart on the board.)

Thinking partners, work together to complete the chart with additional events and allusions.

(Allow time for whole group discussion.)

Event in Sleeping Ugly	Allusion—Story It Reminds You Of	Alike? Different? In What Ways?
Miserella's foot turns to stone.	Midas—He touched things that turned to gold.	Miserella and Midas are both wicked. Midas turns things into gold instead of stone.

 **SHARE THE LEARNING**
Focus on Allusion

Tip for Share the Reading

Read the passage to model fluent reading. Then encourage children to read along. Discuss the allusions to *Snow White* in *Sleeping Ugly.* You might prompt discussion with questions such as: What part does beauty play in the two stories? Why does the prince kiss Snow White? Why does the prince kiss Jane?

Snow White took refuge in the house of seven dwarfs to hide from her stepmother, the Wicked Queen. The Queen was jealous because Snow White was much more beautiful than she. The dwarfs loved Snow White. But one day when the dwarfs were working, the Queen disguised herself as an old peddler and persuaded Snow White to bite a poisonous apple. The dwarfs rushed home to save Snow White, but they were too late. They placed her in a glass coffin. The Prince, who had fallen in love with Snow White, awakened Snow White from the Queen's spell with love's first kiss.

Tip for Readers Theater Script

Read "A Cast of Characters" to the children. Ask students to identify the characters based on their lines. Allow children to read the different roles, and have a team ready to state the name of the character in the allusion before the next line is read. As an extension, children may enjoy creating riddles for additional characters from fairy tales, books, and movies.

A Cast of Characters
By Lynnette Brent

Character 1: I lost my shoe. But when I found it, I found my prince!
I am _____

Character 2: My hair was so long, you could use it as a ladder.
I am _____

Character 3: It's not easy to sleep with peas under the mattress.
I am _____

Character 4: Granny's cookies looked good to me! But the girl with the red cape had other ideas.
I am _____

Character 5: My brothers used sticks and straw, but I think that bricks work best for building houses.
I am _____

EXTEND THE LEARNING

☆ Work with children to list allusions in other books or in movies. In the movie *Shrek*, for example, characters from many tales are part of the movie.

☆ Create a class notebook of allusions. Children can find allusions in magazines and newspapers and write examples of allusions from movies, books, and so on. As children learn more about allusions, they can classify them by source—allusions from fairy tales, popular movies, the Bible, advertisements, and so on.

☆ Read additional titles with allusions, such as *"I Can't" Said the Ant* by Polly Cameron, *Four Dollars and Fifty Cents* by Eric Kimmel, *The Frog Prince Continued* by Jon Scieszka, and *Tar Beach* by Faith Ringgold.

ASSESS THE LEARNING

➤ As thinking partners discuss allusion, listen in to be sure that they can figure out the references. Children should compare and contrast the original source with the allusion. Children who are proficient may be able to discuss the effects of changing the original story.

➤ Look at the charts created by thinking partners. Children should be able to link the story events to events from tales that they know.

INFUSION OF FORMAL LANGUAGE
Test-style language

An *allusion* is
  A. the person who tells the story.
  B. a lesson you learn from reading a story.
  C. something that seems greater than it really is.
  D. a reference to another story or person, place, or thing.

Sleeping Beauty and *Sleeping Ugly* are alike because they both have
  A. a 100-year nap.
  B. a foot that turns to stone.
  C. a prince with no jewels or property.
  D. a plain character who lives in the woods.

Snow White took refuge in the house of seven dwarfs to hide from her stepmother, the Wicked Queen. The Queen was jealous because Snow White was much more beautiful than she. The dwarfs loved Snow White. But one day when the dwarfs were working, the Queen disguised herself as an old peddler and persuaded Snow White to bite a poisonous apple. The dwarfs rushed home to save Snow White, but they were too late. They placed her in a glass coffin. The Prince, who had fallen in love with Snow White, awakened Snow White from the Queen's spell with love's first kiss.

A Cast of Characters

By Lynnette Brent

Character 1: I lost my shoe. But when I found it, I found my prince!

I am _____.

Character 2: My hair was so long, you could use it as a ladder.

I am _____.

Character 3: It's not easy to sleep with peas under the mattress.

I am _____.

Character 4: Granny's cookies looked good to me! But the girl with the red cape had other ideas.

I am _____.

Character 5: My brothers used sticks and straw, but I think that bricks work best for building houses.

I am _____.

Character 6: A little girl sat in my chair, ate my dinner, and even slept in my bed!

I am _____.

Character 7: That apple looked tasty, but I shouldn't take food from strangers.

I am _____.

Character 8: Most beans don't grow that tall! It was fun to climb the beanstalk.

I am _____.

Character 9: I never knew I would get three wishes from rubbing a lamp. I should have started rubbing lamps a long time ago!

I am _____.

Character 10: I am the person who is in charge of your school. I help the teachers and children be the best learners they can be.

I am _____.

When I Was Young in the Mountains
Cynthia Rylant

FOCUS THE LEARNING

Introduction: Memories are like special treasures we each have. A special memory for me is learning to ride a bike. I remember that I got the bike for Christmas and I remember my Dad taking me out on the sidewalk and holding the seat while I tried to get my balance. I also remember that the bike was bright blue and had a red seat. Did you notice how I used repetition and said "I remember" several times? Repetition of important words is a tool we can use to draw attention to our thinking.

Think for a moment about a memory you have. Can you remember your last birthday? The first time you rode a bike? Kicking the ball in a soccer game? Jumping into a swimming pool?

Share a memory with a partner. Try to say "I remember" at least twice while you are sharing your memory.

Cynthia Rylant used repetition in *When I Was Young in the Mountains*. Listen to the repetition and think about how it helps the story.

INTERACTIVE READ-ALOUD
Model and Guide Practice

READ PAGES 1–4. Isn't this interesting? Cynthia Rylant has used the title of the book as a repeating line in the story. "When I was young in the mountains…" It makes it sound a little like a poem. I am going to read pages 1–4 again and enjoy the language. I am also going to start a tally and keep track of how many times she uses the line in the story. We can start with two tally marks because she used the line on page 1 and page 2.

READ PAGE 5. I am catching on to the way Cynthia Rylant is using repetition. She uses the line "When I was young in the mountains" each time she starts telling about a new memory. If she doesn't start the page with that repeating line, then she is continuing to talk about the same memory.

READ ABOUT PUMPING PAILS OF WATER FOR A BATH AND DRINKING HOT COCOA TO GET WARM.

 Thinking partners, think together about this book. What has been your favorite memory so far?

CONTINUE TO THE END. Pause occasionally to give partners time to talk.

END OF STORY REFLECTION

Let's look at our tally marks and see how many times Cynthia Rylant used the phrase "When I was young in the mountains." This book is really beautiful, and I think the repetition of the line made it special. If I were going to write about memories and use what I learned from Cynthia Rylant, I would want to tell several memories from my childhood. I already mentioned my bike so I am going to add digging clams at the beach and helping my grandma make pancakes in funny shapes. My story might sound like this:

When I was young in Oregon, my grandma let me help her make pancakes. Sometimes we made them in the shape of little fish, and sometimes we made them in the shape of letters and spelled our names. When I was young in Oregon, I got to go clam digging. It was cold and I got wet, but it was fun digging in the sand and piling the shells in my bucket.

Your turn. Use the stem "When I was young" and share memories with your partner.

SHARE THE LEARNING
Focus on Repetition

Tip for Share the Reading

Remind the students that repetition can help us connect to the author's view of what is important. Model reading the passage fast. Then read it again slowly with dramatic emphasis. Ask the students which style of reading better matches the emotions the author is trying to convey. Play quiet instrumental music in the background and read the passage again. How does the music affect the meaning? Invite students to read the passage with partners, experimenting with dramatic interpretations.

> When I was young in the mountains,
> we sat on the porch swing in the evenings,
> and Grandfather sharpened my pencils with his pocketknife.
>
> . . .
>
> When I was young in the mountains,
> we listened to frogs sing at dusk and awoke
> to cowbells outside our windows.
>
> . . .
>
> When I was young in the mountains,
> we took long walks in the shade of the big old trees
> and took big gulps of clean mountain air.

Tip for Readers Theater Script

For emergent readers, read "Blue Whale" as the children look at the photograph. Guide a conversation about what they learned from the poem. Invite the children to join in on the "Blue whale" introduction while you read the rest of the line. For developing readers, have one group read just "Blue whale" while another group reads the rest of each line. Switch parts and read it again. Move to reading the poem in partners and individually.

Blue Whale
By Linda Hoyt

Blue whale	the largest animal on earth
Blue whale	grows to 110 feet in length
Blue whale	a deep blue color
Blue whale	likes deep ocean waters where the temperature is cool
Blue whale	eats krill which are like little shrimp
Blue whale	dives straight down after showing its flukes
Blue whale	makes a steeper dive than any other whale
Blue Whale	Blue Whale

EXTEND THE LEARNING

☆ Lead students in an interactive writing experience focused on the repeating line "At the beginning of the year…" or "When summer comes…." Be sure they understand the repeating line needs to appear several times in their writing.

☆ Guide writers in crafting repetitive language focused on their families. "In my family…" could be the lead on each page, creating a predictable structure that even the most emergent students could follow.

ASSESS THE LEARNING

> Listen in as partners tell their memories to see if they can insert the repeating line into their oral communication.

> Confer with readers during independent reading to see if they recognize repetition and its effect in writing.

> Assess students' writing after guided experiences such as those listed in Extend the Learning to see if they understand the power of repetition.

INFUSION OF FORMAL LANGUAGE
Test-style language

When an author uses repetition, it probably means

  A. the repeated line is important to the author's message.

  B. the author couldn't think of enough words.

  C. it is about memories.

  D. the story is true.

What conclusion can you draw from this story?

  A. The girl loved her grandparents.

  B. She loved the mountains.

  C. She has a lot of special memories.

  D. All of the above.

When I was young in the mountains,

we sat on the porch swing in the evenings,

and Grandfather sharpened my pencils with his

pocketknife.

. . .

When I was young in the mountains,

we listened to frogs sing at dusk and awoke

to cowbells outside our windows.

. . .

When I was young in the mountains,

we took long walks in the shade of the big old trees

and took big gulps of clean mountain air.

Blue Whale

By Linda Hoyt

Blue whale	the largest animal on earth
Blue whale	grows to 110 feet in length
Blue whale	a deep blue color
Blue whale	likes deep ocean waters where the temperature is cool
Blue whale	eats krill which are like little shrimp
Blue whale	dives straight down after showing its flukes
Blue whale	makes a steeper dive than any other whale
Blue Whale	Blue Whale

Cloudy With a Chance of Meatballs
Judi Barrett

FOCUS THE LEARNING
Introduction: "I'm so hungry, I could eat a horse!" Do you think I could really eat a whole horse, even if I hadn't had any breakfast or lunch? I don't think so. I was exaggerating. Exaggerating is the same thing as overstating. That means you make something bigger than it actually is. If my sister yawns and I say, "Her mouth is as big as the Grand Canyon," you know her mouth isn't really that big. That's just my way of saying that my sister is really tired and has a big yawn. Sometimes writers exaggerate, too. We will be looking for exaggerations as we read today's story, *Cloudy With a Chance of Meatballs* by Judi Barrett.

INTERACTIVE READ-ALOUD
Model and Guide Practice

LOOK AT THE COVER. At first, I thought I saw hail falling. But then I read the title and looked more carefully. That's a meatball! Can you imagine a weather forecaster saying, "Tomorrow it will be cloudy with a chance of meatballs"? That would be a big surprise!

READ TO "ACROSS THREE DESERTS, AND ONE SMALLER OCEAN...." I am going to reread the first paragraph carefully. The author says that Grandpa told the best tall-tale bedtime story he'd ever told. *Tall tales* are stories that are full of exaggerations.

Thinking partners, what examples of exaggeration do you see on this page? What kind of story do you think this will be? Serious? Funny? Full of facts? Why do you think so?

CONTINUE TO THE END. Pause periodically and discuss exaggeration.

Thinking partners, how can you tell that Grandpa's bedtime story is a tall tale? What kinds of exaggerations does Grandpa include in his story about the amazing town of Chewandswallow? How do the exaggerations affect the text? What do you find humorous? Interesting? Different from other books you have read?

REREAD THE PAGE ENDING "I REMEMBER HIS GOOD-NIGHT KISS."

How is the new town different from Chewandswallow? Do you think the new town will have as many exaggerations? Tell why.

END OF STORY REFLECTION
Grandpa tells a funny and exaggerated bedtime story. I wonder what it would be like to live in Chewandswallow. You could get food almost anytime, but it sure would be messy.

Talk together about the last page of the book. After Grandpa's story, what do the brother and sister see in their own town? What exaggerated tales could they make up about where they live?

SHARE THE LEARNING
Focus on Exaggeration

Tip for Share the Reading

Read the story to the students, asking them to identify the exaggerations. Children can read the story with you or with partners. Model and talk with them about how to emphasize the exaggerations when they read—the tone of voice can make an exaggeration come to life when it's read aloud!

Pecos Bill was a cowboy folk hero. His legend goes something like this:

When Pecos Bill was a baby, he fell out of his parents' wagon. Some coyotes found him and raised him like he was their pup. When Bill grew up, he rode a snarling mountain lion. He also rode a horse that was so wild no other man could ride it. Bill carried a whip, but it wasn't made of leather—it was a live rattlesnake. He married Slue-Foot Sue, a girl he met when she was riding down the river on a catfish the size of a whale. When Pecos Bill's ranch was dry after a long period without rain, he drained the entire river to water his fields. The crops grew so well and so high, they blocked out the sun. Everyone thought it was nonstop night. You should have seen the corn he grew. Each ear was so big it filled the entire back of a pickup truck. One ear could feed nearly a hundred people for a week. Pecos Bill. What a cowboy!

Tip for Readers Theater Script

"Clouds…and Weather" describes real weather. Students can double up to read the descriptions of weather. Developing readers can focus on the "All" lines. Consider having students expand on the script by inserting "nonsense" exaggerations about different kinds of weather. Examples: "Clouds are made of water, air, and *bits of cotton candy.*" "Those big puffy clouds look like *zoo animals in the sky.*"

Clouds . . . and Weather
by Lynnette Brent

All:	Clouds
Reader 1:	Clouds are made of water and air.
Reader 2:	Those big puffy clouds that look like shapes in the sky are called cumulus.
All:	Rain
Reader 3:	Water evaporates and rises up into the air.
Reader 4:	This water falls back to earth as rain.
All:	Snow
Reader 5:	Snowflakes fall to earth when light ice crystals stick together and get heavy.
Reader 6:	One snowflake can be made up of 200 ice crystals.
All:	Wind

EXTEND THE LEARNING

☆ Children will enjoy reading tall tales and other exaggerated stories. Encourage them to talk about what makes these stories "larger than life" and rate the stories to determine their favorites.

☆ Ask students where they can find exaggerations in real life. Prompt them to consider advertisements as exaggeration— if you use a product, you'll become beautiful. If you buy a certain cereal, it will be the best you've ever tasted. Students can clip advertisements and talk about how they use exaggeration.

☆ Students can use *Cloudy With a Chance of Meatballs* as a springboard to write their own exaggerated weather reports. You might give them a sentence to start: "When I went outside, I was so surprised when I saw …"

☆ Model a piece of writing about a familiar classroom event. Use a lot of exaggeration to turn a ho-hum retell into something funny.

ASSESS THE LEARNING

➤ As children discuss *Cloudy With a Chance of Meatballs,* be sure they understand exaggeration. The sentence "It is raining really hard" is not an exaggeration. Can students explain why?

➤ Choose a book that contains exaggerations. Conference with students individually or in small groups. Ask them to identify exaggerations. Students who understand exaggeration can explain the effect that exaggeration has on a piece of writing.

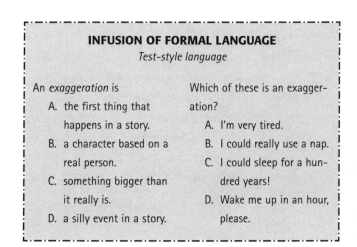

INFUSION OF FORMAL LANGUAGE
Test-style language

An *exaggeration* is
- A. the first thing that happens in a story.
- B. a character based on a real person.
- C. something bigger than it really is.
- D. a silly event in a story.

Which of these is an exaggeration?
- A. I'm very tired.
- B. I could really use a nap.
- C. I could sleep for a hundred years!
- D. Wake me up in an hour, please.

Pecos Bill was a cowboy folk hero. His legend goes something like this:

When Pecos Bill was a baby, he fell out of his parents' wagon. Some coyotes found him and raised him like he was their pup. When Bill grew up, he rode a snarling mountain lion. He also rode a horse that was so wild no other man could ride it. Bill carried a whip, but it wasn't made of leather—it was a live rattlesnake. He married Slue-Foot Sue, a girl he met when she was riding down the river on a catfish the size of a whale. When Pecos Bill's ranch was dry after a long period without rain, he drained the entire river to water his fields. The crops grew so well and so high, they blocked out the sun. Everyone thought it was nonstop night. You should have seen the corn he grew. Each ear was so big it filled the entire back of a pickup truck. One ear could feed nearly a hundred people for a week. Pecos Bill. What a cowboy!

Clouds . . . and Weather

By Lynnette Brent

All: Clouds

Reader 1:   Clouds are made of water and air.

Reader 2:   Those big puffy clouds that look like shapes in the sky are called cumulus.

All: Rain

Reader 3:   Water evaporates and rises up into the air.

Reader 4:   This water falls back to earth as rain.

All: Snow

Reader 5:   Snowflakes fall to earth when light ice crystals stick together and get heavy.

Reader 6:   One snowflake can be made up of 200 ice crystals.

All: Wind

Reader 7:   Wind is air in motion.

Reader 8:   People have used the power of wind for over 5,000 years.

All: Thunder

Reader 9:   Thunder is a loud noise that is caused by electricity.

Reader 10:   If you hear thunder at the same time you see lightning, the storm is right over your head.

All: Move inside!

All: Lightning

Reader 11:   Lightning strikes somewhere on earth about 100 times a second!

Reader 12:   A lightning rod is a big metal pole. When lightning hits it, the electricity goes into the ground.

All: Weather

Reader 13:   A sunny day with a blue sky as far as your eyes can see.

Reader 14:   A blustery day with a wind that chills you to the bone.

Reader 15:   A rainy day with sloshy, wet mud puddles.

Reader 16:   A wintry day with snow you can sink into, pack, and throw.

All: Weather

Doctor De Soto
William Steig

FOCUS THE LEARNING

Introduction: Poetic justice is a tool authors use in which bad is punished and good is rewarded. In poetic justice the "punishment" for the bad is usually really a good match to what the individual did wrong. For example, remember *Strega Nona* by Tomie dePaola? Remember how Big Anthony had to EAT all of the spaghetti and clean up the town to solve the problem he created? That is poetic justice: good is rewarded and bad is punished. Remember our classroom rule that if you make a mess, you need to be the one to clean it up? That is poetic justice.

Think about Cinderella. *Think about the stepsisters. They wanted to marry the prince but they were really mean to Cinderella. Think about poetic justice together. Good is rewarded and bad is punished. What was the poetic justice in that story?*

INTERACTIVE READ-ALOUD
Model and Guide Practice

READ TO WHERE DR. DE SOTO WOULD NOT TREAT EVEN THE MOST TIMID-LOOKING CAT. I am thinking about Dr. De Soto. I know one of the attributes of poetic justice is that good is rewarded. He seems really good, doesn't he? Dr. De Soto helps a lot of animals and works really hard. I am thinking that he will some-how be rewarded for being so good. It is important to notice that the big animals he is treating are not dangerous to mice. These big animals don't eat mice. They eat other things.

READ TO WHERE MRS. DE SOTO YELLS, "WIDE OPEN!"

Remember that in poetic justice, good is rewarded and bad is punished. What are your thoughts about poetic justice? What do you think will happen?

READ TO WHERE THE FOX IS LEAVING THE OFFICE. I am thinking about poetic justice again. This fox is really bad—after they have helped him, he is thinking about eating the De Sotos!

What do you think of this fox?

CONTINUE TO THE END. Pause occasionally to let partners dis-cuss poetic justice.

END OF STORY REFLECTION

I definitely think the fox deserved this poetic justice! He was going to eat the De Sotos, but they sure outsmarted him.

What do you think of the "punishment" the fox received? Is this poetic justice? Does the punishment fit his bad thinking?

SHARE THE LEARNING
Focus on Poetic Justice

Tip for Share the Reading

Remind the students that in poetic justice the punishment must be appropriate to the crime and that there is no long-term injury. Read the shared selection together and discuss the poetic justice. Read it again for fluency and expression, dramatizing the selection.

"Help! Help!" cried a young girl. "I can't get out of this swimming pool."

Thankfully a big, strong boy came along, and just when the girl thought he would help her, he said, "Don't worry. All you have to do is roll on your back and kick. That way you will float."

"I'm afraid! Please get me out of here," she pleaded.

"In a minute. Right now I am going to finish drinking my soda. Then I will help you. In the meantime, just kick, kick and float. You can do it."

The big strong boy sat down and watched the girl struggle. He drank his soda and smiled at her while she splashed and gulped and cried for help.

Finally, he reached down, grabbed her hand, and pulled her out of the water. Just as she was safely out of the water, he lost his balance and fell in.

"Help! Help!" he cried. "I can't swim!"

"Don't worry," said the girl. . . . "Just roll on your back and kick. You will float just fine."

She sat down with a big smile and drank a soda while she watched him flail around in the water. Then she walked calmly to the side and tossed him a life ring.

Tip for Readers Theater Script

Read "A Beautiful Day in the Woods" to the students as a poem. Discuss poetic justice. What would be an appropriate punishment for whoever left the garbage? Recast the poem as a Readers Theater script by dividing into teams and presenting it as a performance. You may want to add lines to reflect an ending the students create to include poetic justice.

A Beautiful Day in the Woods
By Linda Hoyt

Narrator 1:   There is nothing like a hike in the woods
Narrator 2:   on a cool fall afternoon.
Narrator 3:   As I look up I can see the bright blue sky
Narrator 4:   through a canopy of yellow, red, and orange leaves.
Narrator 1:   There is a delicious crunching, shuffling sound
Narrator 2:   as I move along the trail
Narrator 3:   and the fallen leaves crackle under my feet.
Narrator 4:   I take a big breath of the cool, clean air
Narrator 4:   and dip my hands into the bubbling stream
Narrator 1:   that spills around rocks
Narrator 4:   and shares its music with the trees.

EXTEND THE LEARNING

☆ Read a variety of books with poetic justice, including *May I Bring a Friend* by Beatrice De Regniers, *Snail Mail* by Hazel Edwards, and *Chrysanthemum* by Kevin Henkes.

☆ Talk about poetic justice in daily living. If we make a mess, we clean it up. If we don't wear a coat on a cold day, we get cold.

☆ Read *The Tale of Peter Rabbit* by Beatrix Potter and discuss the poetic justice of having Peter sick in bed while his family gets to eat goodies.

☆ Read a variety of fairy tales and consider poetic justice.

ASSESS THE LEARNING

> Have students create illustrations reflecting poetic justice in literature. Have them show how good is rewarded and bad gets an appropriate punishment. Assess their work for understanding.

> During small group instruction, discuss poetic justice and assess children's ability to identify the literary device.

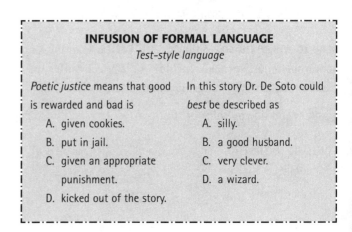

INFUSION OF FORMAL LANGUAGE
Test-style language

Poetic justice means that good is rewarded and bad is

   A. given cookies.

   B. put in jail.

   C. given an appropriate punishment.

   D. kicked out of the story.

In this story Dr. De Soto could *best* be described as

   A. silly.

   B. a good husband.

   C. very clever.

   D. a wizard.

"Help! Help!" cried a young girl. "I can't get out of this swimming pool."

Thankfully a big, strong boy came along, and just when the girl thought he would help her, he said, "Don't worry. All you have to do is roll on your back and kick. That way you will float."

"I'm afraid! Please get me out of here," she pleaded.

"In a minute. Right now I am going to finish drinking my soda. Then I will help you. In the meantime, just kick, kick and float. You can do it."

The big strong boy sat down and watched the girl struggle. He drank his soda and smiled at her while she splashed and gulped and cried for help.

Finally, he reached down, grabbed her hand, and pulled her out of the water. Just as she was safely out of the water, he lost his balance and fell in.

"Help! Help!" he cried. "I can't swim!"

"Don't worry," said the girl. . . . "Just roll on your back and kick. You will float just fine."

She sat down with a big smile and drank a soda while she watched him flail around in the water. Then she walked calmly to the side and tossed him a life ring.

A Beautiful Day in the Woods

By Linda Hoyt

Narrator 1:   There is nothing like a hike in the woods

Narrator 2:   on a cool fall afternoon.

Narrator 3:   As I look up I can see the bright blue sky

Narrator 4:   through a canopy of yellow, red, and orange leaves.

Narrator 1:   There is a delicious crunching, shuffling sound

Narrator 2:   as I move along the trail

Narrator 3:   and the fallen leaves crackle under my feet.

Narrator 4:   I take a big breath of the cool, clean air

Narrator 2:   and dip my hands into the bubbling stream

Narrator 1:   that spills around rocks

Narrator 4:   and shares its music with the trees.

Narrator 3: Then . . . I can hardly believe it.

All: There is a huge pile of garbage

Narrator 1: right in the middle of all this beauty!

Narrator 2: What kind of fool would throw garbage

Narrator 3: and rubber tires right here in the woods?

Narrator 4: This isn't right!

All: Where is poetic justice when we need it!

The Frog Prince Continued
Jon Scieszka

FOCUS THE LEARNING

(Read *The Frog Prince* to the children before reading this story so they can understand the irony.)

Introduction: When there is a contrast between what we expect and what happens, then we have *irony*. Here is an example: If it is raining really hard, we would expect someone to say, "Wow! It is miserable outside today." If instead I say, "Nice day," you know I am using irony because it isn't a nice day at all. If you are eating something that is really delicious, like a warm, gooey chocolate chip cookie and you say, "It's too bad these aren't any good," that is irony as well. Stories have irony when there is a contrast between what we expect and what happens. *The Frog Prince Continued* by Jon Scieszka is a story with irony. To help us notice the irony, it is important to think about what we know about the original story of *The Frog Prince*. Think together. What do you remember?

INTERACTIVE READ-ALOUD
Model and Guide Practice

READ THE FIRST THREE PAGES. This is irony. Everyone assumes that a frog would be happy to be turned into a prince, but this prince really liked being a frog. It sounds like he still acts like a frog since he is jumping on the furniture and sticking out his long tongue. Look at page 1. He is trying to catch flies on the wallpaper!

READ TO WHERE THE WITCH WANTS TO CAST A NASTY SPELL ON HIM. Here is more irony. He goes to a witch for help to become a frog again, and all she wants to do is cast a nasty spell on him to keep him from kissing a princess. It is ironic that he can't get any help. I thought princes were supposed to get anything they wanted.

READ TO WHERE THE WITCH OFFERS HIM THE APPLE. I think it would be another ironic twist if he ate the apple and fell asleep for 100 years.

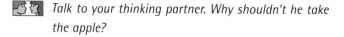 *Talk to your thinking partner. Why shouldn't he take the apple?*

CONTINUE READING AS HE SEARCHES FOR WITCHES TO HELP HIM.

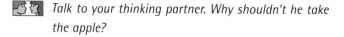 *Think together. What do you think he should do?*

CONTINUE TO THE END. Pause occasionally to wonder about the irony and let thinking partners share their ideas.

END OF STORY REFLECTION
The ending was ironic. The princess is now a frog! We don't expect a princess to turn into a frog, do we? Stories don't usually end like that. It says they lived happily ever after. Does that mean she likes being a frog? That is ironic because stories make it sound like being a princess is the perfect life.

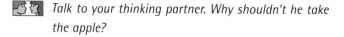 *What do you think of the ending?*

SHARE THE LEARNING
Focus on Irony

Tip for Share the Reading

Show children the pictures in *Rosie's Walk* by Pat Hutchins. Highlight scenes where the fox gets hit with the rake, falls in the pond, and so on. Place the shared reading text on the overhead and have the children read it chorally. Then talk about the irony in *Rosie's Walk*.

(Read *Rosie's Walk* by Pat Hutchins.)

Rosie the hen goes for a walk across the yard, around the pond, over the haystack, past the mill, and so on. The fox wants to get Rosie for his dinner, but every time he leaps to catch her, something happens to him. It is ironic to see how many times the fox has trouble and Rosie never even notices that the fox is chasing her.

Tip for Readers Theater Script

For emergent readers, read "Oh, NO!" to them and have them create illustrations and use them to support a retell. For developing readers, enjoy the script as a three-team experience. With increased proficiency, small groups of three can read the script together for fluency and expression.

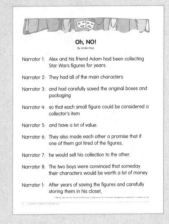

Oh, NO!
By Linda Hoyt

Narrator 1: Alex and his friend Adam had been collecting Star Wars figures for years.

Narrator 2: They had all of the main characters

Narrator 3: and had carefully saved the original boxes and packaging

Narrator 4: so that each small figure could be considered a collector's item

Narrator 5: and have a lot of value.

Narrator 6: They also made each other a promise that if one of them got tired of the figures,

Narrator 7: he would sell his collection to the other.

Narrator 8: The two boys were convinced that someday their characters would be worth a lot of money.

Narrator 1: After years of saving the figures and carefully storing them in his closet,

EXTEND THE LEARNING

☆ Use the terms *irony* and *ironic* to describe daily moments in the classroom so students get used to hearing the terms and thinking about irony.

☆ Read *Pinkerton Behave* by Steven Kellogg and talk about the irony of Pinkerton's bad manners actually saving the day.

☆ Read *Four Dollars and Fifty Cents* by Eric Kimmel and search for irony.

ASSESS THE LEARNING

> Have children create illustrations that show an expected outcome and an ironic ending.

> Listen to partner conversations to assess students' understanding of irony.

INFUSION OF FORMAL LANGUAGE
Test-style language

It was ironic that the Frog Prince wasn't happy as a prince. He just wanted to be
  A. a toad.
  B. a frog.
  C. married.
  D. in the woods.

Which of the following would show irony on a sunny day?
  A. You are wearing rubber boots and a raincoat.
  B. You are wearing sunglasses.
  C. You have a bathing suit for a trip to the beach.
  D. You are going on a long bike ride.

(Read *Rosie's Walk* by Pat Hutchins.)

Rosie the hen goes for a walk across the yard, around the pond, over the haystack, past the mill, and so on. The fox wants to get Rosie for his dinner, but every time he leaps to catch her, something happens to him. It is ironic to see how many times the fox has trouble and Rosie never even notices that the fox is chasing her.

Oh, NO!

By Linda Hoyt

Narrator 1: Alex and his friend Adam had been collecting Star Wars figures for years.

Narrator 2: They had all of the main characters

Narrator 3: and had carefully saved the original boxes and packaging

Narrator 4: so that each small figure could be considered a collector's item

Narrator 5: and have a lot of value.

Narrator 6: They also made each other a promise that if one of them got tired of the figures,

Narrator 7: he would sell his collection to the other.

Narrator 8: The two boys were convinced that someday their characters would be worth a lot of money.

Narrator 1: After years of saving the figures and carefully storing them in his closet,

Narrator 2: Alex finally decided it was time to sell his collection.

Narrator 3: He was getting older and it was time to stop wishing for the action figures to be worth a lot of money.

Narrator 4: He called Adam and told him he could have the entire collection for $10.00.

Narrator 5: When Alex handed over his collection, he was sad but felt that $10.00 was better than nothing.

Narrator 6: A week later, Alex opened the morning newspaper.

Narrator 7: The headline said, "Star Wars Figures Top the Charts, Collectors Make a Fortune."

Narrator 8: Oh, NO!

All: That's irony.

Genre

Genre categories—fiction, nonfiction, fairy tale, drama, and so on—each have a particular kind of content or structure. Exploring the standards in this strand, learners begin to understand the distinguishing features of various genres and learn what to expect from each.

DISTINGUISHING FEATURES OF GENRES
POETRY

Heartland
Diane Siebert

FOCUS THE LEARNING

(Gather samples of a variety of genre including newspapers, magazines, cookbooks, nonfiction resources, poetry books, and fiction before beginning this lesson. Be prepared to create a class list of features of poetry.)

Introduction: Boys and girls, we know that resources have different features that make them unique. Let's start by looking at this newspaper. What are its features? How can we tell just by looking that this is a newspaper? Now let's compare it to this cookbook. How do we know this isn't a newspaper? What are its features? I brought a beautiful book of poetry to share with you. This book *is* a poem. It's called *Heartland* by Diane Siebert.

Think together. What are the features of a poem? How is a poem different from a news article or a fiction story?

INTERACTIVE READ-ALOUD
Model and Guide Practice

READ THE BOOK FROM START TO FINISH. Guide the children in a conversation about the meaning of the poem and the visualizations that they were able to generate as they listened. Explain that you are going to read the book again with a focus on the features that Diane Siebert used in her poem.

READ TO THE THIRD PAGE OF TEXT. I am going to stop reading. We can all agree that the language is beautiful and that Diane Siebert is a master at helping readers to visualize. But let's think about the features of this poem. I notice that the lines don't stretch from margin to margin. Some lines are very brief and aren't attempting to even be a sentence. Sometimes the lines are just a phrase. I also notice that Diane Siebert made the first word in each line a capital letter even if the line isn't the beginning of a new sentence. I am going to write these features on a list so we can keep track.

READ THE NEXT THREE PAGES. I am going to reflect on the illustrations and the way they match the pages of the poem. I am noticing that the illustrations are carefully matched to the meaning of the poem. And I notice that even if there was room for more writing, Diane Siebert was careful to keep the lines on the page limited so they really match the picture. I am going to read the next page to you, but I am not going to show the illustration. Listen and visualize. Be ready to tell your partner what you think should be in the picture.

Thinking partners, share your visualizations. Share your thinking about the illustration and what should be in it. Then I will show you the illustration that is in the book.

CONTINUE TO THE END. Pause occasionally to guide the children in noticing the metaphors, imagery, interesting punctuation, phrasing of lines, the voice inherent in the first-person perspective, rhyming structure, the well-chosen verbs, and so on. This poem is so richly written, you could read it many times and continually notice new things. As children consider features of the poem, be sure to add them to the list.

END OF STORY REFLECTION

Thinking partners, look at the list of features we found in this poem and think together. Which features were the most powerful in this poem?

SHARE THE LEARNING
Focus on Features of Poetry

Tip for Share the Reading

Place the excerpt from *Heartland* on the overhead and guide students in looking closely at the visual features of the text. Encourage them to notice that the first three lines are centered, and recall that this structure repeats throughout the book. Guide them in examining the varied punctuation and noticing the capital letter at the beginning of each line. Encourage them to read the selection with you, focusing on dramatic interpretation that supports visualization and meaning. Add observations to the list of distinguishing features for poetry.

From *Heartland*
by Diane Siebert

I am the Heartland.
On this soil
Live those who through the seasons toil:

The farmer, with his spirit strong;
The farmer, working hard and long,
A feed-and-seed-store cap in place,
Pulled down to shield a weathered face—
A face whose every crease and line
Can tell a tale, and help define
A lifetime spent beneath the sun,
A life of work that's never done.

Tip for Readers Theater Script

Read "Rainbows: A Magic Mix" to the students, or invite them to read it with you chorally. Guide a conversation about the distinguishing features of this piece. What genre do the children think it is? How do they know? Which features support their thinking? Divide into two teams and have teams read alternating paragraphs after rehearsing for fluency and expression. Partners can reread the selection for fluency, taking time to reflect on their oral expression, phrasing, and use of punctuation.

Rainbows: A Magic Mix
by Linda Hoyt

When do rainbows occur?
Conditions need to be just right, but in general, rainbows are a mixture of rain and light. Rainbows happen both during the day and during the night after a rain. The rainbows form when the sun or a full moon sits low in the sky and their light shines through the water droplets hanging in the air.

How is a rainbow created?
When sunlight or moonlight pass through millions of falling raindrops, the raindrops act like tiny prisms and bend the light. As light shines through the raindrops, the white light is split into many colors that are visible to someone watching the sky.

How many colors are in a rainbow?
Raindrops project a total of seven colors against the sky. The top color is red, followed by orange, yellow, green, blue, indigo, and violet.

When can you see a rainbow most clearly?
To get the best view of a rainbow, stand with your back to the sun or the moon and look straight into the rainbow. The colors will be more intense when there is plenty of light flowing through the raindrops.

EXTEND THE LEARNING

☆ Read poetry by Shel Silverstein and Jack Prelutsky and compare the features to the excerpt from *Heartland*.

☆ Read poetry selections that do not rhyme. Discuss distinguishing features that still allow each selection to be considered poetry.

☆ Engage children in writing poetry about topics in science and social studies or about characters in fiction selections.

☆ Look at recipe books, brochures, and a wide array of non-fiction texts and talk about distinguishing features. Create lists of distinguishing features for each text type.

☆ Compare the features of fiction and nonfiction selections.

☆ Have students write a variety of forms and use the appropriate features for each.

☆ During small group instruction, have students read and interpret poetry selections. Then discuss the distinguishing features of the poems.

ASSESS THE LEARNING

➤ Listen as partners discuss distinguishing features to check for understanding.

➤ During small group instruction, have children sort text samples according to the distinguishing features they notice.

➤ Confer with individuals during independent reading to assess their ability to recognize distinguishing features of different genres.

INFUSION OF FORMAL LANGUAGE
Test-style language

A common feature in poetry is
- A. short phrases.
- B. incomplete sentences.
- C. visual images.
- D. All of the above.

In *Heartland*, the phrase "patchwork quilt" means
- A. a bedspread.
- B. a patch of grass.
- C. women sewing.
- D. the farmers' fields.

From *Heartland*

By Diane Siebert

I am the Heartland.
On this soil
Live those who through the seasons toil:

The farmer, with his spirit strong;
The farmer, working hard and long,
A feed-and-seed-store cap in place,
Pulled down to shield a weathered face—
A face whose every crease and line
Can tell a tale, and help define
A lifetime spent beneath the sun,
A life of work that's never done.

Rainbows: A Magic Mix

By Linda Hoyt

When do rainbows occur?

Conditions need to be just right, but in general, rainbows are a mixture of rain and light. Rainbows happen both during the day and during the night after a rain. The rainbows form when the sun or a full moon sits low in the sky and their light shines through the water droplets hanging in the air.

How is a rainbow created?

When sunlight or moonlight pass through millions of falling raindrops, the raindrops act like tiny prisms and bend the light. As light shines through the raindrops, the white light is split into many colors that are visible to someone watching the sky.

How many colors are in a rainbow?

Raindrops project a total of seven colors against the sky. The top color is red, followed by orange, yellow, green, blue, indigo, and violet.

When can you see a rainbow most clearly?

To get the best view of a rainbow, stand with your back to the sun or the moon and look straight into the rainbow. The colors will be more intense when there is plenty of light flowing through the raindrops.

Tomorrow's Alphabet
George Shannon

INTERACTIVE READ-ALOUD
Model and Guide Practice

(As you read, fold the book back so the children can only see the page with the letter until you show the outcome.)

READ "A IS FOR SEED, TOMORROW'S APPLE." What a great pattern. The author chose apple for A but he didn't say A is for apple. He said "A is for seed" because someday that seed will grow into a tree and that tree will grow apples! To understand this book, I have to think about how things start and what they turn into.

READ "B IS FOR EGGS. . . ." What will an egg turn into later? Think together and then I will show the next page.

👥 *Think together. Why would B be for eggs?*

CONTINUE TO THE END. Pause to engage the children in partner conversations to think about the relationships that allow them to solve the puzzles.

END OF STORY REFLECTION

Guide the children in thinking about nonfiction as a genre. Ask: How is this book like and different from other nonfiction selections? What makes this a nonfiction book? In what ways is it unique?

👥 *Think together. Use the nonfiction pattern in* Tomorrow's Alphabet *to describe something. When you and your partner think you have gotten to the heart of it, put your thumb over your heart so I know you are ready to share.*

SHARE THE LEARNING
Focus on Features of Nonfiction

Tip for Share the Reading

Read "Flight" and talk about the features that distinguish this nonfiction selection. How can students tell this is nonfiction? Help them to notice the title, photos, boldface print, and captions. Have students read the selection in unison to focus on fluent interpretation and phrasing that supports the meaning.

Tip for Readers Theater Script

Explain that the Readers Theater script, titled also "Flight," is virtually the same as the Share the Reading selection. It just has been divided into parts so teams can share the reading and emphasize key understandings. Have teams rehearse and then weave their reading together to create an interesting presentation. Have students take a familiar nonfiction selection from small group time, a textbook, or other favorite nonfiction piece, divide it into speaking parts, and present it as a Readers Theater script.

EXTEND THE LEARNING

☆ Gather an array of nonfiction selections. Compare text features and other attributes that make them uniquely nonfiction.

☆ Read an array of nonfiction poetry and discuss nonfiction poetry as a dimension of nonfiction.

☆ Read nonfiction books by Seymour Simon and talk about the power of the photographs vs. other nonfiction books that have line drawings.

☆ During small group instruction, guide children in reading a variety of nonfiction books and discussing their attributes.

☆ Confer with readers during independent reading to ensure they know how to navigate a nonfiction selection.

☆ Read a nonfiction selection and then write a poem about the same subject. Discuss the features of the nonfiction description and the nonfiction poem.

ASSESS THE LEARNING

> Assess children's ability to recognize and navigate a nonfiction book by conferring with individuals during independent reading.

> During small group instruction, assess children's understanding of how to navigate the features of a nonfiction selection, including the table of contents, index, glossary, headings, and so on.

INFUSION OF FORMAL LANGUAGE
Test-style language

Nonfiction books

A. are about real things.

B. include facts.

C. often have features such as headings, bold print, and a table of contents.

D. All of the above.

This nonfiction selection was written mainly to

A. teach.

B. explain.

C. show relationships between things.

D. tell how things should be.

Flight

By Linda Hoyt

Flight is an amazing thing. We know that birds are built to soar through the sky, but how is it that a **machine** can fly without even flapping its wings?

Propeller Planes

Early planes had propellers, which turn really fast and push air across the wings to create lift and move the plane forward. Small aircraft still use propellers to move up and through the sky.

Early propeller plane

Jet Planes

Larger aircraft use **jet-powered** engines to move air across the wings and to create the lift and forward motion that are needed to move the airplane forward. These huge planes can carry large numbers of people or loads of **cargo** and travel great distances.

Jet engine

Commercial aircraft

Flight

By Linda Hoyt

Team 1:   Flight is an amazing thing.

Team 2:   We know that birds are built to soar through the sky,

Team 3:   but how is it that a **machine** can fly

Team 4:   without even flapping its wings?

Team 2:   Early planes had **propellers,**

Team 3:   which turn really fast and push air across the wings

Team 1:   to create **lift** and move the plane forward.

Team 2:   Small aircraft still use propellers to move up and through the sky.

Team 1:   Larger aircraft use **jet-powered engines**

Team 2:   to move air across the wings

Team 3:   and to create the lift and forward motion

Team 4:   that are needed to move the airplane forward.

Teams 1 and 2: These huge planes can carry large numbers of people

Teams 3 and 4: or loads of **cargo** and travel great distances.

All: **Flight is an amazing thing.**

Martin's Big Words
Doreen Rappaport

INTERACTIVE READ-ALOUD
Model and Guide Practice

LOOK AT THE COVER. This is Dr. Martin Luther King, Jr.

 Talk to your thinking partner. What do you know about Dr. Martin Luther King, Jr., already? What do you expect you'll read in his biography?

READ TO "WHEN I GROW UP, I'M GOING TO GET BIG WORDS, TOO." I always think of Martin as an adult, not as a child. The author is helping us to understand his childhood.

 Thinking partners, talk about the biography. What have you noticed about this biography?

READ TO ". . . WILL HAVE TO DISCOVER A WAY TO LIVE TOGETHER." The author has done something special in this text. Can you figure out why some words are different colors?

What is special about the words that are in yellow on this page? Look for words like this throughout the text. How does this help us better understand the biography?

CONTINUE TO THE END. Pause to talk with students about the characteristics of biography in the text. Prompt students to notice dates that signal real events, other historical figures mentioned in the text, details that paint a vivid picture of the place and time King lived, and King's own words throughout the text.

END OF STORY REFLECTION

This was a very helpful look into the life of Martin Luther King, Jr. What facts from his life did you find the most interesting?

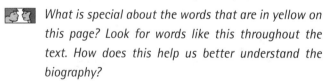 *Talk together about this biography. Why do you think the author wrote this biography? What is her point of view about Dr. King? How can you tell that she feels that way?*

SHARE THE LEARNING
Focus on Biography

Tip for Share the Reading

Read "Rosa Parks" to the students to model fluent reading. Guide a discussion about Rosa Parks. Ask the students to identify features of biography in the selection. Then have the students read the passage chorally to focus on interpretation of this piece.

Rosa Parks

On a December evening in 1955, a woman left work and got on a bus to head home. She was tired after a long day of work. The bus became crowded, and the woman, Rosa Parks, was asked to give up her seat to a man. Parks was African American, and the male passenger was white.

Rosa Parks did not give up her seat.

The driver warned her, "I'm going to have you arrested." She replied, "You may go on and do so." Rosa Parks was arrested. Rosa Parks did not yell or fight or cry on the bus or at her trial. She sat bravely and quietly and sparked other people to be brave.

After the arrest of Rosa Parks, a new group started in Alabama. Dr. Martin Luther King, Jr., was the leader of this group. They set out to peacefully create change.

Tip for Readers Theater Script

Read "Continuing the Dream" to the students to model expressive, fluent reading. Discuss any details that are not clear to the children. Then have three teams practice the narrators' parts to ensure they are delivered with fluency and meaning. You might play soft music in the background as students present the rehearsed script. King's famous "I Have a Dream" speech, delivered in 1963, would be a powerful follow-up to this lesson.

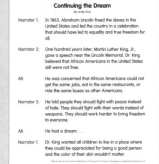

Continuing the Dream
By Linda Hoyt

Narrator 1: In 1863, Abraham Lincoln freed the slaves in the United States and led the country in a celebration that should have led to equality and true freedom for all.

Narrator 2: One hundred years later, Martin Luther King, Jr., gave a speech near the Lincoln Memorial. Dr. King believed that African Americans in the United States still were not free.

All: He was concerned that African Americans could not get the same jobs, eat in the same restaurants, or ride the same buses as other Americans.

Narrator 3: He told people they should fight with peace instead of hate. They should fight with their words instead of weapons. They should work harder to bring freedom to everyone.

All: He had a dream . . .

Narrator 1: Dr. King wanted all children to live in a place where they could be appreciated for being a good person and the color of their skin wouldn't matter.

EXTEND THE LEARNING

☆ Gather biographies for your classroom library. Encourage children to delve into them to find out the rich histories of people's lives. Students can share interesting facts they find.

☆ Have learners make a list of the attributes of their favorite biographies. What are the distinguishing features of a biography? What makes a biography interesting? What would they want to be sure to do in writing a biography?

☆ Introduce writing and visual art activities. For example, students might interview people in their lives and write biographies of them.

☆ Engage students in writing biography poems.

☆ During small group instruction, guide readers in reading biographies.

ASSESS THE LEARNING

> As children discuss biographies with their thinking partners, listen in to see if they are able to identify facts from the text. Assess children's ability to determine the most important facts from a biography and to consider the reason the person is notable.

> Ask children to create a "biography checklist." In pairs or small groups, children can list the traits of biographies and then describe the characteristics of a *great* biography.

INFUSION OF FORMAL LANGUAGE
Test-style language

A *biography* is
   A. a true story of someone's life.
   B. a made-up story that involves a mystery.
   C. a story an author writes to teach a lesson.
   D. a story a famous person tells about himself or herself.

According to this text, the word that *best* describes Martin Luther King, Jr., is
   A. cruel.
   B. selfish.
   C. peaceful.
   D. violent.

Rosa Parks

On a December evening in 1955, a woman left work and got on a bus to head home. She was tired after a long day of work. The bus became crowded, and the woman, Rosa Parks, was asked to give up her seat to a man. Parks was African American, and the male passenger was white.

Rosa Parks did not give up her seat.

The driver warned her, "I'm going to have you arrested." She replied, "You may go on and do so." Rosa Parks was arrested. Rosa Parks did not yell or fight or cry on the bus or at her trial. She sat bravely and quietly and sparked other people to be brave.

After the arrest of Rosa Parks, a new group started in Alabama. Dr. Martin Luther King, Jr., was the leader of this group. They set out to peacefully create change.

Continuing the Dream

By Linda Hoyt

Narrator 1: In 1863, Abraham Lincoln freed the slaves in the United States and led the country in a celebration that should have led to equality and true freedom for all.

Narrator 2: One hundred years later, Martin Luther King, Jr., gave a speech near the Lincoln Memorial. Dr. King believed that African Americans in the United States still were not free.

All: He was concerned that African Americans could not get the same jobs, eat in the same restaurants, or ride the same buses as other Americans.

Narrator 3: He told people they should fight with peace instead of hate. They should fight with their words instead of weapons. They should work harder to bring freedom to everyone.

All: He had a dream . . .

Narrator 1: Dr. King wanted all children to live in a place where they could be appreciated for being a good person and the color of their skin wouldn't matter.

Narrator 3:   He wished that all children everywhere could join hands and be brothers and sisters.

Narrator 2:   He wished that everyone would stand up for freedom together, as a family.

All: He knew things could be different, if we all worked together . . .

Narrator 3:   Dr. King wished that everyone from the east coast to the west coast

Narrator 2:   and from the Canadian border to the Gulf of Mexico

Narrator 1:   would sing out together for peace and freedom and equality.

All: He had a dream that all people everywhere, no matter the color of their skin, would work together, live together, and treat each other with respect.
We share that dream.

Jumanji
Chris Van Allsburg

FOCUS THE LEARNING

Introduction: I love reading fantasy stories because they can take me to different worlds! In fantasy stories, we can meet animals that talk, go to enchanted lands, and find characters we would never meet walking down the street. In fantasy, our imaginations get to run free and to experience things we know could never really happen. Today we will think about the characteristics of fantasy as we read *Jumanji*, a wonderful fantasy story by Chris Van Allsburg.

INTERACTIVE READ-ALOUD
Model and Guide Practice

LOOK AT THE COVER. What an interesting title! I wonder what it means. The illustration is interesting, too. I can't imagine opening my kitchen door to find monkeys on the table!

 Talk to your thinking partner. What clues on the cover tell you that this might be a fantasy story?

READ TO "...UNTIL ONE PLAYER REACHES THE GOLDEN CITY."

 Thinking partners, talk about the story so far. What do you think is unusual about the game? What clues have you noticed that this story might be a fantasy?

READ TO "THE RAIN BEGAN TO FALL IN BUCKETS AS JUDY TOOK THE DICE." I wonder what Peter and Judy's house looks like while they are playing this game! I wonder what would happen if their parents came home.

 Thinking partners, discuss the fantasy so far. How do the animals in this story act? What do they do that is different from real animals?

CONTINUE TO THE END. Pause periodically to allow thinking partners to discuss the characteristics of fantasy in the text. Be sure that students notice how the real setting—playing a game—makes the fantasy come to life. Encourage thinking partners to close their eyes, imagine themselves in the scenes in the book, and describe what they can see and hear. What words does the author use to create vivid pictures that bring this fantasy to life?

END OF STORY REFLECTION

I'm not sure if I would like to play a game like Jumanji. It would be interesting...but also a little scary!

 Talk together about this fantasy. Would you want to play the fantasy game of Jumanji? Why?

SHARE THE LEARNING
Focus on Features of Fantasy

Tip for Share the Reading

Read "At Last" for the children. Guide a conversation about the piece focused on their interpretation of what is happening. Ask them to identify elements of this story that make it a fantasy (landing on a planet, driving a spacecraft, make-believe animals, technology that doesn't exist). Have students read chorally, interpreting moments of tension in the passage.

At Last
By Linda Hoyt

Thomas stepped out of his craft and looked around. After spending months peering out the window into darkness and stars, it was a relief to step out and stretch his legs. Through the mist, he could see strange creatures moving around him. There was a sense of calm, not fear, as he peered at the scene. Everything that met his eye was new and mystical. Plants, animals, and even the soil on which he stood looked different.

He tugged the pack from his back and pulled out his photoranger machine. Transmitting pictures of this incredible scene was his first task and one he was excited to begin. Just then, he heard a scraping sound. As Thomas turned, a regal and beautifully dressed individual slowly approached, looking straight at him through the single eye in the center of his forehead.

At last, he was face to face with the man in his dreams. His mother wasn't going to believe this one! He could hardly wait to dial in his transmitter and send her visuals.

Tip for Readers Theater Script

"Fantasy?" compares fantasy characters to their "real" counterparts. You can put children in small groups to be the "real" and the "fantasy" characters. Have them read the script several times, emphasizing dramatic interpretation, phrasing, and a rate that supports meaning.

Fantasy?
Readers Theater Adaptation by Lynnette Brant

Fantasy Lions:	We like to growl on the top of the piano.
Real Lions:	We like to growl on the plains of Africa.
Fantasy Lions:	Sometimes we squeeze under beds.
Real Lions:	Sometimes we squeeze in twenty hours of sleep in one day.
Fantasy Monkeys:	You might find us throwing bananas in the kitchen.
Real Monkeys:	You might find us eating insects and seeds in the jungle.
Fantasy Rhinos:	You might hear us stampeding down the hallway.
Real Rhinos:	If we're angry, we'll stampede; but we'd rather wallow in the mud.
Fantasy Pythons:	We like to wrap ourselves around mantel clocks.

EXTEND THE LEARNING

☆ Allow children the opportunity to read a wide variety of fantasies and talk about fantasies they've already read. Gather fantasy books for your classroom. You might introduce specific types, such as animal fantasy, science fiction, and fantasy adventure stories.

☆ Watch the movie *Jumanji* and compare it to the fantasy picture book.

☆ Students will enjoy writing fantasies of their own. Have them brainstorm a list of fantasy ideas to use as "sparks" for stories. Supply story maps for planning, reminding students that their stories should include characters, a setting, and a plot with a definite sequence of events.

☆ During small group instruction, guide students in reading fantasy selections and analyzing the attributes of a fantasy.

ASSESS THE LEARNING

➢ Discuss a fantasy story with a small group, focusing on whether children can identify elements that make the story fantasy.

➢ During independent reading, confer with individuals about fantasy and assess their understanding of the genre.

INFUSION OF FORMAL LANGUAGE
Test-style language

A *fantasy* is
  A. a made-up story that involves imaginary situations.
  B. a story that teaches readers a lesson.
  C. a text that contains facts about a topic.
  D. a story created to be acted on stage.

The *first* result of playing the game Jumanji is
  A. monkeys stealing food.
  B. a monsoon in the living room.
  C. a lion appearing on the piano.
  D. a rhinoceros stampede in the hallway.

At Last

By Linda Hoyt

Thomas stepped out of his craft and looked around. After spending months peering out the window into darkness and stars, it was a relief to step out and stretch his legs. Through the mist, he could see strange creatures moving around him. There was a sense of calm, not fear, as he peered at the scene. Everything that met his eye was new and mystical. Plants, animals, and even the soil on which he stood looked different.

He tugged the pack from his back and pulled out his photoranger machine. Transmitting pictures of this incredible scene was his first task and one he was excited to begin. Just then, he heard a scraping sound. As Thomas turned, a regal and beautifully dressed individual slowly approached, looking straight at him through the single eye in the center of his forehead.

At last, he was face to face with the man in his dreams. His mother wasn't going to believe this one! He could hardly wait to dial in his transmitter and send her visuals.

Fantasy?

Readers Theater Adaptation by Lynnette Brent

Fantasy Lions:	We like to growl on the top of the piano.
Real Lions:	We like to growl on the plains of Africa.
Fantasy Lions:	Sometimes we squeeze under beds.
Real Lions:	Sometimes we squeeze in twenty hours of sleep in one day.
Fantasy Monkeys:	You might find us throwing bananas in the kitchen.
Real Monkeys:	You might find us eating insects and seeds in the jungle.
Fantasy Rhinos:	You might hear us stampeding down the hallway.
Real Rhinos:	If we're angry, we'll stampede; but we'd rather wallow in the mud.
Fantasy Pythons:	We like to wrap ourselves around mantel clocks.

Real Pythons:	We like to wrap ourselves around a log in the middle of the grassland or around a small animal we're going to eat for lunch.
Fantasy Volcanos:	We can erupt anywhere, even in your living room.
Real Volcanos:	We spew hot gases through cracks in the earth.
Fantasy Monsoons:	We don't need clouds. We can just fall from the ceiling.
Real Monsoons:	We can make an entire season wet and rainy.
All Fantasy:	Where can you find us?
All Real:	Where can you find us?
All:	Are we real or in your imagination?

Rumpelstiltskin
Paul O. Zelinsky

INTERACTIVE READ-ALOUD
Model and Guide Practice

SHOW THE COVER AND READ THE FIRST PAGE. This story doesn't start with "Once upon a time," but it's close! Let's start a list. We'll call it Elements of Fairy Tales. First, I'll write "Once upon a time." As we read *Rumpelstiltskin*, we'll add some more details to our list.

READ TO "… ALL THE STRAW WAS SPUN AND ALL THE SPOOLS WERE FULL OF GOLD."

Thinking partners, what are some traits of this fairy tale that you have heard or read in other fairy tales?

(Elicit students' ideas, such as "happened long ago," "make-believe," "a magic character," and "royalty [a prince]." Add ideas to the list.)

READ TO "… AND SHE BECAME A QUEEN."

 Thinking partners, how many times did the miller's daughter have to spin straw into gold? What other fairy tales have this same important number?

(Add relevant ideas to the list.)

CONTINUE TO THE END. Pause periodically to have partners talk about important elements of fairy tales. Your class list might include previous ideas along with "good and evil characters," "problems that need to be solved," "three tries to solve a problem" (or other ideas having to do with threes), "a lesson to teach the readers," and "happy endings."

END OF STORY REFLECTION

Let's review our list of fairy tale elements. Remember, we should think about elements that are true of many fairy tales, not just *Rumpelstiltskin*.

Put your heads together and talk about other fairy tales you know. What elements from our list are in these fairy tales?

(Allow time for partners to share their findings with the whole group.)

SHARE THE LEARNING
Focus on Features of Fairy Tales

Tip for Share the Reading

Put "The Princess and the Pea" on an overhead and read it to the children. Guide a conversation about elements of fairy tales the children find in this shared reading. Read the selection chorally and then dramatize the story.

The Princess and the Pea
Retold by Linda Hoyt

Once upon a time, there was a prince. He traveled around the world to find a princess, but there was something wrong with each one. One evening in the middle of a storm, somebody knocked at the palace gate. The king answered and saw a girl who said she was a real princess. The queen went into the bedroom and put a pea on the bed. Then she took twenty mattresses and piled them on top of the pea. The next morning, the girl said she'd had a horrible night—something was in the bed. The queen knew she was a real princess. Only a princess would have skin that delicate. So the prince had found his princess.

Tip for Readers Theater Script

As students perform "Goldilocks and the Three Bears," have readers wear signs indicating their roles. If possible, you might videotape the performance and have students discuss strategies for improving fluency and dramatic interpretation.

Goldilocks and the Three Bears
Readers Theater Adaptation by Lynnette Brent and Linda Hoyt

Narrator 1:	Once upon a time, there was a little girl named Goldilocks.
All:	She was a very naughty girl and seldom did what she should.
Narrator 2:	In the center of a clearing, she came upon a house. No one was home so she marched right in.
Narrator 3:	At the table in the kitchen, there were three bowls of porridge. Goldilocks was hungry. She didn't think about being polite. She picked up a spoon and tasted the porridge.
All:	You know what happened.
Narrator 4:	One was too hot. One was too cold. One was just right.
All:	So she ate the whole bowl of porridge!
Narrator 1:	After she'd eaten breakfast, she decided she was feeling a little tired. So she invited herself into the living room where she saw three chairs.
Narrator 2:	Goldilocks sat in the first chair to rest her feet.
Goldilocks:	This chair is too big!
Narrator 3:	So she sat in the second chair.
Goldilocks:	This chair is too soft.

EXTEND THE LEARNING

☆ Provide a variety of fairy tales in the classroom library. Students will enjoy reading familiar and not-so-familiar tales. They can share their favorites with classmates.

☆ Provide a story map that students can use to write their own fairy tales. Aside from including characters, setting, and plot, encourage them to choose at least four elements from the class list. Students can illustrate their tales and share them with the group.

☆ Read some "fractured" fairy tales, such as Jon Scieszka's *The True Story of the Three Little Pigs* or *The Stinky Cheese Man and Other Fairly Stupid Tales*. Invite students to select a fairy tale, such as *Rumpelstiltskin* or *The Princess and the Pea*, and challenge them to write a "fractured" version with a new setting, a new character, or a different point of view.

☆ During small group instruction, guide students in reading a series of fairy tales and discussing attributes of the tales.

ASSESS THE LEARNING

➤ Listen in as partners discuss fairy tales. Be sure they can identify story elements that fairy tales have in common.

➤ Students might create a checklist titled "Is it a fairy tale?" They can write a list of yes/no questions that would help a reader decide whether a story is a fairy tale or not. Assess their checklists for understanding of fairy tale features.

INFUSION OF FORMAL LANGUAGE
Test-style language

A *fairy tale* is
- A. a story that explains how something came to be.
- B. a text that contains facts about someone's life.
- C. a made-up story with a magical character.
- D. a rhyming verse that tells about a single topic.

In *Rumpelstiltskin*, the queen promised her first child to the little old man because
- A. he spun straw into gold.
- B. he helped her fix her ring.
- C. he saved her from a wicked man.
- D. she gave him his unusual name.

The Princess and the Pea

Retold by Linda Hoyt

Once upon a time, there was a prince. He traveled around the world to find a princess, but there was something wrong with each one. One evening in the middle of a storm, somebody knocked at the palace gate. The king answered and saw a girl who said she was a real princess. The queen thought, "Well, we'll see if that's true." The queen went into the bedroom and put a pea on the bed. Then she took twenty mattresses and piled them on top of the pea. The next morning, the girl said she'd had a horrible night—something was in the bed. The queen knew she was a real princess. Only a princess would have skin that delicate. So the prince had found his princess.

Goldilocks and the Three Bears

Readers Theater Adaptation by Lynnette Brent and Linda Hoyt

Narrator 1:	Once upon a time, there was a little girl named Goldilocks.
All:	She was a very naughty girl and seldom did what she should.
Narrator 2:	In the center of a clearing, she came upon a house. No one was home so she marched right in.
Narrator 3:	At the table in the kitchen, there were three bowls of porridge. Goldilocks was hungry. She didn't think about being polite. She picked up a spoon and tasted the porridge.
All:	You know what happened.
Narrator 4:	One was too hot. One was too cold. One was just right.
All:	So she ate the whole bowl of porridge!
Narrator 1:	After she'd eaten breakfast, she decided she was feeling a little tired. So she invited herself into the living room where she saw three chairs.
Narrator 2:	Goldilocks sat in the first chair to rest her feet.
Goldilocks:	This chair is too big!
Narrator 3:	So she sat in the second chair.
Goldilocks:	This chair is too soft.

Narrator 4:	So she tried the last and smallest chair.
Goldilocks:	Ahhh, this chair is just right!
Narrator 1:	But Goldilocks weighed too much for the little chair.
All:	It broke all to bits and she didn't even try to fix it!
Narrator 2:	Goldilocks was very tired by this time, so she went upstairs to the bedroom.
All:	Being naughty wears you out, you know!
Narrator 1:	She lay down in the first bed, but it was too hard.
Narrator 2:	Then she lay in the second bed, but it was too soft.
Narrator 3:	Then she lay down in the third bed, and it was just right. Goldilocks fell asleep. As she was sleeping, the three bears came home.
All:	What do you think will happen now?
Papa Bear:	Someone's been eating my porridge.
Mama Bear:	Someone's been eating my porridge.
Baby Bear:	Someone's been eating my porridge, and they ate it all up!
Papa Bear:	Someone's been sitting in my chair.
Mama Bear:	Someone's been sitting in my chair.
Baby Bear:	Someone's been sitting in my chair, and they've broken it all to pieces.
All:	When they got upstairs to the bedroom, Papa Bear growled.
Papa Bear:	Someone's been sleeping in my bed.
Mama Bear:	Someone's been sleeping in my bed, too.
Baby Bear:	Someone's been sleeping in my bed, and she's still here!
Narrator 4:	Just then, Goldilocks woke up and saw the three bears. She screamed, then jumped up and ran away into the forest.
All:	And she learned not to enter if no one is home.

Ashanti to Zulu: African Traditions

Margaret Musgrove

FOCUS THE LEARNING

(Be prepared to create an "alphabox" as described in this lesson.)

Introduction: This beautiful Caldecott-winning book is nonfiction. The author has used an alphabet book format to help us learn about traditions that are important to people in the country of Ghana, which is in Africa. The title is *Ashanti to Zulu*, and the author is Margaret Musgrove.

Think together. What do you know about Africa?

I am going to start an alphabox to record the important things I will learn about Africa in this alphabet book. Using an alphabet book format to teach about a topic is a great way to help us learn and think.

INTERACTIVE READ-ALOUD
Model and Guide Practice

READ THE FIRST PAGE. This is really interesting. It sounds like the patterns for the cloth are saved and repeated. They must have a lot of respect for those who design and weave the cloth for their kente. I am going to add "kente" to the K box in the alphabox to remind myself that the beautiful cloth is called kente. I am also going to add "drape" to the D box to remind myself they drape themselves with the kente.

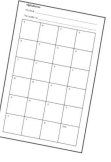

READ THE NEXT PAGE. Oh, my. Can you imagine giving a baby to a crocodile?

Think together. Is this a fact or is this a folktale from Africa? Why do you think so? Are there any important words or ideas we want to add to the alphabox?

READ TO THE "C" PAGE. This is really interesting. It says that children grow up in groups with other children the same age and sex. I wonder if that means that eight-year-old girls and eight-year-old boys would be together, but they wouldn't be in a class like ours with both boys and girls.

What do you think of that? Are there any words or ideas you want to add to our alphabox?

CONTINUE TO THE END. Pause occasionally to wonder about the content being learned and to reflect on additions for the alphabox.

END OF STORY REFLECTION

Our alphabox is loaded with words and ideas to help us remember what we learned about traditions in Africa. Listen as I use some words from the alphabox to help me summarize what I learned. I am going to use "bird" from the B box and "honey" from the H box. These words remind me that there is a tradition that when a bird leads a person to honey, the bird gets to have some of the honey as a reward.

Look at the alphabox and choose words you can link together to help yourself summarize important ideas. Write your ideas down and be ready to share with others.

SHARE THE LEARNING
Focus on Features of Alphabet Books

Tip for Share the Reading

Read the selection to the students. Then have them join you in reading in unison. This page is the "O" page in *Ashanti to Zulu*. With the alphabet as the organizer for the book, is there another focus letter that might make sense to the students? What would they think about choosing "M" for "market" or "B" for "bargain"? Encourage them to think about how the alphabet book structure helps them to notice key ideas.

> **o**
>
> A Ouadai *(wah-dy)* market is held under leaf canopies. The sun is very hot, so palm leaves are woven together and stretched over sticks. Market women sit under these shelters and sell dates, meat, cloth, and other things. Their shrill voices call out as their hands and eyes beckon. Customers must bargain with them for fair prices. People shake their heads and walk away, but they come back. Bargaining is serious business, but it's a lot of fun, too.

Tip for Readers Theater Script

"Ashanti to Zulu" summarizes information within an alphabet book structure. Props can turn the Readers Theater performance into a presentation that could be shared with parents or other classes. As students rehearse and lift the fluency of their reading, encourage them to use careful phrasing and select a rate that matches the meaning of the selection.

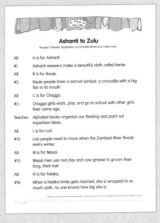

Ashanti to Zulu
Readers Theater Adaptation by Lynnette Brent and Linda Hoyt

All:	A is for Ashanti.
#1:	Ashanti weavers make a beautiful cloth called kente.
All:	B is for Baule.
#2:	Baule people have a sacred symbol: a crocodile with a big fish in its mouth.
All:	C is for Chagga.
#3:	Chagga girls work, play, and go to school with other girls their same age.
Teacher:	Alphabet books organize our thinking and point out important ideas.
All:	L is for Lozi.
#12:	Lozi people need to move when the Zambezi River floods every winter.
All:	M is for Masai.
#13:	Masai men use red clay and cow grease to groom their long, thick hair.
All:	N is for Ndaka.
#14:	When a Ndaka bride gets married, she is wrapped in so much cloth, no one knows how big she is.

EXTEND THE LEARNING

☆ Read *The Z Was Zapped* by Chris Van Allsburg and *The Ocean Alphabet Book* by Jerry Pallotta. Compare the alphabet books.

☆ Ask students to think of and examine books, documents, and procedures in which alphabetical order is important. Students might list dictionaries, encyclopedias, indexes, phone books, and so on. Talk with students about how alphabetical order is helpful.

☆ Work with students to create an alphabet book. You might focus the alphabet book on a topic of class study in science or social studies. Each student could craft text based on a letter or set of letters. Encourage students to consider how facts, art, and well-crafted writing are combined in *Ashanti to Zulu*. Students can keep these ideas in mind as they create their pages.

☆ Have students use an alphabox to gather ideas on a topic. Then have them attempt to use words from the alphabox in a summary.

ASSESS THE LEARNING

> Analyze student writing samples to determine if the students are able to use the alphabet to focus on key ideas and vocabulary.

> As students use materials that are arranged alphabetically, assess their ability to efficiently locate information using alphabetical order.

INFUSION OF FORMAL LANGUAGE
Test-style language

Which sentence *best* tells about the kente cloth?

  A. The cloth is beautiful.

  B. Each pattern is given a different name.

  C. People wear the kente cloth.

  D. Beautiful designs are woven into kente and worn by the Ashanti people.

Which of the following do Uge people collect?

  A. large fish

  B. palm leaves

  C. kola nuts

  D. None of the above.

O

A Ouadai *(wah-dy)* market is held under leaf

canopies. The sun is very hot, so palm leaves

are woven together and stretched over sticks.

Market women sit under these shelters and sell

dates, meat, cloth, and other things. Their shrill

voices call out as their hands and eyes beckon.

Customers must bargain with them for fair

prices. People shake their heads and walk away,

but they come back. Bargaining is serious

business, but it's a lot of fun, too.

Ashanti to Zulu

Readers Theater Adaptation by Lynnette Brent and Linda Hoyt

All: A is for Ashanti.

#1:   Ashanti weavers make a beautiful cloth called kente.

All: B is for Baule.

#2:   Baule people have a sacred symbol: a crocodile with a big fish in its mouth.

All: C is for Chagga.

#3:   Chagga girls work, play, and go to school with other girls their same age.

Teacher: Alphabet books organize our thinking and point out important ideas.

All: L is for Lozi.

#12:   Lozi people need to move when the Zambezi River floods every winter.

All: M is for Masai.

#13:   Masai men use red clay and cow grease to groom their long, thick hair.

All: N is for Ndaka.

#14:   When a Ndaka bride gets married, she is wrapped in so much cloth, no one knows how big she is.

Teacher: Alphabet books are good models for writing as they can be used with any topic.

All: V is for Vai.

#22: Vai people carry almost everything in bowls on their heads—and almost never drop anything!

All: W is for Wagenia.

#23: Wagenia fishermen trap fish in the dangerous rapids of the Congo River.

All: X is for Xhosa.

#24: Xhosa people in South Africa wear blankets to keep warm.

Teacher: Alphabet books can become part of *our* writing.

All: Y is for Yoruba.

#25: Yoruba artists carve beautiful statues to honor mothers and children.

All: Z is for Zulu.

#26: Zulu dancers have beautiful and complicated dances for all special occasions.

Group 1: From A to Z,

Group 2: From Ashanti to Zulu,

All: traditions are the heart of life in Africa.

Teacher: *You* can write an alphabet book, too.

Writing Traits

Engaging, well-written texts provide outstanding models for beginning writers. Standards in this strand explore ideas, organization, voice, and so on, so learners can begin to emulate that writer's work and incorporate those traits into their own writing.

Snowflake Bentley

Jacqueline Briggs Martin

FOCUS THE LEARNING

Introduction: Often our best ideas for writing come from things we experience or know a lot about. For example, we know a lot about our school. If we were to write about our school, we would have a lot of ideas to work with. We know a lot about weather, too. On a sunny day, wouldn't we have a lot to say about walking and playing in the sunshine?

 Turn to your partner. What ideas do you have about our weather today?

Today we are going to read *Snowflake Bentley* by Jacqueline Briggs Martin. You will notice that the author knows a lot about her topic. She must have done a lot of thinking and learning to get her ideas ready for this book.

INTERACTIVE READ-ALOUD
Model and Guide Practice

READ PAGES 1–3. I am thinking about the ideas in this book. The descriptions are so clear I am wondering if the author lived on a farm in the snow and experienced something like "watching snowflakes fall on mittens . . . and the dark metal handle of the barn door."

 Have you ever been in the snow? Was it like that for you?

READ TO WHERE WILLIE TELLS HIS MOTHER THAT HE WANTED THE CAMERA. I am still thinking about ideas in this book. I am thinking now that experience with snow would help but the author must have done a lot of reading about Willie to know so much about his life. That reminds me that writers can use a combination of experiences and reading to get ideas for their writing.

CONTINUE TO THE END. Pause occasionally to give partners time to talk about the ideas in the book.

 Turn to your thinking partner. How do you think the author got the ideas for this book?

END OF STORY REFLECTION

If I was to write about ideas and what I learned from this book, I would say that snow and Snowflake Bentley are great topics. If I was to write using these ideas, I could use my experiences with snow to help me and I could read to get more information so my writing would be interesting. I really liked the author's idea of adding information in the margins.

 Where do you get your ideas for the writing we do in our writers workshop?

SHARE THE LEARNING
Focus on Ideas

Tip for Share the Thinking

Guide the children in visualizing being in the snow using all of their senses and lots of details. Record the words and phrases that they use as they describe their visualizations. Next, have them think about what they learned about snow from reading the book (especially the side notes). Record their ideas from reading in the second box. Then model the beginning of a piece of writing showing how you can get ideas from the words and phrases you have listed.

Experience	+	Reading	=	Great Ideas!
Words that tell about our experiences with snow:	+	What we learned from reading about snow...		Let's write!

Tip for Readers Theater Script

For emergent readers, read "Snowflake Bentley" to them using it as a support to summarizing and reflecting on the story line. Encourage them to dramatize as they listen and to consider illustrations they could create after listening to the script. For developing readers, read the script once through to model fluent, expressive reading. Then have teams of four meet to rehearse a presentation of the script.

Snowflake Bentley
Readers Theater Adaptation by Linda Hoyt

Narrator 1:	Long ago there lived a boy who loved snow.
Narrator 2:	He was happiest when there was a snowstorm
Narrator 3:	and he could watch the beautiful flakes fall.
Narrator 4:	He wanted to share his love of snowflakes with others,
Narrator 2:	but there was no way to keep them.
Narrator 1:	They always melted before anyone could take a look.
Narrator 3:	When other children played in the snow, Willie studied snowflakes
Narrator 4:	and tried to understand their shapes and designs.
Narrator 2:	When Willie was 16, his parents bought him a camera
Narrator 1:	with a microscope inside.
Narrator 3:	He had many failures
Narrator 4:	but eventually figured out how to capture the snow crystals in a picture.
Narrator 2:	Willie was a farmer who was also known as Snowflake Bentley.
Narrator 1:	His memory lives on in a museum,
Narrator 3:	and in the monument that was built for him,
Narrator 4:	and in the book of photographs that he finally published when he was 66.
Everyone:	Snowflake Bentley loved snow more than anything else.

EXTEND THE LEARNING

☆ Have children draw to show something they have experienced. Talk to them about ideas that come from their drawings and how much drawing helps writers.

☆ Encourage children to talk to partners about their ideas for writing before they attempt to create text.

☆ Model getting ideas for writing from simple, everyday moments. Show the students how you can even turn your grocery list into a poem!

☆ Provide children with experiences such as blowing bubbles or eating popcorn slowly. Create lists of words to capture their experience. Then write using their wonderful ideas.

☆ Read lots of nonfiction aloud and encourage students to use what they are learning in their own writing.

ASSESS THE LEARNING

> Confer with writers to see if they have strategies for selecting ideas for writing.

> Have children tell you about their writing before they begin so you can assess the clarity of their focus and the level of detail in their thinking.

INFUSION OF FORMAL LANGUAGE
Test-style language

The most important ideas in this book were about
  A. snow.
  B. Snowflake Bentley.
  C. studying snow crystals.
  D. All of the above.

There is enough information to suggest that
  A. Snowflake Bentley was a scientist.
  B. he was a dairy farmer.
  C. he got rich.
  D. people wanted to meet him.

Experience   +   Reading   =   Great Ideas!

Words that tell about our experiences with snow:	+	What we learned from reading about snow...	→	Let's write!

Snowflake Bentley

Readers Theater Adaptation by Linda Hoyt

Narrator 1:   Long ago there lived a boy who loved snow.

Narrator 2:   He was happiest when there was a snowstorm

Narrator 3:   and he could watch the beautiful flakes fall.

Narrator 4:   He wanted to share his love of snowflakes with others,

Narrator 2:   but there was no way to keep them.

Narrator 1:   They always melted before anyone could take a look.

Narrator 3:   When other children played in the snow, Willie studied snowflakes

Narrator 4:   and tried to understand their shapes and designs.

Narrator 2:   When Willie was 16, his parents bought him a camera

Narrator 1:   with a microscope inside.

Narrator 3:   He had many failures

Narrator 4:   but eventually figured out how to capture the snow crystals in a picture.

Narrator 2:   Willie was a farmer who was also known as Snowflake Bentley.

Narrator 1:   His memory lives on in a museum,

Narrator 3:   and in the monument that was built for him,

Narrator 4:   and in the book of photographs that he finally published when he was 66.

Everyone: Snowflake Bentley loved snow more than anything else.

When I Was Young in the Mountains
Cynthia Rylant

FOCUS THE LEARNING

Introduction: Our memories are special treasures that we can use as writers. When we write about our memories, it is a chance to savor them and enjoy them one more time. The author of *When I Was Young in the Mountains*, Cynthia Rylant, lived with her grandparents in a cabin in the mountains of West Virginia until she was eight. The house had no electricity or running water. This book is a wonderful celebration of her memories from those special years.

 Think back to when you were little. Can you think of a memory that is special to you? Share your memories with your thinking partner.

INTERACTIVE READ-ALOUD
Model and Guide Practice

READ THE FIRST PAGE. Isn't this a good reminder? Our memories aren't just about big things like trips and special events. The author is writing about Grandpa coming home from work with clean lips for a special kiss on her head. That is a small thing, but what a wonderful memory to use as a writer! I am going to start a list of things to remember when I am looking for ideas. I want to start with "focus on small things."

READ TO WHERE THEY ARE IN THE SWIMMING HOLE. This is another reminder about ideas for writing. Swimming is a great topic. Everyone likes to swim. I am going to add "swimming" and "fun things to do" on my list.

 Do you have a special memory of going swimming? Share your thinking.

READ THE PAGE WHERE THEY ARE AT MR. AND MRS. CRAWFORD'S STORE. This is another good reminder about ideas for writing. The people in our lives! We all know people we can write about. We have our friends in class, our neighbors, our family members, and even the principal! Thinking about people we know is a great way to get ideas for writing. I am going to add that to our list.

 If you were going to write about a person, who would you write about?

CONTINUE TO THE END. Pause occasionally to help the children think about ideas for writing and to add suggestions to the list.

END OF STORY REFLECTION

I feel like I am just bursting with ideas for writing. I could write about special people in my life, about the fun of cooking and working on food with someone, about just sitting outside and listening to night noises.... I could go on and on.

 What ideas are you ready to write about after hearing this book? Share your thinking.

 # SHARE THE LEARNING
Focus on Ideas

Tip for Share the Reading

Read the passage to the students, or invite them to read it with you chorally. Then have them reflect with a partner about the memory in the selection. Guide a conversation about generating writing from small ideas.

> When I was young, I remember my grandfather making popcorn. He had this funny old popcorn popper that sat on top of the stove. He would add oil and popcorn kernels and then put the lid on. Then Grandpa would smile really big and ask who would like to help. Of course, my brother and sister and I all wanted to be first.
>
> The popcorn popper had a lid with a handle. When the pan started to get hot, we could take turns standing on a stool by the stove and we would turn the handle around and around while the popcorn cooked. The pan was hot so we had to be careful, but oh how we loved to be the one to turn that handle.
>
> Standing on the stool, I felt almost as tall as Grandpa. I could see the whole top of the stove and smell the oil as the pan got hotter and hotter. We had to wear a big oven mitt on our hand so we didn't get burned, but that didn't slow us down. Even with that big mitt, we could grab the little handle and turn and turn and turn.
>
> There was nothing better than the sound of the first kernels as they started popping. Pop! Pop! Then pop-pop-pop-pop really fast!
>
> What a wonderful memory!

Tip for Readers Theater Script

For emergent readers, read "Field Trip Fiasco" to them and have them create illustrations and use them to support a retell. They may enjoy dramatizing the crazy events in the script. For developing readers, have them meet in teams of two to rehearse and plan how to present the script. Then have students meet in teams of four and perform for each other.

> ### Field Trip Fiasco
> Readers Theater by Brendon Host
> Adapted from *The Day Jimmy's Boa Ate the Wash* by Trinka Hakes Noble
>
> Mom: Hi, Sam. How was your field trip to the farm?
> Sam: It was pretty boring . . . until the cow got hurt.
> Mom: A cow got hurt?
> Sam: Yeah. A haystack fell on it.
> Mom: What made the haystack fall?
> Sam: The farmer crashed into it with his tractor.
> Mom: Are you sure? I thought farmers were good tractor drivers.
> Sam: He was busy looking at the pigs that had gotten on the school bus.
> Mom: Pigs on the bus!
> Sam: Yeah. They were eating our lunches.
> Mom: The pigs were eating your lunch? Why?
> Sam: We threw their corn at each other, and they didn't have anything else to eat.
> Mom: Why were you throwing corn?
> Sam: Because we ran out of eggs.
> Mom: You were throwing eggs! Why would you do that?
> Sam: Because of the boa constrictor.
> Mom: A BOA CONSTRICTOR!

EXTEND THE LEARNING

☆ Read many stories and poems and wonder with the children about the author's idea for the piece. What might have helped the author come up with this idea?

☆ Have the students write about content area studies and remind them that their science and social studies content is a great source of ideas for writing.

☆ Have students keep a personal list of ideas for writing in their writing folder and add to it often.

☆ Bring in a photo album of your own and share a few photos and special memories. Then model a piece of writing about a memory while the children watch you write.

ASSESS THE LEARNING

> Confer with writers to consider the range of ideas they have already written about. Help each student to expand his or her own personal list of ideas.

> Gather small groups of students together and encourage them to share the ideas they have for writing. Assess their ability to gather ideas from personal experience and mentor texts.

INFUSION OF FORMAL LANGUAGE
Test-style language

In *When I Was Young in the Mountains,* you could infer that

A. the grandparents loved the children.

B. the children were happy.

C. they had a good life even without electricity.

D. All of the above.

"We stopped at Mr. Crawford's for a mound of white butter." In this sentence, the word *mound* means

A. mountain.

B. something creamy.

C. a rounded pile.

D. a cube.

When I was young, I remember my grandfather making popcorn. He had this funny old popcorn popper that sat on top of the stove. He would add oil and popcorn kernels and then put the lid on. Then Grandpa would smile really big and ask who would like to help. Of course, my brother and sister and I all wanted to be first.

The popcorn popper had a lid with a handle. When the pan started to get hot, we could take turns standing on a stool by the stove and we would turn the handle around and around while the popcorn cooked. The pan was hot so we had to be careful, but oh how we loved to be the one to turn that handle.

Standing on the stool, I felt almost as tall as Grandpa. I could see the whole top of the stove and smell the oil as the pan got hotter and hotter. We had to wear a big oven mitt on our hand so we didn't get burned, but that didn't slow us down. Even with that big mitt, we could grab the little handle and turn and turn and turn.

There was nothing better than the sound of the first kernels as they started popping. Pop! Pop! Then pop-pop-pop-pop really fast!

What a wonderful memory!

Field Trip Fiasco

Readers Theater by Brenden Hoyt

Adapted from *The Day Jimmy's Boa Ate the Wash* by Trinka Hakes Noble

Mom: Hi, Sam. How was your field trip to the farm?

Sam: It was pretty boring . . . until the cow got hurt.

Mom: A cow got hurt?

Sam: Yeah. A haystack fell on it.

Mom: What made the haystack fall?

Sam: The farmer crashed into it with his tractor.

Mom: Are you sure? I thought farmers were good tractor drivers.

Sam: He was busy looking at the pigs that had gotten on the school bus.

Mom: Pigs on the bus!

Sam: Yeah. They were eating our lunches.

Mom: The pigs were eating your lunch? Why?

Sam: We threw their corn at each other, and they didn't have anything else to eat.

Mom: Why were you throwing corn?

Sam: Because we ran out of eggs.

Mom: You were throwing eggs! Why would you do that?

Sam: Because of the boa constrictor.

Mom: A BOA CONSTRICTOR!

Sam: Yeah. Jimmy took his pet snake on the trip because he thought it would like to see all of the animals. It was pretty cool. Jimmy took the snake into the henhouse. The chickens saw the snake and started squawking and flying all around.

Mom: Oh my! What happened next?

Sam: One hen got excited and laid an egg on Jenny's head! It broke right in her hair.

Mom: Poor Jenny! What did she do?

Sam: She picked up an egg and threw it at Jimmy, and Jimmy dropped the boa constrictor. Jimmy grabbed another egg and threw it back at her. It looked like fun, so everyone joined in.

Mom: So let me see if I've got all of this right. The hens are squawking, and the snake is on the loose! Everyone starts throwing eggs, and then you run out of eggs so you throw the pigs' corn. Right?

Sam: That's it!

Mom: The pigs are still hungry so they climb into the bus and start eating your lunches. Now, the pigs are on the bus, and the kids are throwing eggs and corn. The cow gets hurt, and the farmer is mad. Where WAS your teacher?

Sam: I'm not sure, but he wanted to get out of there fast and told the kids to get on the bus. We left in such a hurry that Jimmy left without the boa constrictor, and one of the pigs was still on the bus! By the way, Jimmy's mom said that if we give Jimmy a ride back to the farm to get his boa constrictor, then I can keep the pig! Can we?

Mom: If this keeps up, I just may need a vacation.

Tuesday
David Wiesner

INTERACTIVE READ-ALOUD
Model and Guide Practice

READ THE FIRST PAGE AND SHOW THE NEXT SEVEN PAGES. I am thinking about how David Wiesner used time in organizing this book. It starts with "Tuesday evening, around eight." That tells me exactly what time the story is starting, but I notice other ways he tells me time is passing as well. I am looking at the moon in this picture with the turtle. I notice that it is pretty low in the sky. As I turn pages and get over to the page with the birds, I notice that the moon is really high now. The moon has moved. That tells me that time has gone by since the story started. I am going to go back to the beginning and turn the pages really slowly. Look closely. Do you see anything else that tells us that time has gone by? Watch the faces of the frog s.... Notice the number of frogs.... Look at the lights in the houses.

Think together. What did you notice?

CONTINUE TO WHERE THE MAN IS EATING AT 11:21 P.M. The lights in the houses were dark earlier and now they are on.

What does that tell us?

CONTINUE TO WHERE THE FROGS ARE WATCHING TELEVISION.

Look closely at the clock on the table. What time is it? How much time has passed?

TURN TO WHERE THE CHIMNEY AND THE ROOFTOPS ARE FEATURED. Look closely at this illustration. What do you notice? Has time passed again? What are the clues?

CONTINUE TO THE END. Pause on the picture with the police to wonder what time of day it might be.

END OF STORY REFLECTION
David Wiesner organized *Tuesday* around exact times of the night. Let's look at some other books that also use time as an organizer. (Display copies of *Diary of a Worm* by Doreen Cronin, *Snowflake Bentley* by Jacqueline Briggs Martin, and *The Relatives Came* by Cynthia Rylant. Page through these books asking students to look for evidence that time is passing. Help them to notice changes in shadows, notations of time as headings, characters getting older, etc.)

Writers, our important question is: What did we learn about using passage of time to organize our writing?

Think together. What have we learned and how can we use passage of time to improve the organization of our writing?

(Record their ideas on a chart.)

Tip for Share the Reading

Read the poem expressively to the students, asking them to listen and think about clues that time is passing. After a discussion about the meaning and the clues, ask the students if they got any additional ideas for using passage of time in their writing that could be added to the chart they started earlier. Invite the students to practice reading the selection expressively with a partner.

Listen
By Linda Hoyt

Peaceful
I lie still
Listening to the sounds of silence
Wondering what is and what could be
Bits of moonglow drift over me
The dark is alive
Yet the quiet is strong

The wind yawns through the trees
As the sun gently caresses the leaves
And whispers, "Wake"
Birds take flight
Pale light on their wings
A newly born day
Listen

Tip for Readers Theater Script

Read "Storm" and discuss: What did the author do to organize the piece? Is there a sense of beginning, middle, and end? Passage of time? A strong lead and ending? Have the students first practice performing the script in two teams to emphasize the changing voices and use the sound effects to punctuate the meaning. As they gain proficiency, have them perform the script with partner pairs.

Storm
Readers Theater by Linda Hoyt

Team One	Team Two
One wild winter's evening	
Clouds race across the sky	
Thunder roars	Boom!
Lightning flashes	Crr-ack!
Wind and rain rattle at the windows	Whoo, whoo, swoosh!
Trees bend in the wind and scratch across the roof	Scritch . . . creak!
Then crack	Bang!
Somewhere in the distance	Way over there
A branch falls	Crash!
Animals scurry	Clickety, clickety, shhh
The lights go out	Oh, no!
Darkness	This is creepy
The dog growls low in his throat	Grrrrrr
Fists beat on the door	Bang, bang, bang
Voices shout	Hey!
A light at the window	Flash!
Are you okay?	Phew . . .

EXTEND THE LEARNING

☆ Read books from the DK *Watch Me Grow* collection and note the organization used to show passing of time.

☆ Read *Diary of a Wombat* by Jackie French, *The Journey of Oliver K. Woodman* by Darcy Pattison, and other books organized in diary format to help children become comfortable with the format.

☆ Pause during read-alouds to reflect on passage of time and the tools the author is using to make it evident.

☆ Confer with writers about the way they will organize their work. If their piece involves passing of time, how will they use that to support their organization?

☆ Model writing an observation in which you observe something daily, date your writing, and write a description. Let the students watch you organize and craft language using the passage of time as a tool to hold your ideas together.

☆ Have students keep a diary or an observation log for a week and make entries each day.

☆ During small group instruction, guide students in discussing and applying different techniques for showing passage of time.

ASSESS THE LEARNING

> During small group instruction, assess students' ability to identify the organizing structure of a piece of writing and point out passage of time if it is evident.

> Confer with writers to examine the organizational structures they have in their writing folders or notebooks. Check to see if they have used or can add passage of time in a piece.

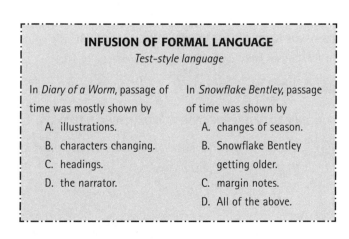

INFUSION OF FORMAL LANGUAGE
Test-style language

In *Diary of a Worm*, passage of time was mostly shown by

  A. illustrations.

  B. characters changing.

  C. headings.

  D. the narrator.

In *Snowflake Bentley*, passage of time was shown by

  A. changes of season.

  B. Snowflake Bentley getting older.

  C. margin notes.

  D. All of the above.

Listen

By Linda Hoyt

Peaceful

I lie still

Listening to the sounds of silence

Wondering what is and what could be

Bits of moonglow drift over me

The dark is alive

Yet the quiet is strong

The wind yawns through the trees

As the sun gently caresses the leaves

And whispers, "Wake"

Birds take flight

Pale light on their wings

A newly born day

Listen

Storm

Readers Theater by Linda Hoyt

Team One	**Team Two**
One wild winter's evening	
Clouds race across the sky	
Thunder roars	Boom!
Lightning flashes	Crrr-ack!
Wind and rain rattle at the windows	Whoo, whoo, swoosh!
Trees bend in the wind and scratch across the roof	Scritch . . . creak!
Then crack	Bang!
Somewhere in the distance	Way over there
A branch falls	Crash!
Animals scurry	Clickety, clickety, shhh
The lights go out	Oh, no!
Darkness	This is creepy
The dog growls low in his throat	Grrrrrr
Fists beat on the door	Bang, bang, bang
Voices shout	Hey!
A light at the window	Flash!
Are you okay?	Phew . . .

The Important Book
Margaret Wise Brown

FOCUS THE LEARNING

Introduction: Authors organize their books in many ways. They might organize a book as an alphabet book and use the alphabet to guide their writing and thinking. They might write a book that tells how to do something and organize their writing around the steps in the process. We know that writers of stories have a beginning, middle, and end plus a problem and solution. Today we are going to read a book that is organized in a different way. *The Important Book* by Margaret Wise Brown is organized to make main ideas really clear to the reader. It has a sense of poetry within its overall structure.

INTERACTIVE READ-ALOUD
Model and Guide Practice

READ THE FIRST TWO PAGES. I notice that this book has a sense of organization to each page as well as a connection between pages. It uses the phrase "The important thing about . . ." to begin and end every page.

 What are your thoughts about that? What do you notice about the way this book is organized?

READ TO THE PAGE ABOUT RAIN. I am noticing something else about the organization on each page. Margaret Wise Brown starts with a main idea, and then she provides details that help us to create sensory images. She then repeats her main idea. I am going to read this page again.

Think together about the details you noticed.

CONTINUE TO THE END. Pause occasionally to talk about the organization of each page as well as the overall structure of the book.

END OF STORY REFLECTION

This is an organizational pattern we can use in lots of ways. Here is an example:

"The important thing about our school is that we are learning. We work hard. We do a lot of reading, writing, and math. We are kind to each other and take good care of our classroom. But, the important thing about our school is that we are learning."

Think together. Use the organizational pattern to talk about something you know. The important thing about _____.

SHARE THE THINKING
Focus on Organization/Main Ideas and Details

Tip for Share the Thinking

Place the template on the overhead and engage the students in sharing the applications they thought of during the End of Story Reflection. Record some examples on the overhead so students can see how the text is arranged on the page and notice the repetition of the first and last sentences.

Engage the students in reading the work of their peers. Then challenge them as writers to craft additional paragraphs based on a current topic of study.

The Important Thing . . .
(Adapted by Linda Hoyt from *The Important Book* by Margaret Wise Brown.)

The important thing about _____

is that _____.

It is true that _____

_____

_____

But the important thing about _____

is that _____

_____

Tip for Readers Theater Script

Read "The Octopus" to the students and discuss the way it is organized. Help them to notice the headings and the way that each paragraph is focused on the topic identified by the heading. Invite students to read the script in partner teams, working on fluency, pacing, phrasing, and rate. Encourage them to then read into a tape recorder and listen to self-assess fluency.

The Octopus
by Linda Hoyt

The Body
An octopus is a sea animal that seems to be all head and arms. The eight arms, or tentacles, are long, waving extensions, each carrying two rows of suction cups that can hold tight to almost anything. The huge head features two eyes and a strong jaw that can crack right through a crab shell.

Hiding Places
The octopus likes to squeeze in between underwater rocks for protection and to surprise its prey. It is really a very shy animal and not likely to hurt a human. While in its hiding place, it can observe as small fish and small animals, such as crabs and lobsters, swim by. Then it can dart out and grab its dinner.

EXTEND THE LEARNING

☆ Create visual maps of stories and nonfiction texts to assist students in thinking about different patterns of organizing a piece of writing.

☆ Model writing in front of the students using a variety of organizational patterns. You might want to model a set of directions, a descriptive piece, a persuasive piece, a poem, or a story with problem/solution structure. In all cases, be sure to model that good writing has a clear beginning and ending.

☆ During small group instruction, guide readers in conversations about the organizational structure of the piece.

☆ Guide writers in making conscious decisions about organizational patterns for their own writing. Writers should be able to identify the organizational structure of their own work.

☆ Look at recipe books, brochures, and a wide array of nonfiction texts and talk about the organization of each.

ASSESS THE LEARNING

➤ Confer with individuals during independent reading to assess their ability to describe and identify the organizational structure of their reading selection.

➤ Confer with writers during writers workshop. Assess the range of organizational patterns that have been explored in each child's writing.

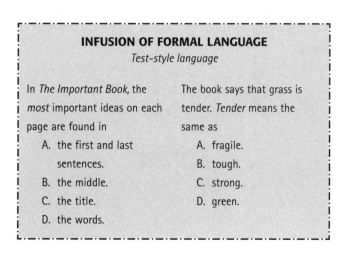

INFUSION OF FORMAL LANGUAGE
Test-style language

In *The Important Book*, the *most* important ideas on each page are found in

  A. the first and last sentences.

  B. the middle.

  C. the title.

  D. the words.

The book says that grass is tender. *Tender* means the same as

  A. fragile.

  B. tough.

  C. strong.

  D. green.

The Important Thing...

(Adapted by Linda Hoyt from *The Important Book* by Margaret Wise Brown.)

The important thing about _____

is that _____.

It is true that _____

_____

_____.

But the important thing about _____

is that _____

_____.

The Octopus

By Linda Hoyt

The Body

An octopus is a sea animal that seems to be all head and arms. The eight arms, or tentacles, are long, waving extensions, each carrying two rows of suction cups that can hold tight to almost anything. The huge head features two eyes and a strong jaw that can crack right through a crab shell.

Hiding Places

The octopus likes to squeeze in between underwater rocks for protection and to surprise its prey. It is really a very shy animal and not likely to hurt a human. While in its hiding place, it can observe as small fish and small animals, such as crabs and lobsters, swim by. Then it can dart out and grab its dinner.

Size

Most octopuses are only about two or three feet long. Divers have found evidence of some that are much larger. Some have been found to be as much as thirty feet across. These huge creatures are rare but definitely worth staying away from!

Protection

The octopus protects itself in several ways. It can squeeze its soft body in between rocks, making it very difficult for a predator to reach it. The octopus can wrap all eight of its arms around another animal and use the suction disks to hold tight. It also carries a supply of dark, inky fluid that it can spray into the water. This makes the water so dark that the octopus may be able to swim away before the predator can see again.

Officer Buckle and Gloria
Peggy Rathmann

FOCUS THE LEARNING

Introduction: When writers show voice in their writing, they are giving us a glimpse into who they are. Voice is the ability of the writer to add humor and personality to a piece of writing, to add something unique that is theirs alone. In *Officer Buckle and Gloria* by Peggy Rathmann, the author's voice comes through in her humor, in the funny things that happen, and in her message.

INTERACTIVE READ-ALOUD
Model and Guide Practice

READ PAGE 1. This is great. The humor of the author really shows here. The text says that Safety Tip #77 is Never Stand on a Swivel Chair, but that is exactly what Officer Buckle is doing, and there goes the chair. The voice of the author shows, and it is funny.

READ PAGES 2 AND 3. The kids are snoring, doing puzzles, playing with their food, and throwing paper airplanes. The author is helping us to understand that Officer Buckle is trying, but no one is listening...even the principal ignored Officer Buckle when he said not to stand on a swivel chair!

 What do you think of that?

READ TO WHERE OFFICER BUCKLE SAYS NOT TO SIT ON A THUMB-TACK. I can really tell the author has used voice now. What a great imagination she has to think of having a dog act out the rules when Officer Buckle explains them. This is really funny.

READ TO WHERE OFFICER BUCKLE REALIZED THAT GLORIA WAS GETTING ALL OF THE ATTENTION. Now the author has helped us to understand that Officer Buckle is really sad.

 Think together. What do you think of this part? What do you think the author will have happen next?

CONTINUE TO THE END. Pause occasionally to give partners time to talk.

END OF STORY REFLECTION

I think I would like to meet Peggy Rathmann, the author of this book. I can tell from this story that she has a great sense of humor and also understands how important it is to stick with your buddies.

If you could meet the author, what would you say to her?

🎭 SHARE THE LEARNING
Focus on Voice

Tip for Share the Thinking

🖋️ Explain to the children that if we care a lot about something, it is easier for our voice as writers to shine through. Think about something in your school that you feel strongly about creating, changing, or celebrating. Then write in front of the children, showing them how you could express your thinking to the principal. Don't hesitate to celebrate something wonderful and tell why. Be sure to explain that you want your voice and your strong feelings to show through so you are going to choose words and punctuation that will make your feelings very clear. Have the students read the letter with you when you are finished drafting.

Dear Principal,

Sincerely,

Tip for Readers Theater Script

📖 For emergent readers, read "Four-Legged Friend" to them several times. Talk about the meaning of each line, and connect the lines of the poem to their experiences with dogs. Guide their attention to the voice of the writer. The writer's feelings about dogs provide strong voice in this piece. Talk to the students about what the writer has done to help voice be clear. For developing readers, have them first experience the poem as an echo poem (teacher reads and students echo) and then by trading lines or partner reading.

Four-Legged Friend
By Linda Hoyt

Wagging tail
Trusting eyes
Leaning close for a hug.

When I'm sad
You're always there
Wet nose and a comforting paw.

Ready to go
Always my friend
Walking side by side.

EXTEND THE LEARNING

☆ Help the children create safety posters to place around the school. Have them express voice by telling why the rule is important.

☆ Write poetry about things the children care about, emphasizing that poetry can often reflect strong voice.

☆ Write a sentence on the board, such as "Children, finish your homework." Show the children how voice can shine through by reading it as if you are really mad, in a hurry, acting lovingly, and so on.

☆ Confer with writers about the voice in their writing. Help them to understand that their pictures can express voice through the expressions of the people, humor that is shown, and so forth.

ASSESS THE LEARNING

➤ Confer with readers during independent reading to see if they understand and recognize voice in the selection.

➤ Confer with writers about voice in their own writing. Assess the writing and give feedback to help the writer grow in use of voice.

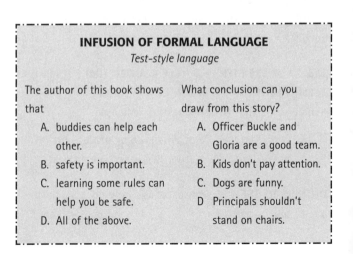

INFUSION OF FORMAL LANGUAGE
Test-style language

The author of this book shows that

   A. buddies can help each other.

   B. safety is important.

   C. learning some rules can help you be safe.

   D. All of the above.

What conclusion can you draw from this story?

   A. Officer Buckle and Gloria are a good team.

   B. Kids don't pay attention.

   C. Dogs are funny.

   D Principals shouldn't stand on chairs.

Dear Principal,

Sincerely,

Four-Legged Friend

By Linda Hoyt

Wagging tail

Trusting eyes

Leaning close for a hug.

When I'm sad

You're always there

Wet nose and a comforting paw.

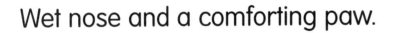

Ready to go

Always my friend

Walking side by side.

Heartland
Diane Siebert

INTERACTIVE READ-ALOUD
Model and Guide Practice

READ TO THE PAGE WHERE THE FARMER IS DRIVING THE TRAC-TOR. I am noticing some of the things Diane Siebert has done to add voice to her writing. She says the farms are "like treasures in my fertile hand." If she calls a farm a treasure, she is showing us how much she cares about the farms. I think word choice helps a writer to show voice so I am going to write "word choice" on this chart. I am also noticing that Diane Siebert has made the "heartland" come alive by having the heartland be the speaker in the poem. She says, "I am the heartland." This makes the farmland seem like it is alive. This helps us to connect. I think that voice is also about helping readers connect to the writing. I am going to write "use I" and "help readers connect" as ideas for voice.

 Thinking partners, do you have any other ideas to add to our chart? What do you think about the author's voice?

READ TO WHERE THE FARMER IS LOOKING AT HIS FIELD. I am thinking that the illustrations are helping the author's voice come alive.

 Thinking partners, what do you notice in the illustration? How does it help the author's voice to come through? What should we add to our chart?

CONTINUE TO THE END. Pause to point out personification and point of view as additional tools in bringing voice to the selection.

END OF STORY REFLECTION
The voice of the author was really clear in this poem, wasn't it? Look for a moment at the chart we created. Can you think of anything else we can add that would help us think about voice and using voice in writing?

Tip for Share the Reading

Place the poem on the overhead and read it expressively to the students. Guide a conversation about the voice of the writer. What do the students notice? What did the writer do that gave this piece strong voice? Are there any attributes of voice that they want to add to the chart they started earlier?

To My Teacher
By Linda Hoyt

You knew there was a flower waiting inside
Bursting to grow, to know and to learn.

Your caring heart and loving way

Helped me to bloom.

When things were hard,

You smiled and encouraged.

When I did well,

You shared my joy and helped me see why.

I can do it now.

Thank you for believing.

Tip for Readers Theater Script

Explain that the two sections of "Frog, Frog" represent two different points of view. Read the selection to the students and ask them to talk with partners to consider the voice of each section. Have students read the selection in teams, dramatizing and reading as expressively as possible. After presenting the script, have the students review the chart on voice and ask if there are any attributes they would like to add.

Frog, Frog
Readers Theater by Linda Hoyt

Voice 1
I am a frog.

I slide deeply into the mud to protect my sensitive skin.

My disk-shaped eyes roll patiently from side to side.

My long sticky tongue is poised . . . Ready . . .

Snap! My wonderful tongue flashes out, catching an unsuspecting fly. Oh, I am good.

There's a worm over there. This could be my lucky day.

Shh. Just one big leap of these powerful hind legs and . . . Got it!

Voice 2

Oh, yuck!—Not a frog.

Mud. Who wants to wallow in mud?

Have you ever seen eyes like that? Big, bulging, and slimy!

Sticky? Why would anyone want a sticky tongue?

How gross! The frog just ate a fly! This is disgusting!

That frog's looking at a worm. He can't be thinking of eating it!

That's it! No more frogs for me.

EXTEND THE LEARNING

☆ Use the format of *Heartland* to write nonfiction selections. Examples: I am a volcano. I am a frog. I am a golden eagle. I am the mayor. I am the turbine in a hydro-electric dam.

☆ During small group instruction, guide conversations about voice. Analyze the voice of the writer and consider the attributes listed on the chart started in the read-aloud segment of this lesson.

☆ During independent reading, confer with learners about voice in their selections.

☆ During independent writing, confer with writers about voice in their writing. Reread completed pieces to consider voice and improvements that could be made.

☆ Read persuasive pieces such as *Letters to the Editor* or *Should There Be Zoos?* by Tony Stead and talk about the voice of the writers.

☆ Have students write poetry to parents and encourage the students to bring strong voice to their work.

ASSESS THE LEARNING

> Listen as partners discuss voice to assess their understanding.

> During small group instruction, have children sort books according to those with strong voice and those without.

> Confer with individuals during independent reading to assess their ability to recognize voice and describe its attributes.

INFUSION OF FORMAL LANGUAGE
Test-style language

Voice in writing is the sense that

  A. a real person is speaking to you and cares about the message.

  B. something really bad is about to happen.

  C. pictures are the most important thing.

  D. if you write a lot, it is always better.

The author most likely wrote this piece because she

  A. grew up on a farm.

  B. likes pigs.

  C. knows a lot about farming.

  D. wants readers to understand the importance of the topic.

To My Teacher

By Linda Hoyt

You knew there was a flower waiting inside

Bursting to grow, to know and to learn.

Your caring heart and loving way

Helped me to bloom.

When things were hard,

You smiled and encouraged.

When I did well,

You shared my joy and helped me see why.

I can do it now.

Thank you for believing.

Frog, Frog

Readers Theater by Linda Hoyt

Voice I

I am a frog.

I slide deeply into the mud to protect my sensitive skin.

My disk-shaped eyes roll patiently from side to side.

My long sticky tongue is poised . . .
Ready . . .

Snap! My wonderful tongue flashes out, catching an unsuspecting fly.
Oh, I am good.

There's a worm over there. This could be my lucky day.

Shh. Just one big leap of these powerful hind legs and . . .
Got it!

Voice 2

Oh, yuck!—Not a frog.

Mud. Who wants to wallow in mud?

Have you ever seen eyes like that? Big, bulging, and slimy!

Sticky? Why would anyone want a sticky tongue?

How gross! The frog just ate a fly! This is disgusting!

That frog's looking at a worm. He can't be thinking of eating it!

That's it! No more frogs for me.

Owl Moon
Jane Yolen

INTERACTIVE READ-ALOUD
Model and Guide Practice

READ THE FIRST PAGE. I am trying to get a picture in my mind, and the words Jane Yolen has chosen are really helping me: "The trees stood still as giant statues. The moon was so bright the sky seemed to shine." Wow! Isn't that amazing? She could have said, "There was snow on the ground." That would have been okay, but I wouldn't have felt the experience so clearly. I am going to start a chart listing the beautiful words and phrases she uses in this book. I will start with trees . . . "giant statues." Her words really help me see them in my mind. I am going to read it again. Please listen carefully and see if there are any words or phrases you think we could add to our chart.

READ THE SECOND AND THIRD PAGES. I really liked the word "crunched." She said their feet "crunched" over the snow, and I could almost hear the sound of their feet breaking through the crust on the top of the snow. I also really liked "my shadow bumped after me." That makes me realize that it didn't float smoothly along but that it bounced and bumped along the way a little person would walk in the snow. I am going to write those words on my chart.

Turn to your thinking partner and talk about the words that helped you to visualize. Should we add any words to our chart?

CONTINUE TO THE END. Pause frequently to encourage partner talk about words and phrases. Record the children's ideas on the chart.

END OF STORY REFLECTION

Let's read our words and phrases from the story. They are almost like a poem and will help us really think about the story and what was happening.

☺☺ SHARE THE LEARNING
Focus on Word Choice

Tip for Share the Reading

Place the page on the overhead projector and read both versions aloud with expression. Ask the students which version they like better and why. Guide their attention to words and phrases that help them to visualize and become part of the experience.

Version 1

I got a bike. My dad helped me. We were on the sidewalk. It was fun.

Version 2

My hand reached for the rubber grip, and I held on as the breath seemed to back up in my lungs. I raised my right leg and placed my foot on the pedal as I settled myself on the seat. The fear and excitement rushed together so fast I could hardly think, and then my dad gave me a big shove. I was off. Cruising down the street, my bicycle and I . . . King of the mountain!

Tip for Readers Theater Script

Read "Chocolate" and "Frog" with fluency and expression. Guide a conversation about word choice. Which of the words are the best? Why? On a second reading, have students read chorally or in partners with the goal of emphasizing important words. Then have the students write list poems about characters in books, topics of study, or each other!

Chocolate
By Linda Hoyt

Smooth,
Brown,
Silky,

Creamy,
Melting,
Sweet on my tongue.

Chocolate

Frog
By Linda Hoyt

Sitting,
Blinking,
Nestled in mud.

Sticky tongue darts
A fly for his dinner.
Splash!

Frog

EXTEND THE LEARNING

☆ Create an illustration with a lot of detail, thinking aloud as you sketch. Then, begin adding words and phrases that describe and extend the illustration, showing the children how words make a big difference.

☆ Engage the children in creating an illustration that draws the reader into the moment. Encourage them to add words and phrases to support their thinking.

☆ Model word lists when you engage in science experiments, take a class trip, or listen to a wonderful read-aloud. Use the lists to power up word choices in students' writing.

☆ Begin lists of powerful synonyms for common words and post them around the room.

☆ Read, read, read from beautifully crafted literature, which will expand oral vocabulary.

☆ Post a sheet of butcher paper on the door of the classroom and begin a list of wonderful words to use in writing.

ASSESS THE LEARNING

➤ Confer with writers and focus on word choice.

➤ Confer with readers during small group and independent reading to consider word choice. Can they identify well-chosen words or substitute words of their own that would have added power to the writing?

INFUSION OF FORMAL LANGUAGE
Test-style language

Silent means the same as
   A. soundless.
   B. quiet.
   C. hushed.
   D. All of the above.

The *most* important idea of this selection is that
   A. it is cold when you go owling.
   B. owling happens at night.
   C. it is important to appreciate owls and nature and being outdoors.
   D. snow is cold.

Version 1

I got a bike. My dad helped me. We were on the sidewalk. It was fun.

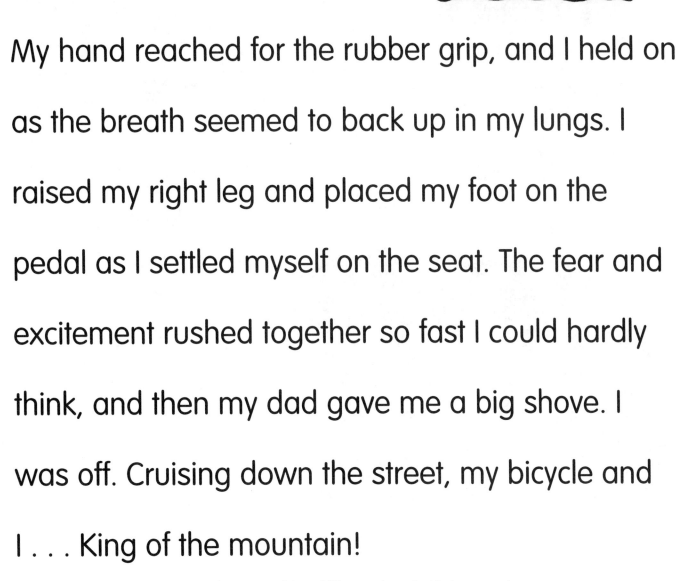

Version 2

My hand reached for the rubber grip, and I held on as the breath seemed to back up in my lungs. I raised my right leg and placed my foot on the pedal as I settled myself on the seat. The fear and excitement rushed together so fast I could hardly think, and then my dad gave me a big shove. I was off. Cruising down the street, my bicycle and I . . . King of the mountain!

Chocolate

By Linda Hoyt

Smooth,

Brown,

Silky,

Creamy,

Melting,

Sweet on my tongue.

Chocolate

Frog

By Linda Hoyt

Sitting,

Blinking,

Nestled in mud.

Sticky tongue darts

A fly for his dinner.

Splash!

Frog

Jumanji
Chris Van Allsburg

FOCUS THE LEARNING

Introduction: Word choice is really important in writing. When we select words that are colorful and precise, they help our readers to visualize what is happening. I am going to read *Jumanji* by Chris Van Allsburg. We may already know the story and what happens. Today as I read, I am going to ask you to focus on the words the author uses, especially the adjectives that describe and clarify. To help us get ready, let's think about adjectives. Get your imagination ready. "Pink" is a color. It is an adjective that describes things. Picture a "pink elephant." That sure is a different kind of elephant from the kind you see in photographs and at the zoo, isn't it?

 Share your thinking. What does your pink elephant look like?

INTERACTIVE READ-ALOUD
Model and Guide Practice

(Place an easel or chart within reach and record adjective/noun pairings that catch your attention. Be sure to underline the adjective to make it stand out.)

READ THE FIRST THREE PAGES. I am going to pause and think about the adjectives, the describing words the author has chosen. It says they spread the game on a card table. *Table* is the noun and *card* tells what kind of table it is. A card table is a place where you play cards. I know they are square, so it isn't very big, and everyone can reach the center of the table easily. I am going to write "card table" on this chart so we can remember how much the choice of adjective told us about the table.

I notice it also said "jungle adventure."

 Think together. Jungle is the adjective that tells about the kind of adventure. What do you think that means?

READ THE NEXT PAGE. I am thinking about adjectives again. The ones the author chose are really interesting. The first one is "bored" yawn. *Bored* tells what kind of yawn.

 Show your partner a "bored yawn." What does that mean?

On this page I also noticed the adjectives "unexcited," describing Peter's voice, and "absolute" horror, describing the look on Judy's face.

 What do unexcited *and* absolute *mean? Are these good word choices to describe Peter's voice and the look on Judy's face?*

CONTINUE TO THE END. Pause to notice adjective/noun pairs and add them to the chart.

END OF STORY REFLECTION

What a good reminder of how important it is to choose adjectives that describe and clarify. The adjectives that Chris Van Allsburg chose really helped us to visualize and understand this story.

 Think together. Look at the chart and select your favorite adjective/noun pairing. Get ready to act it out for the group.

SHARE THE LEARNING
Focus on Word Choice

Tip for Share the Reading

Read the passage to the children asking them to visualize as you read. Invite partners to discuss which words best helped them to visualize. Using an overhead pen, underline the adjectives in the passage. Show children how well-chosen adjectives make the nouns so much more meaningful. Have the children read the passage with expression. Then dramatize the action.

From the kitchen came the sound of banging pots and falling jars. The children ran in to see a dozen monkeys tearing the room apart. With an anguished cry, Judy ran into the kitchen waving her thin arms and trying to chase the misbehaving monkeys away. The children gazed in horror at smashed glasses, crushed plates, spilled juices, and gooey messes all over the floor.

Tip for Readers Theater Script

Read "Favorite Jokes" and discuss the word choices that make the jokes funny. Have the children underline the important words and then practice reading with fluent expression to interpret the jokes and responses.

Favorite Jokes
Readers Theater by Linda Hoyt

Why is a river like a dollar bill?
Because it goes from bank to bank.

What starts with t, ends with t, and has t in it?
A teapot.

Why is the ocean restless?
Because it has rocks in its bed.

If you were facing east, what would be on your left hand?
Fingers.

Why is a river so rich?
Because it has two banks.

What has a face and hands but no body or legs?
A clock.

What happens when you tell an egg a joke?
It cracks up!

EXTEND THE LEARNING

☆ Read many stories and poems looking for well-chosen words, especially adjectives.

☆ Model a piece of nonfiction writing to show how carefully selected adjectives can lift a piece of informational text.

☆ During small group instruction, guide learners in watching for precisely chosen words or discussing more powerful words that an author might have selected.

☆ Have students watch for interesting adjective/noun pairings to add to the chart started during the reading of *Jumanji*.

☆ Read stories to watch for carefully chosen verbs and show students how verbs can be the engine of a sentence.

ASSESS THE LEARNING

> Confer with writers to examine well-chosen words in their writing and assess adjective use.

> During small group instruction, assess readers as they identify well-chosen words and adjectives in passages.

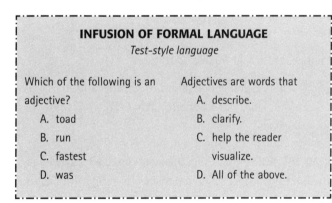

INFUSION OF FORMAL LANGUAGE
Test-style language

Which of the following is an adjective?
  A. toad
  B. run
  C. fastest
  D. was

Adjectives are words that
  A. describe.
  B. clarify.
  C. help the reader visualize.
  D. All of the above.

From the kitchen came the sound of banging pots and falling jars. The children ran in to see a dozen monkeys tearing the room apart. With an anguished cry, Judy ran into the kitchen waving her thin arms and trying to chase the misbehaving monkeys away. The children gazed in horror at smashed glasses, crushed plates, spilled juices, and gooey messes all over the floor.

Favorite Jokes

Readers Theater by Linda Hoyt

Why is a river like a dollar bill?

Because it goes from bank to bank.

What starts with t, ends with t, and has t in it?

A teapot.

Why is the ocean restless?

Because it has rocks in its bed.

If you were facing east, what would be on your left hand?

Fingers.

Why is a river so rich?

Because it has two banks.

What has a face and hands but no body or legs?

A clock.

What happens when you tell an egg a joke?

It cracks up!

How do you fix a cracked pumpkin?

With a pumpkin patch!

What did the pork chop say to the steak?

Nice to meat you!

What did the teddy bear say when he was offered dessert?

No thanks, I'm stuffed!

Why don't they serve chocolate in prison?

Because it makes you break out!

What happens to a hamburger that misses a lot of school?

He has a lot of ketchup time!

Why are cooks mean?

Because they beat the eggs and whip the cream!

What did the hamburger name his daughter?

Patty!

If a carrot and a cabbage ran a race, who would win?

The cabbage, because it is a head!

Why can't the magician tell her magic secrets in the garden?

The corn has ears and the potatoes have eyes!

Why did the tomato turn red?

Because he saw the salad dressing!

Why doesn't the corn like the farmer?

Because he picks their ears!

Why did the cookie go to the hospital?

He felt crummy!

What kind of lettuce did they serve on The Titanic?

Iceberg!

How did Ronald McDonald celebrate his engagement to Wendy?

He gave her an onion ring!

Why did the orange stop in the middle of the road?

Because she ran out of juice!

Dogteam
Gary Paulsen

FOCUS THE LEARNING

Introduction: Sentence fluency is the rhythm and flow of the language, the sound of word patterns, and the way the writing sounds to a listener. The best test for sentence fluency is to read a piece of writing aloud and see how it sounds. It should be easy to read out loud, with the sentences flowing smoothly from one to another. Sentence fluency also means having sentences of different lengths and with different beginnings. *Dogteam* by Gary Paulsen is written with wonderful sentence fluency.

INTERACTIVE READ-ALOUD
Model and Guide Practice

READ THE FIRST FOUR PAGES. Isn't the sentence fluency incredible! I am noticing that the lines pull me along as a reader. The short sentences followed by a longer sentence, and even the repetition, draw me along and help me to pick a reading pace that matches the book. Listen to this repetition: "They want to run, breathe to run, eat to run, live to run . . ."

 What do you think of the repetition? What effect does that have on the sentence fluency?

READ THE PAGE THAT BEGINS "THE DANCE." Wow! I am noticing so many things that Gary Paulsen did as a writer. I really like these short sentences, like "The dance. But silent." They cause me to pause and to focus. Then Gary Paulsen slides into a sentence that is long and rich with sensory images. Did you notice the onomatopoeia, "shusshh-whine"? I am going to read this page again just to savor it.

 Talk to your thinking partner. What do you like about this writing?

CONTINUE TO THE END. Pause occasionally to point out attributes of sentence fluency and appreciate the imagery.

END OF STORY REFLECTION

This book is so beautifully written. I am going to read it again so we can really focus on the craft of the writer. We are going to create a checklist for sentence fluency to help us as writers. We will read the book again and think about what we can learn from Gary Paulsen about how to be a fluent writer.

(Read the book again, page by page, asking the students to discuss sentence fluency. What are the elements of sentence fluency? What can we do as writers to have fluency in our writing? List the ideas from the students and add your own. The following chart may help you guide the children in creating a checklist that they can use to lift their own writing.)

Elements of Sentence Fluency Checklist	Book _____ √ if element is present	Book _____ √ if element is present	Book _____ √ if element is present	Book _____ √ if element is present
Sentences vary in length.				
Sentences flow together.				
The piece appeals to the ear when read aloud.				

 **SHARE THE LEARNING**
Focus on Sentence Fluency

Tip for Share the Reading

Have the students read "The Dark" chorally and then visually dissect the passage for elements of sentence fluency. Apply the checklist made earlier to the passage. How many elements are present? Does the passage provide ideas to add to the Elements of Sentence Fluency Checklist? Would you want to revise "The Dark" to improve its sentence fluency?

The Dark
By Linda Hoyt

Have you ever felt afraid at night? Darkness has the power to make you feel alone. Even a familiar and safe environment, such as your bedroom, can look strange and unfamiliar in the dark. Without light, your imagination can make you think that harmless things are suddenly scary.

Things are different for nocturnal animals. Nocturnal animals love the dark because they can see very well. Their eyes are especially large, and this extra size helps them to reflect even a small bit of light. Nocturnal animals also have a thin layer of material in their eyes that reflects light back into the eye, making it easier to see. This ability to reflect light is why you can often see the eyes of a cat or a deer in the dark.

Tip for Readers Theater Script

Read "Silver Tranquility" Reading #1 to the students and ask them to apply the Elements of Sentence Fluency Checklist they created to this passage. Engage them in reading the passage chorally, emphasizing phrasing and pauses for drama. Next, divide into teams and rehearse Reading #2 before weaving the voices together as a performance. Be sure to play soft music in the background to support their Readers Theater performance.

Silver Tranquility
Readers Theater by Linda Hoyt

Reading #1:
Darting like flashes of underwater neon, they school together, quivering and alert. Fins slice smoothly through clear water, waiting. Waiting for a minnow, the flash of an unsuspecting insect, or the floating eggs of a frog.

The water swirls around and overhead, but they remain tranquil, suspended in stillness, unaffected by the pulsing current. Then the moment is right. In a flashing burst of power, they carve a strong path. So quickly it seems like an illusion, jaws snap. Hunger is satisfied . . . for the moment.

EXTEND THE LEARNING

☆ Pause during read-alouds and consider the Elements of Sentence Fluency Checklist. How does this book rate on the checklist? What does the author do well? What suggestions might we make about sentence fluency?

☆ Engage children with poetry and apply the Elements of Sentence Fluency Checklist to the poems.

☆ Have the children use the Elements of Sentence Fluency Checklist they created on a piece of their own writing and then revise to try to hit more of the elements of the checklist.

☆ Model a piece of writing in front of the students and think aloud as you deliberately integrate each element of the Elements of Sentence Fluency Checklist the children created.

ASSESS THE LEARNING

> Confer with readers during small group instruction to assess their understanding of sentence fluency.

> Confer with writers during writers workshop and help them self-assess sentence fluency in their own work.

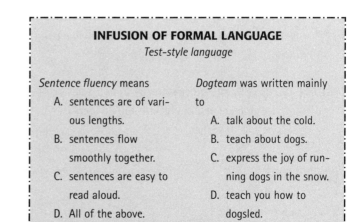

INFUSION OF FORMAL LANGUAGE
Test-style language

Sentence fluency means
  A. sentences are of various lengths.
  B. sentences flow smoothly together.
  C. sentences are easy to read aloud.
  D. All of the above.

Dogteam was written mainly to
  A. talk about the cold.
  B. teach about dogs.
  C. express the joy of running dogs in the snow.
  D. teach you how to dogsled.

The Dark

By Linda Hoyt

Have you ever felt afraid at night? Darkness has the power to make you feel alone. Even a familiar and safe environment, such as your bedroom, can look strange and unfamiliar in the dark. Without light, your imagination can make you think that harmless things are suddenly scary.

Things are different for nocturnal animals. Nocturnal animals love the dark because they can see very well. Their eyes are especially large, and this extra size helps them to reflect even a small bit of light. Nocturnal animals also have a thin layer of material in their eyes that reflects light back into the eye, making it easier to see. This ability to reflect light is why you can often see the eyes of a cat or a deer in the dark.

Silver Tranquility

Readers Theater by Linda Hoyt

Reading #1:

Darting like flashes of underwater neon, they school together, quivering and alert. Fins slice smoothly through clear water, waiting. Waiting for a minnow, the flash of an unsuspecting insect, or the floating eggs of a frog.

The water swirls around and overhead, but they remain tranquil, suspended in stillness, unaffected by the pulsing current. Then the moment is right. In a flashing burst of power, they carve a strong path. So quickly it seems like an illusion, jaws snap. Hunger is satisfied . . . for the moment.

Silver Tranquility

Readers Theater by Linda Hoyt

Reading #2:

Voice 1:   Darting like flashes of underwater neon,

Voice 2:   they school together, quivering and alert.

Voice 3:   Fins slice smoothly through clear water,

Voice 4:   waiting.

Voice 1:   Waiting for a minnow,

Voice 2:   the flash of an unsuspecting insect,

Voice 3:   or the floating eggs of a frog.

Voice 4:   The water swirls around and overhead,

Voice 1:   but they remain tranquil,

Voice 2:   suspended in stillness,

Voice 3:   unaffected by the pulsing current.

Voice 4:   Then the moment is right.

Voice 1:   In a flashing burst of power,

Voice 2:   they carve a strong path.

Voice 3:   So quickly it seems like an illusion,

Voice 4:   jaws snap.

All: Hunger is satisfied . . . for the moment.

The Relatives Came
Cynthia Rylant

FOCUS THE LEARNING

Introduction: Good writers think about sentence fluency when they are writing. They wonder how their writing would sound if someone read it out loud. They wonder if their sentences flow together smoothly, and they wonder if they are remembering to vary the length of their sentences. Cynthia Rylant uses wonderful sentence fluency in *The Relatives Came.* As we listen to this book today, your job is to pay special attention to the length of the sentences.

INTERACTIVE READ-ALOUD
Model and Guide Practice

(Have a large piece of paper close at hand. You are going to count the number of sentences on each page so the children can have a visual record of the varying number of sentences used on each page of the book.)

READ THE FIRST PAGE EXPRESSIVELY. I am thinking about the sentence fluency on this page. Did you notice how the sentences flowed together? Reading them out loud was easy because the sentences match the way we talk. Listen. I am going to read the page again. Notice how the first sentence is pretty long, and then the next sentence is really short. After that there is a really long sentence with a pause (a clause) near the end. I am going to count the sentences on this page and tally the number on this big paper.

READ THE SECOND PAGE. Did you notice? The first paragraph was all one sentence with the word "and" connecting all of the parts. We wouldn't want to do that very often, but now and then it creates really good sentence fluency. I am going to read it again. Listen to how long that sentence is … try to count the number of "ands" that you hear. Our first page had three sentences. This one has only 2! I am going to write "2" on the chart so we can remember that this page had a different number of sentences.

Think together. How many times did the author use "and" in that sentence?

READ TO WHERE IT SAYS "THEY HUGGED US FOR HOURS."

What did you notice about the sentence fluency? Share your thinking about the length of the sentences.

We are going to read these pages again. This time we will stop on each page and count the number of sentences so we can add the total to our list.

CONTINUE TO THE END. Look at this chart. It's interesting to see how the number of sentences varies so much from page to page. This tells us a lot about how sentence fluency is helped when there is a lot of variety to sentences. Some are short, and some are really pretty long.

END OF STORY REFLECTION

Think together. What did you notice about the sentence fluency in this book? What can we take into our work as writers?

SHARE THE LEARNING

Focus on Sentence Fluency

Tip for Share the Reading

Place the text on the overhead projector and read it expressively with the children joining in as they are ready. Guide a conversation about sentence length, variety, and how commas help us know when to pause to create interest in the message. Read it again so students

> Then it was hugging time. Talk about hugging! Those relatives just passed us all around their car, pulling us against their wrinkled Virginia clothes, crying sometimes. They hugged us for hours.
>
> Then it was into the house and so much laughing and shining faces and hugging in the doorways. You'd have to go through at least four different hugs to get from the kitchen to the front room. Those relatives!

can emphasize the punctuation and add interest to their oral interpretation.

Tip for Readers Theater Script

Guide a conversation about the sentence fluency of "Tadpoles," having the students work in pairs to analyze sentence length and variety. Divide the students into teams or groups of four to practice reading the piece. Make it clear that even though the narrator may

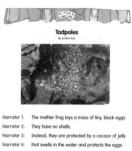

Tadpoles
By Linda Hoyt

Narrator 1:	The mother frog lays a mass of tiny, black eggs.
Narrator 2:	They have no shells.
Narrator 3:	Instead, they are protected by a cocoon of jelly
Narrator 4:	that swells in the water and protects the eggs.
Narrator 1:	This jelly holds the eggs together
Narrator 2:	and creates a mass that floats to the surface.
Narrator 3:	Once the ball of jelly reaches the surface,
Narrator 4:	the sun warms the frog spawn.

shift in the middle of a sentence, their performance needs to be so smooth that the sentence retains its fluency. As the groups or teams become proficient with the piece, add quiet instrumental music in the background to support the sentence fluency and oral interpretation.

EXTEND THE LEARNING

☆ Pause often during read-alouds to talk about sentence fluency and notice sentence length.

☆ During small group instruction, guide readers in discussions about sentence fluency.

☆ During writers workshop, confer with writers about their sentence fluency to ensure they are keeping it at a conscious level.

☆ Do a modeled write in front of the students and think aloud about your sentence fluency. Count the number of words in a sentence and help the children understand that you consciously follow a long sentence with a shorter one.

☆ Place writing samples on the overhead, with the permission of the student author, and have the class consider sentence fluency.

ASSESS THE LEARNING

> Listen as partners discuss sentence fluency during the read-aloud.

> During small group instruction, assess the ability of individuals to identify sentence fluency in a piece of writing.

> Review student writing samples to identify students who do and do not exemplify sentence fluency in their writing.

INFUSION OF FORMAL LANGUAGE

Test-style language

Stories with sentence fluency have sentences that
  A. are good.
  B. have lots of words.
  C. vary in length.
  D. have commas.

You do all the following *except*:
  A. Read the passage out loud.
  B. Make sure sentences are different lengths.
  C. Check to see if the sentences sound like people talk.
  D. Start each line with a capital letter.

Then it was hugging time. Talk about hugging!
Those relatives just passed us all around their car,
pulling us against their wrinkled Virginia clothes,
crying sometimes. They hugged us for hours.

Then it was into the house and so much laughing
and shining faces and hugging in the doorways.
You'd have to go through at least four different
hugs to get from the kitchen to the front room.
Those relatives!

Tadpoles

By Linda Hoyt

Narrator 1:   The mother frog lays a mass of tiny, black eggs.

Narrator 2:   They have no shells.

Narrator 3:   Instead, they are protected by a cocoon of jelly

Narrator 4:   that swells in the water and protects the eggs.

Narrator 1:   This jelly holds the eggs together

Narrator 2:   and creates a mass that floats to the surface.

Narrator 3:   Once the ball of jelly reaches the surface,

Narrator 4:   the sun warms the frog spawn.

Narrator 1:   Within this warm space, tadpoles begin to grow,

Narrator 2:   curled tightly inside their eggs.

Narrator 3:   Growing,

Narrator 4:   expanding,

Narrator 1:   getting ready to hatch,

All: this warm mass is tempting food for hungry ducks and fish.

Narrator 2:   After two weeks,

Narrator 3:   the tadpoles that survive will hatch—

Narrator 4:   wriggling free of their eggs

Narrator 1:   and swimming freely in the water,

All: ready to become frogs.

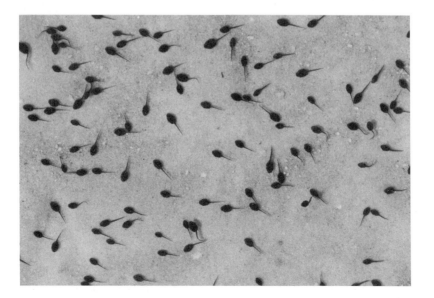

Yo! Yes?

Chris Raschka

FOCUS THE LEARNING

Introduction: Conventions are the tools we use to make writing easier to follow. They include our spelling, punctuation, grammar, capital letters, and so on. *Yo! Yes?* by Chris Raschka is a Caldecott-winning book that invites thinking about conventions and reminds us how much punctuation can affect meaning.

Think together. When you think of punctuation, what do you think of?

INTERACTIVE READ-ALOUD
Model and Guide Practice

READ THE FIRST TEN PAGES. I get it. They are talking to each other. The boy in the white shirt is trying to get the boy in the green shirt to talk. I am amazed how much the boy in the white shirt is communicating when he is only using one or two words at a time. I am going to go back and look at just the pages with the boy in the white shirt. I see on page 1 that "Yo!" has an exclamation mark. I see him saying this kind of loud. "Hey!" and "You!" have exclamation marks, too. I am thinking these might be even louder. Now, he says, "Yes, you." It only has a period, so I am thinking that he is speaking more softly because the boy in the green shirt is paying attention.

What do you think of this book so far? How are the conventions—the punctuation—helping you understand what is happening?

READ TO WHERE IT SAYS "NO FRIENDS."

The punctuation is different now. Talk together. What is happening here?

CONTINUE TO THE END.

Think together. This book has very few words, but a lot of meaning is conveyed. Why is the punctuation so important here?

END OF STORY REFLECTION

Read the story again and explain to the children that you are going to be the boy in the white shirt and read his pages as though you are in the story. They need to read the pages that represent the boy in the green shirt. You and the students need to ACT like the role you are reading. Read it a third time after placing double thickness of sticky notes over the punctuation in the book. This time have the students decide what punctuation they would like to add on each page.

SHARE THE LEARNING
Focus on Conventions/Punctuation

Tip for Share the Reading

Have the students think together about punctuation that could be added to the dialogue to make it storylike and express characters' feelings. Begin by modeling and thinking aloud about where you would place punctuation marks. Then give partners copies of the dialogue and have them dramatize and punctuate together until they feel that there is meaning and characters' feelings are expressed. Celebrate their work by dramatizing different versions.

Hey	Yo
What's up	Nothing
Play	No
Why	Can't
Why	No ball
Mine	Yours
Yes	OK

Tip for Readers Theater Script

Sing "Punctuation Song" to the students. Then have them join in singing it chorally until it is familiar. Have small groups and teams rehearse the song, and then challenge students to take it home and sing it to their parents. After singing the song, students can assess a piece of writing for conventions listed in the song.

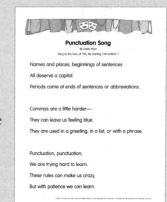

Punctuation Song
By Linda Hoyt
(Sing to the tune of "Oh, My Darling Clementine.")

Names and places, beginnings of sentences
All deserve a capital.
Periods come at ends of sentences or abbreviations.

Commas are a little harder—
They can leave us feeling blue.
They are used in a greeting, in a list, or with a phrase.

Punctuation, punctuation,
We are trying hard to learn.
These rules can make us crazy,
But with patience we can learn.

EXTEND THE LEARNING

☆ Make transparencies of pages from familiar read-alouds after you enlarge the text, and guide the students in talking about the punctuation. Is there any punctuation that could be modified to make it better?

☆ Place the writing of a volunteer student author on a transparency and have the class talk with the writer about possible punctuation to consider.

☆ Edit the writing of volunteers on the overhead for spelling, punctuation, and capitalization after revisions are complete. Be sure the volunteers understand what will happen to their work.

☆ Engage writers in interactive editing. On a chart, place a piece of writing that you have filled with errors in spelling, grammar, punctuation, and capitalization. Have small groups meet and discuss editorial changes.

☆ During small group instruction, discuss the role of punctuation in oral reading. Demonstrate and practice pausing for commas and periods.

ASSESS THE LEARNING

> Confer with writers during writers workshop to review conventions in their writing and consider strategies for improvement.

> Observe and assess as learners discuss conventions during whole-class editing of work on the overhead.

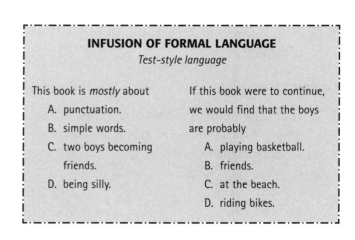

INFUSION OF FORMAL LANGUAGE
Test-style language

This book is *mostly* about
A. punctuation.
B. simple words.
C. two boys becoming friends.
D. being silly.

If this book were to continue, we would find that the boys are probably
A. playing basketball.
B. friends.
C. at the beach.
D. riding bikes.

Hey	Yo
What's up	Nothing
Play	No
Why	Can't
Why	No ball
Mine	Yours
Yes	OK

Punctuation Song

By Linda Hoyt

(Sing to the tune of "Oh, My Darling Clementine.")

Names and places, beginnings of sentences

All deserve a capital.

Periods come at ends of sentences or abbreviations.

Commas are a little harder—

They can leave us feeling blue.

They are used in a greeting, in a list, or with a phrase.

Punctuation, punctuation,

We are trying hard to learn.

These rules can make us crazy,

But with patience we can learn.

The Ghost-Eye Tree
Bill Martin, Jr., and John Archambault

FOCUS THE LEARNING

(Prepare a chart that says: Ooo… I dreaded to go… I dreaded the tree… Why does Mama always choose me?)

Introduction: We know that punctuation is important. We practice using capitals, question marks, exclamation marks, and periods whenever we write. As we read *The Ghost-Eye Tree* by Bill Martin, Jr., and John Archambault, I am going to ask you to think about a special kind of punctuation called an ellipse. We know that a period tells us to pause. We sometimes take a breath when we come to a period. An ellipse is a series of three periods. This tells the reader to take a longer pause. Listen to me as I read this chart with some lines from the story. (Read the four lines of the chart aloud using expression and suspenseful pauses at each ellipse.)

 Think together. What did you think of my reading? How did the ellipses affect the way that I read?

INTERACTIVE READ-ALOUD
Model and Guide Practice

READ THE FIRST PAGE. Did you notice those ellipses? Did you hear the way they changed my reading? Ellipses are a tool writers use to add meaning.

READ PAGES 2 AND 3. Did you notice the ellipses on page 3? What happened when I read that page?

TURN TO PAGE 4. I just realized something about these ellipses … they are not always at the end of the sentence! I am going to read the first paragraph as though the ellipses were not there. Then I am going to read it again with the ellipses in place. Listen and see what you think. (Read paragraph 1.)

 Think together. What did you notice about the two readings? What are your thoughts about the ellipses?

CONTINUE TO THE END. Pause occasionally to point out ellipses and help the children compare how the reading sounds with and without the ellipses.

END OF STORY REFLECTION

Weren't those ellipses a great punctuation tool! I really like the way that Bill Martin, Jr., and John Archambault used them to guide my reading.

 Partners, let's look at the passage on our chart again and practice reading using ellipses. Practice together and think about how you want it to sound.

Tip for Share the Thinking

Display the template and point out the conventions of a friendly letter. Create a friendly letter as the students watch you write. (Think of an authentic purpose, such as inviting the principal to be a guest reader.) As you draft the letter, invite student input on ideas as well as conventions such as capital letters, periods, etc. Be sure to deliver the letter and encourage the recipient to write a response using the conventions for a friendly letter.

_____ (date)

Dear _____ ,

_____

_____

_____

_____

Sincerely,

Tip for Readers Theater Script

Remind students that punctuation can help them read aloud with expression. For emergent readers, demonstrate reading aloud Version 1 of the script before having partners practice reading together. For developing readers, use Version 2. Have partners read the script together and decide where they want to add periods, exclamation marks, question marks, ellipses, and commas. Then have partners read the script, applying the marks they have inserted, before performing for others.

Jack and Jill
Readers Theater by Linda Hoyt

Version 1

Jack (knocking):	Hello! Anybody home?
Jack (louder):	HELLO! Anybody home?
Jack (slowly):	I . . . SAID . . . HELLO! IS . . . ANYBODY . . . HOME?
Jill (faintly):	Jack? Is it you?
Jack:	Jill! Where ARE you?
Jill (still faintly):	Jack! Come in, come in! I'm stuck.
Jack (entering):	You're in a truck?
Jill:	No, silly. I'm stuck in a pail.
Jack (seeing Jill):	What are you doing with that pail over your head?
Jill:	I was getting ready to go up the hill . . .
Jack:	. . . to fetch a pail of water.
Jill:	Of course! Help me get this off!

EXTEND THE LEARNING

☆ Have the students write friendly letters. Mail the letters with return stamped envelopes to encourage responses.

☆ Read *The Jolly Postman or Other People's Letters* by Janet and Allan Ahlberg and examine the conventions in the various pieces of mail.

☆ Encourage the students to include ellipses in their own writing to add drama and emphasis.

☆ Model writing that uses exclamation marks to support sound effects and points of emphasis.

☆ Look at recipe books, brochures, and a wide array of non-fiction texts and talk about the conventions in each.

☆ During small group instruction, guide students in examining conventions in the text. Encourage them to wonder if they could improve the punctuation.

ASSESS THE LEARNING

➤ Confer with writers to review writing samples for conventions. Celebrate the conventions that are being well used and set goals for improving conventions in the next piece of writing.

➤ During small group instruction, assess the learners' ability to identify conventions in print.

INFUSION OF FORMAL LANGUAGE
Test-style language

An *ellipse* is

  A. a series of three periods.

  B. a star in the solar system.

  C. a dash.

  D. the same as an exclamation mark.

Find the sentence with correct punctuation and spelling.

  A. You are wearing boots, a raincoast and a hat.

  B. you are wering boots, a raincoat, and a hat

  C. You are wearing boots a raincoat and a hat.

  D. You are wearing boots, a raincoat, and a hat.

_____ (date)

Dear _____ ,

_____

_____

_____

_____

Sincerely,

Jack and Jill

Readers Theater by Linda Hoyt

Version 1

Jack (knocking):   Hello! Anybody home?

Jack (louder):   HELLO! Anybody home?

Jack (slowly):   I . . . SAID . . . HELLO! IS . . . ANYBODY . . . HOME?

Jill (faintly):   Jack? Is it you?

Jack: Jill! Where ARE you?

Jill (still faintly):   Jack! Come in, come in! I'm stuck.

Jack (entering):   You're in a truck?

Jill: No, silly. I'm stuck. I'm stuck in a pail.

Jack (seeing Jill):   What are you doing with that pail over your head?

Jill: I was getting ready to go up the hill . . .

Jack: . . . to fetch a pail of water.

Jill: Of course! Help me get this off!

Jack and Jill

Readers Theater by Linda Hoyt

Version 2

Jack (knocking): Hello__ Anybody home__

Jack (louder): HELLO__ Anybody home__

Jack (slowly): I___ SAID___HELLO___IS___ANYBODY___HOME__

Jill (faintly): Jack__ Is it you__

Jack: Jill__ Where ARE you__

Jill (still faintly): Jack__ Come in__ come in__ I'm stuck__

Jack (entering): You're in a truck__

Jill: No__ silly__ I'm stuck__ I'm stuck in a pail__

Jack (seeing Jill): What are you doing with that pail over your head__

Jill: I was getting ready to go up the hill___

Jack: ___to fetch a pail of water__

Jill: Of course__ Help me get this off__